Mr. Lancaster's System

Mr. Lancaster's System
The Failed Reform That Created America's Public Schools

Adam Laats

JOHNS HOPKINS UNIVERSITY PRESS   BALTIMORE

© 2024 Johns Hopkins University Press
All rights reserved. Published 2024
Printed in the United States of America on acid-free paper
9 8 7 6 5 4 3 2 1

Johns Hopkins University Press
2715 North Charles Street
Baltimore, Maryland 21218
www.press.jhu.edu

Library of Congress Cataloging-in-Publication Data

Names: Laats, Adam, author.
Title: Mr. Lancaster's system : the failed reform that created America's public schools / Adam Laats.
Description: Baltimore : Johns Hopkins University Press, 2024. | Includes bibliographical references and index.
Identifiers: LCCN 2023050483 | ISBN 9781421449364 (hardcover) | ISBN 9781421449371 (ebook)
Subjects: LCSH: Educational change—United States—History—19th century. | Public schools—United States—History—19th century. | Education, Urban—United States—History—19th century. | Lancaster, Joseph, 1778–1838.
Classification: LCC LA215 .L33 2024 | DDC 370.973—dc23/eng/20231201
LC record available at https://lccn.loc.gov/2023050483

Special discounts are available for bulk purchases of this book. For more information, please contact Special Sales at specialsales@jh.edu.

For Bill, with gratitude

Contents

Preface ix
Acknowledgments xiii

Introduction 1

1 Borough Road 10
2 Children of the City 21
3 Mr. Lancaster's System 36
4 A Numbers Game 61
5 A Growing Disorder 83
6 The Truant Plan 102
7 Public School Society 137
8 The Next Big Thing 171

Conclusion 189

Notes 201
Index 241

Preface

America has never been willing to learn its lesson. In every generation—going all the way back to the very first years of the United States—school reformers have trumpeted their errors, their flawed schemes, and their impossible notions as marvelous new discoveries, new possibilities of a new modern world. Our generation is no exception.

In 2019, for example, then secretary of education Betsy DeVos told a group of education reporters that America needed a "new definition of public education." The endless crisis of public schooling could be solved, DeVos said, by breaking the government monopoly on public schooling. If only parents had the right to choose the schools their children attended, DeVos argued, then the tyranny of one-size-fits-all schooling could be done away with once and for all.[1]

We also saw it in 2010, when Facebook's Mark Zuckerberg convinced himself—along with Oprah Winfrey and then governor of New Jersey Chris Christie—that he had solved the centuries-old challenge of urban public schooling. Zuckerberg's alleged revelation came from sitting next to the brilliant young politician Cory Booker at a fundraising event. At the time, Booker was mayor of Newark, and Zuckerberg was so wowed by Booker's smarts and charisma that Zuckerberg thought that Booker could fix all of America's problems, starting in Newark, if only he had the right support. Zuckerberg thought that $100 million of Facebook money—delivered to Booker directly—could save America by revolutionizing public schooling.[2]

The examples are endless, and they include all kinds of pundits and politicians. They come from the political left, right, and center. For instance, New York City's mayor Eric Adams dismayed New Yorkers in 2021 with his claim that "new technology" had changed the game in public schooling. You didn't need a traditional classroom anymore, Adams asserted confidently. One teacher could teach "300–400 students."[3]

The problem, as we'll see in the pages of this book, is that these half-baked schemes had failed centuries earlier. Secretary DeVos's dream of sending tax dollars to privately run schools is not a "new definition of public education" but rather a description of the existing state of public schooling in the United States throughout the early 1800s. We don't need to wonder whether DeVos's miracle cure might work because the history is starkly clear: it already *didn't* work. It proved so unmanageable, inefficient, and inadequate that our modern public schools were created to save public schooling from DeVos's "new definition."

Mark Zuckerberg's mistakes were not a new product of the internet age but rather the oldest error of US public education. Zuckerberg was only the latest overrich, overconfident person to assume that he could somehow discern true greatness, to assume the right to sidestep regulations and oversight. Eerily similar to the elite men in the early 1800s who embraced Joseph Lancaster with unwarranted self-assurance, Zuckerberg assumed that his successes meant that old rules didn't apply to him.

Mayor Adams's gaffe, too, echoes the claims of his predecessors in the early 1800s. Back then, the mayors of cities like New York, Philadelphia, Boston, Baltimore, and Savannah thought that new technology would revolutionize public schooling; they assumed that the advances of their transformative age meant that old limitations no longer applied. City leaders in every decade—in every century—have stumbled into the patently obvious mistake of thinking that one adult could reasonably teach hundreds of children at once if only the right equipment were available.

The real tragedy of these endless shortsighted solutions is not only that they fail to make a difference but also that their flaws are so obvious. There is, in the end, no secret to school reform. To truly work, any school needs two things: it needs adequate resources, and it needs to provide the kind of schooling that the local community wants. The recipe is simple, but the challenges are enormous. How can politicians provide adequate funding to schools for low-income students? How can families outside the charmed circle of political influence ever force policymakers to listen to their needs?

Instead of tackling those difficult challenges, reformers in every generation have done what DeVos, Zuckerberg, Adams, and, yes, Joseph Lancaster tried to do. They built careers and squandered resources with inflated promises and impossibly simple silver-bullet solutions. They assured audiences—desperate families, taxpayers, and voters looking for some way out of seemingly intractable social problems—that they could overcome entrenched challenges with miraculous modern solutions. They promised the American people over and over again that they could cure poverty and overcome baked-in inequalities without ever forcing difficult conversations about the haves and the have-nots.

The story of Joseph Lancaster and his ill-fated, overhyped school reform is about more than the early 1800s. It is about more than the first heartbreakingly ill-managed school reform to sweep through America's cities. Lancaster's tale is the origin story of modern US public education and the flawed foundation on which American reform efforts have been built ever since—it explains the built-in errors of convenience that have stymied reformers for two full centuries.

To be fair, today's overconfident school reformers can't be blamed for not knowing Lancaster's story. They can't fairly be blamed for not acknowledging the earlier generation of Americans who made the same avoidable mistakes. After all, outside of academic circles, few people know the story of Joseph Lancaster. Like all failures, once the system crashed, its former supporters wanted the embarrassing story to disappear. They publicized the promise, but they buried the flop. As a result, most people don't know the true story of the birth of American public education, the patched-together solutions to fix the problems introduced by the narcissistic schemes of Joseph Lancaster and his overzealous followers. They don't know that American public schools were only created when hard-pressed city families refused to go along with the smug assumptions of naive city leaders. They don't know that the real heroes were not the urban elites who claimed to have solved the problems of poverty but rather the low-income families who refused to accept second-class status in public education.

It's not fair to take today's pundits and politicians to task for not knowing this history, even though it was one of the most revolutionary developments of America's past. But it is fair to point out that today's failures are not all that surprising. Today's debacles and mistakes are not exceptions to the regular functioning of American public education; rather, they are part of its DNA. They are the predictable results of America's eternally simplistic ideas about public education, the results of two full centuries of stubborn refusal to acknowledge the obvious. We can't make sense of today's failures without understanding that today's problems are only the latest incarnations of America's profound unwillingness to address the real challenges of public schooling, an unwillingness inaugurated at the birth of America's modern public schools.

The ignorance and unwarranted confidence of DeVos, Zuckerberg, and

Adams are not mere personality quirks. They are deeply embedded flaws resulting from the unquestioned and often unrecognized assumptions that Americans have always made about the relationship between public schools and the public good. Reformers have always assumed that there must be a shortcut somewhere; they have always assumed that tweaking public schools—using new technology and new ideas to transform schools—can solve social problems without actually challenging the causes of those problems themselves. And the American public has always been willing to believe them, to divert their eyes from the patent implausibility of school reform schemes, and to invest in ill-fated plans that promise to solve every social problem by making quick changes to public schools.

Solutions have never been that simple. As the story of Mr. Lancaster's failed system makes painfully clear, Americans have never been able to shake their addiction to the fantasy of getting something for nothing, the dream of solving society's complex problems without ever addressing their true causes. If we want to understand the nature of American public schools and the eternally frustrated quest for public school reform, we need to understand the ways in which the pattern was laid out from the very beginning.

Acknowledgments

Like any book, this one hogged the time of more than just one person. I'm very grateful to have a community of historians to work with. Many of them read and commented on sections of the manuscript. Some wrote recommendation letters to help fund the research. All of them offered both encouragement and correction. Thank you to Jon Zimmerman, Ben Justice, Laura Michel, Marcelo Caruso, Johann Neem, Victoria Cain, Mark Boonshoft, Cam Scribner, Larry Cuban, and Diane Ravitch. Thanks especially to Bill Reese, who read the entire manuscript and was endlessly generous with his time and expertise. Members of the Society for the History of the Early American Republic gave great feedback too, including Craig T. Friend, Lorri Glover, Caleb McDaniel, Jeffrey C. Stewart, Erik Freeman, and Jesse Chariton.

I also owe a debt to the institutions and archivists who made the research possible. At the American Antiquarian Society, I benefited from the Alstott Morgan Fellowship and the help of Laura E. Wasowicz and Nan Wolverton. At the Historical Society of Pennsylvania and the Library Company of Philadelphia, a McNeil Fellowship allowed me to benefit from the expertise of Christina Larocco and Connie King, and Fran Dolan made it possible to live next door while I worked. At the New-York Historical Society, archivists helped me crack into dusty boxes of bound records, literally unsealing the red tape from centuries-old school records. Finally, the archivists at the British Library tracked down documents even when I wasn't exactly sure what I was looking for.

Greg Britton and Johns Hopkins University Press shaped this book as well. I appreciate the insights of the anonymous reviewers, and I'm grateful for Greg's suggestions and enthusiasm.

Last but definitely not least, I need to thank Lucy for helping me find the right words.

Mr. Lancaster's System

Introduction

We will never know if it was anything other than a tragic accident. When Joseph Lancaster stepped out in front of a rushing horse carriage on the streets of New York on October 24, 1838, his violent death might not have been on purpose. But Lancaster could be forgiven if he felt a deep despair that day, a terrible temptation to end his misery by taking that fateful final step.

After all, for a few glorious years he had enjoyed a reputation—promoted by no one more assiduously than himself—as the world's greatest innovator and reformer of education. Beginning in 1803, he had told an eagerly listening world about his modern, scientific "system" of education, a system that would bring schooling to the mobs of impoverished city children roaming urban streets. Lancaster promised more than just school reform; he promised that his system would literally bring heaven to earth—it would *"utterly exterminat[e] ignorance"* from the entire planet.[1]

His proposals were simple: Instead of paying expensive teacher salaries, Lancaster imagined schools in which children—called "monitors"—taught other children for free. Instead of small classrooms for dozens of students, Lancaster proposed vast educational factories for hundreds. As world-changing ideas go, it was not much, but Lancaster styled himself as a unique genius who had solved modern social problems. He had declared himself the peerless "Patron of Education and Friend of the Poor."[2]

As a young adult, he was sponsored by kings and feted by presidents. His system was adopted by modernizing reformers the world over, from his home in London to the bustling cities of the United States; to Paris and St. Petersburg; to Caracas, Constantinople, and Kolkata; to Monrovia, Montreal,

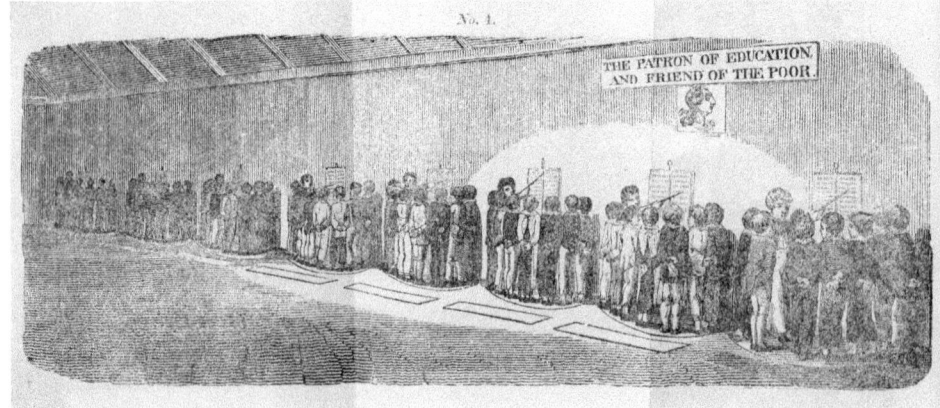

Joseph Lancaster liked to call himself "The Patron of Education and Friend of the Poor." From Joseph Lancaster, *The British System of Education: Being a Complete Epitome of the Improvements and Inventions Practised at the Royal Free Schools, Borough-Road, Southwark* (London: Royal Free School, 1810). Courtesy of the Library Company of Philadelphia.

and Mexico City. He became the darling of the nineteenth century. Yet by 1838, it all lay in tatters.

Twenty years earlier, when he first emigrated to New York by special invitation in 1818, he was whisked away by the city's elites on a luxury cruise ship to the state capital in Albany. He was embraced by the governor and cheered by the legislature. The Americans didn't know yet the sordid details of Lancaster's career in London. They did not know that he had sexually abused his students and pocketed vast sums of well-intended donations. American reformers would find out soon enough that Lancasterian reform was shackled to the monstrous, unmanageable egotism of Lancaster himself. But when he first arrived in New York, America's elites welcomed him with open arms. As he toured his new country, he shook hands with the president and leaders who called him "the benefactor of the human race . . . a blessing sent down from Heaven to redeem the poor and distressed of this world from the power and dominion of ignorance."[3] States such as Pennsylvania passed laws mandating that his system be used in their public schools.[4] He was one of the most famous people in the world, and he planned greedily for a cushy future of riches and public adulation. Yet just two decades later, in 1838, it was all over. As one obituary put it, "Few men have attained more celebrity . . . than Joseph Lancaster, . . . but . . . his latter days were clouded by misfortune."[5]

By the time of his death, Lancaster's eponymous school reform had been rejected by as many schools as had once clamored to adopt it. His enormous debt had chased him from London to New York to Philadelphia to Caracas to Baltimore to Montreal, and by the end, none of his old friends responded to his increasingly desperate pleas for money and attention. Given all that, we have to wonder, did he jump in front of that carriage? After all, everyone who knew the man beyond his carefully crafted public image knew he suffered from frequent bouts of ferocious despair—a "gloomy" tendency, as one disciple wrote him in 1823, full of "melancholy expressions which wind about [your] soul like dark clouds."[6]

The extraordinary life of Joseph Lancaster is one of the stories this book will tell. That life, however, dramatic as it was, would not have been more than a historical footnote if it had not spurred—by sheer accident, distortion, and delusion—a dramatic transformation in American society. That transformation was a profound American revolution, a shift in fits and starts from a haphazard market of city schools to the first awkward attempts at modern public school systems. The brief Lancasterian enthusiasm transformed American cities, but not in the ways elites had imagined. The failed promise forced them to recognize the profound social changes afoot in their growing cities; they were forced to acknowledge that their comfortable traditions of "paternalistic voluntarism" were no longer able to handle the demands of modern urban life.[7]

Observers and historians have struggled to explain what historian Thomas Boese called in 1869 the Lancasterian "delusion."[8] As Boese pondered, it seemed impossible "that thousands of intelligent men believed that a final and immediate remedy had been found for the evils of popular ignorance, and that the era of universal intelligence had begun."[9] It certainly defies an easy explanation. It is too simple to dismiss the enthusiasm of Lancasterian reformers as merely ignorant or deluded. They did press for evidence and proof, but they were all too ready to believe in flimsy assurances when those promises matched their shortsighted assumptions about children and their poor urban neighbors. Even more puzzling, Lancasterian methods worked very well in a few high-profile cases. It didn't happen often, but in places such as New Haven and Boston, well-funded, community-supported Lancasterian schools thrived for decades.

Those rare successes help demonstrate the central uncomfortable truth of the Lancasterian experience: there are a lot of ways to improve schools, and if they are used in a thoughtful manner and backed up with adequate resources, most of them can help. But no reform can work if it promises a shortcut around fundamental structural problems. No simple scheme can eliminate the need for well-funded and well-organized school systems. Yet school reformers in every generation, beginning with Lancaster's generation and continuing through our own, have rushed to avoid that difficult—and expensive—obvious fact.

As it happened, buying into Lancaster's scheme was America's original school reform sin, the unfortunate model reformers would repeat so many times over the generations. Instead of probing into the complex mix of problems facing cities and schools, instead of investing the resources schools needed to truly thrive, instead of finding out what kind of schools would best serve community needs, reformers allowed themselves to be convinced by complicated-looking blueprints and optimistic-sounding promises. They invested in the Lancasterian system—as their successors have invested in simplistic systems ever since—because they wanted to believe that it would work; they wanted to believe that their problems could be solved with a high-tech modern miracle.

At first, Lancaster and his supporters played a desperate numbers game, hoping to create a network of schools for poor children who could not afford to pay tuition. They thought they could use Lancasterian methods to sidestep the obvious truth—that every school needed enough resources to thrive. Instead, they dreamed of a new kind of educational system that could cram thousands of poor children into schools without costing thousands of dollars. But they left some vital factors out of their equations. For one thing, well-heeled reformers were slow to comprehend that schooling involved a sacrifice for lower-income families. School had to be more than tuition-free; it had to be attractive enough to be worth children's precious time.

In addition, Lancasterian reformers simply didn't understand that Lancaster's dream was out of step with the nineteenth century. Reformers assumed they were on the cutting edge, but they were behind the times, imagining schools that would fill a gap, that would provide basic education for children who otherwise would never learn to read and write and do simple math. By the time parents and pundits rejected Lancasterian schools in the 1820s, those ideas about public education had been outpaced by broad changes in the ways Americans thought about both schools and the very idea of the "public." For city families at the time, it wasn't Lancasterian schools or nothing. For white students and their parents, it was Lancasterian schools or an increasingly popular vision of what public schools should be.[10] For Black children in northern cities, the equation was always different; it was difficult to find any public institution that respected community desires and impossible to find any with adequate financial resources. But shifts in demography and citizenship status for urban African Americans also led to rapidly changing attitudes about the power of education for liberation.[11]

By the time Joseph Lancaster butted into reformers' conversations, ideas about public education were changing fast. So were cities. More and more people crowded into seaports and river towns. There were more Catholics, more people who didn't speak English, and overall more people on the streets.[12] Between 1810 and 1830, the number of people in New York City more than doubled. The same was true in Washington, DC. Boston, Baltimore, and Philadelphia were all bursting. Cincinnati grew in that period from an ambitious town of 2,500 residents to become the Queen City of the West with 24,831 people.[13] Urban reformers looked at those numbers with dread, but they also dared to hope. Yes, modern cities had a reputation as hotbeds of crime and dismay, as the growing number of low-income residents overwhelmed traditional networks of philanthropy and control. But reformers also believed that their modern cities could avoid that fate, if only education could be done right.[14] Unfortunately for them and the children they crammed into Lancasterian schools, reformers' assumptions about how to do schools right were all wrong. As the history of the Lancasterian movement shows in sad abundance, urban reformers asked the wrong people and looked in the wrong directions to figure out what it would mean to create modern public education systems.

It was a complicated process, and later historians have had no more luck explaining it than did Thomas Boese. They have looked long and hard at the ways in which cities modernized other institutions, such as prisons, hospitals, and almshouses, and found that reformers' assumptions tended to fare badly.[15] There's no doubt that white urban elites in the era, as one historian noted of Philadelphia, yearned for a modern city "in which the troublesome poor were neither seen nor heard but rather controlled by and confined within civic institutions."[16] But it is still a mystery how urban public schools fit into that effort. Despite the still-powerful myth that Horace Mann and the reformers of the 1840s were the "Fathers" of America's public schools, we know in fact that the earlier Lancasterian movement somehow created modern public school systems, modernizing America's cities.[17] We just don't know how.

The foundations of modern public school systems have been well known among historians for decades. In his Pulitzer Prize–winning examination of the roots of American public schools, for example, Lawrence Cremin pointed out that the Lancasterian "system proved odious" to parents and teachers by the 1830s. Yet somehow that failed system succeeded in creating modern public schools, which emerged, Cremin noted, "particularly in urban areas where the Lancasterian system had been most widely applied."[18] In his authoritative study of the origins of public schools, the late Carl F. Kaestle deemed the Lancasterian mania "the most widespread and successful educational reform in the Western world" at the time.[19] It didn't last, Kaestle noted, but somehow it "provided the nucleus of later public school systems."[20] Somehow, Kaestle recognized, "the seeds of school bureaucracy were borne on the wings of Lancaster's instructional scheme."[21] Somehow.

This book explains how: how the abject, embarrassing, expensive failure of Lancasterian reform ended up creating the nation's first modern public school systems and modernizing the nation's growing cities. The evolution is difficult to trace because, unlike the voluminous self-aggrandizement of Joseph Lancaster himself, the real debates and incremental changes were not preserved in reams of archived pamphlets. And unlike elite Lancasterian reformers, the real decision-makers often left only shadows and oblique references behind.

The key to unlocking the mysteries of the Lancasterian movement can be found in digging past the Lancasterian sleight of hand that fooled urban reformers of the time. It's not easy to do—the archives are bursting with the razzle-dazzle, with Lancasterian manuals and brochures that lay out endless details about classroom methods and educational promises. It is all too easy to read those sources as if they represented the real importance of the Lancasterian movement. They don't. The details of Lancasterian classroom teaching took up all the oxygen in the debates of the early 1800s. But in practice, the methods themselves hardly mattered. In a few cases, well-funded, responsive schools used Lancasterian methods with great success for decades. Almost everywhere else, though, the methods were an immediate and catastrophic failure. They were often not used at all, even in schools that bragged about their "Lancasterian" promise. In the end, the story of the birth of modern public school systems has been obscured by that false promise. It was not the minutiae of Lancasterian pedagogy that mattered. Modern public schools emerged not from the promise but from the wreckage of the Lancasterian movement, tacked together in unplanned ways to make public schools that would serve the needs of families and cities.

It was a complicated evolution, and the outline is worth repeating: Lancasterian ideas did not create modern urban public school systems, at least not simply or directly. To the contrary, Lancasterian dreams were far more stunted and divisive than the systems that emerged. Lancaster himself was only a distraction, a narcissistic sideshow clown who diverted attention from the real work of creating public schools. But Lancasterian promises provided the lure, the promise of schooling for all, that hooked politicians and reformers on the possibility that every child, rich or poor, could attend school. Though Lancasterian ideas were a delusion, a sort of reform fever dream, they convinced elites that governments could find a way to provide schools for all. Once that door was open, families pushed their way through: Black and white, working class and middle class. They demanded a new kind of institution to match a new understanding of public education. In the process, they created modern public school systems by patching the inadequacies of Lancaster's delusional system with newly popular assumptions about what a public school should be.

To tell this complicated story, this book will have to leave out a few things. It is not a traditional biography of Joseph Lancaster himself, though the world could use one. The existing biographies are wildly inaccurate in their celebratory conclusions.[22] When I began this research, I expected to discover in Joseph Lancaster an earnest but naive young Quaker reformer, maybe a little overly optimistic about his chances to improve schools, but overall a sympathetic character. I couldn't have been more wrong. I found myself on the trail of a monster—a cruel parent who left his fourteen-year-old daughter in charge of her mentally ill mother while he sported off to give lectures about his system; an abuser who beat and sexually assaulted the children he claimed to be saving; a deluded narcissist who separated the world into only two categories: sycophantic admirers and deadly enemies. Although his movement was based on deceit, Joseph Lancaster was just as deluded by its promise as anyone else. He truly believed that he was different from the herd, a better sort of person specially gifted with a unique revelation about proper education. A book about Lancaster himself would be fascinating, but in the end, the man himself had little to do with the movement he sparked. He quickly worked his way into irrelevance, becoming a nuisance and embarrassment to the real work of school reform.

One of the most noteworthy aspects of Lancaster's early career will also be left out. In Britain, Lancaster's reforms came to be synonymous with a bitter fight over the proper role of religion in schools.[23] In the United States, in contrast, Lancaster's religious vision was so widely shared that it never became an issue of debate. Like Lancaster, school reformers and the schoolgoing public in American cities generally agreed that public schools must exclude controversial religious ideas yet still teach a broad, generic introduction to Christian principles. For many Americans at the time, the ideas of Christianity, republicanism, and capitalism were so intertwined that their relationship and necessary role in education needed no further discussion; it seemed obvious to them that public schools must teach a certain kind of Protestant religion they called "non-sectarian."[24] Unlike the feuds over teaching and funding that spelled the death knell for Lancaster's promises, the role of religion in the first American public schools was, perhaps surprisingly, not one of the reasons for Lancaster's rise or fall, so it will only be in the background of this book.

Similarly, this book will not attempt a full history of all the different roots of public education throughout the United States. As historian Carl F. Kaestle has demonstrated so powerfully, rural and small-town schools had a very different experience from urban ones. Southern schools were very different from northern ones.[25] Yet the Lancasterian movement brought together these different strands and made a new vision of systematic public schooling seem both possible and necessary. The Lancasterian movement accidentally created the first modern public school systems in a complicated way: No thanks to Lancaster's skimpy plans, city leaders figured out ways to train and pay teachers from tax funding. They realized they needed to run things with elected superintendents instead of well-meaning philanthropists, to include richer and poorer students in the same schools, and to offer more advanced academic classes to all. They created modern school systems without planning to, by combining their improvised solutions to Lancasterian shortcomings with new assumptions about public education from the countryside. It was only in a later generation that those systems were rationalized, made truly systematic, and expanded beyond cities. It took even longer for them to move outside the Northeast.[26] This book will only tell the story of the urban birth of those systems.

This book will also focus only on the experience of US cities, not the global expansion of Lancasterian reform. From the very beginnings, Lancaster's ideas had an international flavor, coming originally from India through London and quickly spreading around the world. Indeed, as historians have noted, the evolution of the Lancasterian dream might be the best example of the way global intellectual networks worked at the turn of the nineteenth century.[27] Lancasterian ideas whipped around the planet, exciting and connecting a generation of reformers. A book tracing and examining those connections would be very welcome, but it would require a much different focus. In order to track the complicated relationships between Lancasterian rhetoric and reality, this book will limit its ambitions to a study of the evolution of city schools in the United States.

This book will attempt to tell that story in all its complexity. It will not ignore the sources that most histories have focused on—the endless self-promoting pamphlets cranked out by Joseph Lancaster and his many followers—but it will paste them over the lumpy realities of big-city school reform. If we are to have any chance of explaining this process, of explaining how a failed school reform accidentally led to the birth of modern public school systems, we need to understand a few things first: We need to know what the reform plan was, at least in theory. We need to know why so many otherwise-rational reformers fell so hard for it. And we need to know something about Lancaster himself, about how an abusive, narcissistic blowhard could convince the world to accept his outlandish delusions. We'll start with that story: the story of Lancaster's first experience with undeserved success, long before he ever set foot in the United States.

1
Borough Road

There wasn't much to see at first. In 1798, nineteen-year-old Joseph Lancaster took two students into his parents' home in London. To prepare for his new career as a teacher, Lancaster read one book about education, John Locke's *Some Thoughts Concerning Education* (1690). He assumed that it would be enough. If success is measured by enrollments, perhaps it was. Within a year, Lancaster had over a hundred students and his own school building on Borough Road.[1] By the time Lancaster was twenty-five, he had become a world-famous author and education reformer. He had met King George III and received fan mail from around the world.[2]

It went straight to his head. Before he ever traveled to the United States in 1818, young Joseph Lancaster had already had a tumultuous career. Lancaster had not meant to start a new kind of school. His family did not have much money, and young Lancaster did not enjoy many opportunities. As a boy, he worked for a while with his father making chairs. At the tender age of fourteen, he joined the navy for a short nine-week career at sea. Back on land, he assisted in a nearby school until he felt ready to take his own students in 1798.[3]

At first, he had only meant to make a living. When he noticed the disheveled state of some of his students in early 1799, he appealed to his immediate circle of the Society of Friends—the Quakers—for donations. At the time, the Quakers were well known for their philanthropic efforts, including opposition to slavery. Lancaster's relationship with the faith was always troubled. He followed his father into the denomination in 1801, but like so much else in his life, Lancaster found it impossible to remain in any group that did not acknowledge his own unique superiority. By 1814 he had left Quakerism behind, though he never stopped hoping for financial support from their international philanthropic network.[4]

In his early days, with Quaker help, Lancaster hoped to provide tuition payments and better clothes for all his students. In the beginning, families at the Borough Road School who could pay tuition did so. Those who could not did not.[5] For a short while, the school thrived. Low-income families embraced the opportunity to send their children to school, and philanthropists embraced the chance to help. At first, Lancaster threw himself into the work with energy and dedication. He adopted an idea fashionable among London's school reformers at the time—promoting talented students to be "monitors," taking on the role of assistant teachers. The idea had come from India via the educational ideas of London's Andrew Bell. And though Lancaster always claimed to have come up with the idea independently, he and Bell became embroiled in a long dispute over both originality and the proper role of religion in their schools.[6]

Following the traditions of apprenticeship, Lancaster took his monitors into his home and under his wing. He sketched out an elaborate system of schooling based on his monitorial method, with detailed descriptions of activities and new technology. He promoted his imagined system as a transformational modern marvel, able to educate the very poor without costing very much. For a few years, the Borough Road School seemed like a beacon of hope in a modern city plagued by industrial tensions and urban anxiety.

Lancaster's rapid success launched a pattern of behavior he would follow for the rest of his life. Based on his growing reputation as a successful school reformer, Lancaster began borrowing heavily to publish reams of promotional materials lauding himself and his school. He planned to expand his building on Borough Road and expand his fame with his publications. By 1803, his efforts had sunk him deeply in debt. Expecting the gratitude of a grateful London public, Lancaster found himself instead dodging the sheriff, who had a warrant for Lancaster's arrest.[7]

Desperate, Lancaster tried to publicize his way out. He published a flyer depicting himself as a courageous reformer, offering education to the beleaguered poor and guarding all of London from the "pernicious and dangerous" effects of poverty. He called for the creation of an "Education Society" to support his efforts.[8] It was a strategy of last-ditch desperation rather than one of thoughtful foresight, but in this instance it worked. Indeed, the overwhelming success of this gambit might have been the pivotal moment of Lancaster's career. Its success saved his Borough Road School but ruined Lancaster's life. He had buried himself in debt without any realistic plan to pay it off. He had told the world that he had invented something new, something crucial. He had styled himself as a self-sacrificing benefactor of the poor, providing free education for London's street urchins. And he had dodged his creditors long enough to appeal for help, without a reasonable expectation of receiving any. This one time—this crucial, formative time—Lancaster's foolhardy tactics worked.

The publicity attracted the curiosity of the Duke of Bedford and Lord Somerville, two high-ranking members of the royal family. In 1803, they paid a visit to Lancaster's Borough Road School. What they saw—or, to be more precise, what they *thought* they saw—changed the history of urban education in London and around the world. They saw a vast open schoolroom, with hundreds of children diligently working in seemingly perfect order. There were modern-looking reading placards adorning the walls, taking the place of expensive individual books. Monitors could hold up signs with messages such as "Ex," telling the teacher that students were ready for examinations. There was no corporal punishment, but only an elaborate and apparently beloved system of rewards and demerits. The students were from the poorest classes of London, yet they appeared neat, tidy, and obedient.

The visitors really did see all those things. What they didn't see was the vast investment of time, money, and intimidation needed to create the apparent success of the Borough Road School. In fact, the high energy and high spirits of Lancaster's famous school were merely the exhaust pumped out by a cruel, abusive system, a system that burned vast reservoirs of resources. As we'll see in chapter 7, the success of the Royal Borough Road School could be repeated in other cities, but only when schools managed to secure adequate resources to thrive. The scheme never worked when reformers tried to run schools only on the skimpy funding that showed up in the official books. But Lancaster concealed those truths, even from himself. Instead, Lancaster explained that his guests were witnessing a transformational modern system of education. In Lancaster's telling, his school plans were more than just ingenious. They were absolutely a new presence for goodness in the world, "a novelty in the history of education."[9] Lancaster explained—falsely—that his school succeeded even though it lacked funding or other resources. In Lancaster's telling, his school thrived because of the way he organized it; he convinced the visiting royalty that he had invented some-

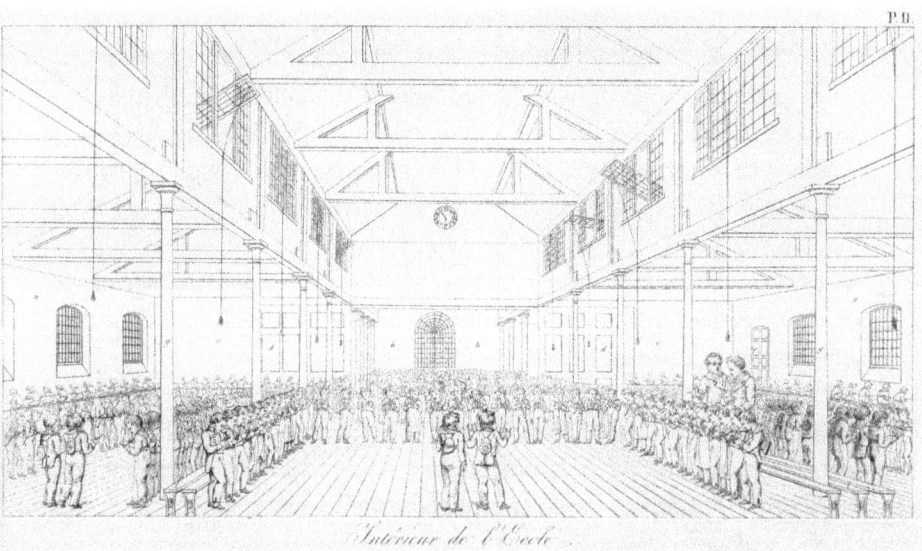

A fantasy of what a Lancasterian classroom should look like. These depictions appeared in an 1818 book translated into French from German: Joseph Hamel, *L'enseignement mutuel ou Histoire de l'introduction et de la propagation de cette méthode* (Paris: L. Colas, 1818). Courtesy of the Gutman Library, Harvard University.

thing breathtakingly new and vitally important: a detailed method to teach poor children cheaply. Lancaster told his visitors that his success could be boxed up and shipped around the world. With Lancaster's manuals to guide them, reformers in any city anywhere could establish a similarly successful school for poor children, with no additional funding required. Without the experience to know any better, Lancaster's elite visitors believed him.

They would soon discover their gullibility, but for a short time that did not matter. The Duke of Bedford and Lord Somerville liked what they saw and believed what they heard. They donated enough money for Lancaster to pay off his debts. The approval of these two leading members of London society turned the tide for young Joseph Lancaster. For a short while, Lancaster's perennial debt burden was lifted. For a while, the money flowed in from around England and around the world. The king himself eventually donated a hundred pounds.[10] More importantly, the king gave the school his official imprimatur and granted Lancaster the right to call his institution the "Royal" Borough Road School.[11]

Against all odds, Lancaster's desperate plea for help was an overnight success. Thanks to the curiosity of the Duke of Bedford and Lord Somerville, Lancaster's fame soared; he suddenly became the talk of the town. It became fashionable to support the school, and Borough Road was soon overwhelmed by well-heeled visitors and buoyed up by their donations. By the end of 1803 Lancaster's school had the financial support of London's elite, including three dukes, dozens of titled gentry, and ambassadors from around the world.[12] Lancaster's close circle of early supporters organized themselves into a committee to support his educational efforts, initially calling themselves the Royal Lancasterian Society.[13]

London's elites were not the only ones to be impressed. One earnest Quaker reformer traveled from New York City to London to witness the school firsthand. When he returned home, Thomas Eddy gathered a group of the city's elites to start their own philanthropic society. Like the founders of the Royal Lancasterian Society in London, founding members of the New York Free School Society hoped in 1805 to rescue children in "indigent circumstances" by starting a Lancasterian school in which "habits of industry and virtue may be acquired."[14]

Lancaster's methods quickly became a global phenomenon. Lancasterian societies popped up all over Europe and Asia. By 1815, there were Lancasterian schools from Uruguay to Egypt.[15] Lancaster received letters and visits from ministers and ambassadors from all around the world.[16] As early as 1808, Lancaster's Borough Road School was described in tour books as a must-see destination for travelers.[17] Borough Road became a tourist attraction for elites from India, Denmark, Spain, New Zealand, Brazil, Russia, and elsewhere.[18] At the time, London liked to think of itself as the most modern city in the world, with a million inhabitants careening toward a steam-powered modern future. Lancaster's new school took its place as a pillar of that modern promise, supposedly revolutionizing education and giving cities a new way to thrive.

Eventually, Lancasterian methods became so widespread that they no longer needed any introduction. For a few decades in the early part of the 1800s, Lancasterian education was simply equated with education as a whole. One early children's novel, for example, used Lancasterian schools as a way to describe the unlikely success of its "deformed" protagonist Dickey Shepard. In spite of Shepard's twisted spine, the author related, "at the Lancaster school where he was monitor . . . he was treated with as much deference as if he . . . had had the limbs of Apollo."[19] Other children's literature at the time made similar assumptions, and the image of a Lancasterian monitorial school, with children teaching other children, became synonymous with school itself.[20]

Perhaps the only person who was not surprised by the sudden fame thrust upon the Lancasterian system was Lancaster himself. Joseph Lancaster always presumed that his educational ideas deserved to be world-famous. From his earliest years at the Borough Road School, long before the Duke of Bedford and Lord Somerville lent him their support, he assumed that his supporters would always bail him out of any debt or crisis. He grew accustomed to receiving donations from supporters rich and poor. At first, he tried to be responsible about it. Between April 20, 1800, and March 22, 1801, Lancaster kept careful records of donations received and costs incurred. He paid himself a reasonable salary for the time, noting all his expenditures down to the last penny. In those early days, Lancaster happily subjected himself to the oversight of his supporters.[21]

He couldn't do so for long. As his fame spread, Lancaster received reams of fan mail. His admirers often tucked in donations alongside praise. He pocketed the money and soon stopped keeping track of it.[22] Instead, he spent it even more quickly than it came in. As one of his first disciples later remembered, "the money came in very freely and it was as freely spent."[23] Lancaster did not scruple to use the money for distinctly noneducational purposes. As his follower recalled, Lancaster quickly grew "luxurious, extravagant, and indolent."[24] Worst of all, Lancaster did not limit his reckless spending to funds on hand. He realized he could use his royal patronage and growing reputation to borrow even more money, and he did so thoughtlessly, always assuming he would soon be so rich he could pay it all back.

Instead of listening to the concerns of the disciples and friends who had gathered around him, Lancaster tended to listen to the adoring fans who glorified him from a distance. As one supporter wrote, Lancaster was more than just another teacher. His reform plans promised a total transformation of society. As this poet wrote to Lancaster,

> Knowledge extending wide her genial reign;
> Virtue, religion, learning, heavenly truth,
> Implanted in the minds of British youth,
> By thee whose liberal acts and fruitful mind,
> Proclaim thee-BENEFACTOR OF MANKIND.[25]

Lancaster wasted no time on false modesty. He agreed wholeheartedly with the adulation he received.

Though Lancaster never recognized the dangers of his reckless spending and endless borrowing, the sober-minded reformers who had gathered around him in the Royal Lancasterian Society soon realized they had a problem. Lancaster's mounting debts and public behavior promised to create a major scandal and ruin the reputation of the Borough Road School and Lancasterian education as a whole. By 1806, Lancaster had stopped focusing on the day-to-day administration of his school. Instead, he flitted about giving speeches and opening new schools. He rarely put in the hard work of making sure his new schools were administered well. Soon, as one aggrieved parent complained, students in at least one of Lancaster's boarding schools were utterly neglected, infested with lice and clothed in rags. Students learned nothing, and even the monitors were "slovenly."[26] Lancaster could not—he would not—maintain a public image as a devoted and humble servant of London's poor. He loved to be seen riding about town in expensive hired carriages, treating himself and his retinue to ridiculously extravagant bottles of "champaigne."[27] Even more worrisome, Lancaster's private behavior was more than scandalous; it was criminal. As Lancaster's supporters discovered, in the early years of his career Lancaster forced his students—his top students, the ones who lived with him and served as teachers in his school—to submit to a gruesome regime of physical, emotional, and sexual abuse.

Even before they became aware of these abuses, the members of the committee decided to act. At first, the committee was primarily worried about Lancaster's tendency to accept donations and take on debt in the name of the school. In 1807, they sat Lancaster down and told him to change. During this first intervention, Lancaster seemed shocked, but he eventually agreed. He broke down in tears and begged the committee for help. They put him on a strict budget, and he promised he would no longer solicit any donations or take on any debt. This first intervention seemed to work. He cried. They all hugged; they "fell on one another's shoulders in tears."[28] Lancaster promised to stop opening new schools and to focus on the existing ones. He agreed to it all. He promised he would change.[29]

He didn't. His behavior only got worse. For several years, the committee tried to clean up his messes: paying off his debts, calming aggrieved parents, and promoting the idea of universal Lancasterian education for all poor children. In 1812, Lancaster finally exhausted their efforts when he broke his promises by opening yet another school in Tooting, just south of London. Once again, the committee confronted Lancaster and opened up the financial books. After much complaint, Lancaster agreed that he could not manage himself. Following yet another tumultuous meeting, he agreed to sign over his control of Borough Road School to the committee. He even agreed to work there as a superintendent for a salary.[30] Perhaps he was relieved that so far no responsible adult had discovered the full extent of his abuses.

The 1812 agreement was a good deal for Lancaster. He would receive a steady income and still have time to make speeches and promote his publications. At the end of this meeting, there were more tears, hugs all around, and another round of seemingly heartfelt promises by Lancaster to abide by the new rules. But it didn't last either. Almost as soon as he left the room, Lancaster began railing against the committee, charging them with stealing his school and kicking him out without any cause.[31] Lancaster howled that the committee had put him in "danger of his life" by forcing him to work in a subpar school building, "in a room neither wind, nor weather tight."[32] He complained to the London public that the committee had left him "hungry, cold and damp." He wrote with ferocious underlining that he had taken on endless "sufferings and oppressions" only in the hope that his agony might somehow help the children of the poor.[33]

By August 1813, the desperate committee called for royal arbitration. Sponsored by the king, Lancaster's earliest royal supporters—the Duke of Bedford and Lord Somerville—agreed to hear both sides. Unfortunately for Lancaster, there really weren't two sides. The committee explained the tortuous history of Lancaster's increasingly outrageous behavior. Lancaster had nothing to say for himself. The decision was clear. Even without knowledge of Lancaster's abusive treatment of his monitors, the royal arbitrators agreed with the committee on every point.

The committee soon realized that things were much worse than they feared. In early 1814, a former apprentice told one committee member that Lancaster habitually abused his live-in monitors. As the boy related, Lancaster—the same man who had ostentatiously forbidden corporal punishment in his famous school—"used to flog his apprentices for his own amusement."[34]

Even the long-frustrated committee members found these revelations shocking. They had grown accustomed to Lancaster's self-defeating behavior, his tendency to borrow extravagantly and spend lavishly. They knew he would eventually apologize if confronted, that he would promise to mend his financial ways and rededicate himself to the mission of education. By 1814, though, they also knew that Lancaster would turn right around and do it all again. They knew that Lancaster's tears and apologies would be followed by bitter public recriminations and a resumption of his follies.

The stories of physical abuse seemed to constitute a different magnitude of sin. The committee formed a formal subcommittee to investigate. They wanted Lancaster to cooperate, so they convinced committee member Francis Place to lead the investigation. By the 1810s, Place was already well-known in London as an ardent social reformer. He had gotten involved with Lancaster's school as yet another way to level the playing field between rich and poor—between worker and owner. More important than his radical past, Place became the perfect go-between with Lancaster because, unlike the rest of the committee members, he had been able to maintain a reasonably friendly relationship with Lancaster.[35]

The subcommittee interviewed as many monitors and former monitors as they could find. They made sure to interview "lads" who had taught at the

Borough Road School but did not personally know the monitor who had first brought these charges to light. In the end, the charges against Lancaster escalated far beyond mere physical abuse. To the subcommittee's dismay, boys told dismally similar stories about Lancaster's behavior. Eventually, the committee felt they had heard enough. They had so much testimony from so many disparate sources that, in Place's evaluation, it "put the matter beyond all doubt."[36]

Though one of Lancaster's claims for his system was that it abolished the need for traditional corporal punishment, it turned out that he had long beaten advanced students "with a rod when they displeased him." These beatings took place at his home, not in the school, and they took a disturbing sexual turn. According to several witnesses who had lived and worked with Lancaster, he could be suddenly "displeased" at any time, seizing on his anger as an excuse to beat the boys. He sometimes turned the beatings into a sexual assault. "His practice," Francis Place explained, "was to hug and caress and kiss [the boys] to induce them to consent to be flogged. Sometimes one boy kissed another, sometimes he laid them down upon the sopha [sic] and sometimes several of them stood before the line with their trousers down and their shirts tucked up around their waists while Lancaster flogged them."[37] According to Place's investigation, this abuse took place over years, with the victims ranging in age from twelve to eighteen years. It was part of the price to be paid by Lancaster's apprentices for their training in Lancaster's system.

The committee confronted Lancaster in early 1814 with the overwhelming evidence. They hoped, in Francis Place's recollection, that Lancaster "might be induced to withdraw himself." They dreamed of paying Lancaster off with a pension. That way, they could continue the good work of building tuition-free schools for all. They could expand the network of Lancasterian schools without subjecting students to the abuses of Lancaster himself.[38]

Lancaster would not budge. He refused to admit to anything. He was, as Place recalled, "very callous." In the end, the committee failed. "Nothing was concluded" about Lancaster's abuse. The committee was so eager to maintain the good name of Lancasterian education that it aided and abetted Lancaster's crimes.[39] By April 1814, at the end of a long process of arbitration and investigation, the committee allowed Lancaster to go his own way. They separated themselves legally and publicly from Lancaster, renaming themselves the British and Foreign School Society. Arbitrators recognized their legal control over all the school properties, including Borough Road, and Lancaster was banned from all its schools. He was prohibited from taking donations or borrowing money in the name of Borough Road. But that was the extent of his punishment by the committee. Lancaster was free to move on, to open new schools, and to accept the invitation in 1818 to supervise the implementation of Lancasterian reform in the United States.

2
Children of the City

The reformers who invited Lancaster to bring his supposed miracle to the United States were similar, in many ways, to the Londoners who tried to save Lancasterianism from Lancaster himself. Roberts Vaux never ran for elected office, but as the product of Philadelphia's Quaker elite, Vaux had a hand in every philanthropic program of his time. He poured himself into every manner of charitable work, hoping to bring his city into the modern age. He helped organize hospitals for the sick, asylums for the poor, and museums for the curious.[1] But none of those institutions were as vital, Vaux believed, as new modern public schools. Those schools held the key to transforming Philadelphia into a true republican utopia by turning its hordes of youthful street urchins into productive, respectful citizens. As a young man just beginning his career, Vaux had briefly volunteered at a city Lancasterian school.[2] His experience teaching for America confirmed Vaux's conviction that Lancaster's system could transform Philadelphia. Later, as president of the Controllers of Philadelphia's public schools, Vaux agonized about the threat of unschooled children, whom he called "beggars or petty depredators." Without some way to corral and control these "vicious children," Vaux warned, the city itself would be doomed.[3]

Luckily for Philadelphia, Vaux believed, the Lancasterian system would solve all their problems at once. If they imported the "system of Lancaster," Vaux told Pennsylvania's leaders in 1817, they could slash the costs of public schools, bringing the dream of universal education within the commonwealth's financial reach. Lancaster's system was not only cheaper, Vaux assured them; it was also better. It taught "habits of attention, order, and obedience." It "inclined" students to act in accordance with the "christian religion." And there were plenty of "accurate data" that proved that the system worked, according to Vaux. It was more than just a tweak; it was a "sort of miracle" that could solve all of their problems at once, for less. The children of the poor, even the crowds of waifs that thronged Philadelphia's streets, would soon develop "correct national feeling and character."[4] Like city leaders around the world at the time, Vaux thought that Lancasterian schools represented the possibilities of a new modern age, one in which ancient problems of poverty and vice could be swept away by the wonders of science and technology. "The Lancasterian System," Vaux believed, was more than just a new method to teach literacy and math. It was a truly revolutionary solution to the problems of modern city life, "a branch of that wonderful Providence, which is destined to usher in the millennial day."[5]

Vaux's enthusiasm and his anxiety were shared by elite reformers in other US cities, reformers similarly apprehensive about their cities' youth and similarly transfixed by the vision of a cheap Lancasterian solution. In New York City, for example, Mayor De Witt Clinton led the campaign to revolutionize the city's schools. Clinton never wondered whether he was the right person for the job. As the nephew of the prominent governor and vice president George Clinton, De Witt was born into a family of wealth and influence. His career seemed to confirm his destiny to lead: from state senator to US senator to mayor and then to governor, Clinton spent his adult life in charge.

And no one—not even Roberts Vaux—was more enthusiastic about the possibilities of Lancasterian reform in American cities than Mayor Clinton. As Clinton put it in 1809, Lancaster had done nothing less than "form and perfect a system" that would bring the "light of Heaven" to "the humble and the depressed."[6] For Clinton, the modern world embodied new possibilities, and Lancasterian methods simply put those possibilities to work in the realm of public education.

Vaux and Clinton were anything but unusual in their quick embrace of Lancasterian education as a solution to their intense urban anxieties. As Clinton remembered, at the turn of the nineteenth century a host of "benevolent persons" grew concerned about the "neglected education of the poor."[7] Yet the interest of Vaux, Clinton, and their Lancasterian allies was never solely benevolent. They certainly feared for the young people exposed to the dangers lurking in modern cities, but they also worried about the dangers those young people could cause. Their fear was the driving force behind

The streets of New York City held plenty of dangers for any young person. From *Some Very Gentle Touches* (1806), a book meant to warn New York's children of the rural dangers of modern urban life. Courtesy of the American Antiquarian Society.

American enthusiasm for Lancasterian reform. Lancaster's simplistic ideas about schools made such a big impact in the United States because they promised a solution—a cheap solution—to that fear. Lancaster's ideas offered a supposedly modern, systematic answer to the problems that plagued America's cities in the first decades of the 1800s. They promised to patch the holes in the amateurish educational safety net that elites had begun to construct.

Moreover, the allure of Lancaster's system—for city leaders in the mold of Clinton and Vaux—was that it promised a radical improvement in city life without calling for radical changes in city leadership. Like so much else about Lancaster's vision, it was a false promise. Elites like Vaux and Clinton always assumed that they were the ones who had the power and the benevolence to solve their cities' modern problems, but by the end of their lives, in 1828 for Clinton and 1836 for Vaux, the collapse of the Lancasterian experiment proved that the enthusiasm of benevolent elites was nowhere near sufficient to tackle the challenges of modern city life.

All Alive with the Swine

At the time, US cities were more than just an ocean away from London. In the first years of the 1800s they were a world apart in their status as modern urban centers. Unlike London, with its ancient roots and modern industrial innovations, American cities were just growing out of their role as jumbled colonial towns. The pressures of modern urban life were still pushing cheek by jowl against the traditions of rural villages. Yes, reformers like De Witt Clinton worried specifically about the threats posed to children and by children in "Great cities," which he called the "nurseries and hot-beds of crimes," but there was no disguising the fact that the greatness of New York and other American cities in the early 1800s could not compare with that of London.[8] They remained, in many ways, provincial backwaters. As late as 1806, for instance, New Yorkers had to be on the alert for attacks from herds of vicious wild pigs. As one aspiring poet put it, in 1806 New York was "a City most wise and most fine," yet it still had "streets all alive with the swine."[9]

Unlike London's well-heeled reformers who nursed an arrogant pride in their world-leading city, America's urban leaders knew that their cities remained muddy, provincial, and merely ambitious. Yet the fears of urban elites in America and England shared some common elements. Modern life brought a host of new realities, notably including a new set of ideas about the nature of childhood. Like their partners and friends in London, reformers in New York, Philadelphia, Boston, and other American cities worried about the special susceptibility of children to the dangers of a modern city. Yes, packs of aggressive hogs were a threat—to adults and children alike. But just as a boar might be a mere nuisance for a fully grown adult but a life-threatening menace for a small child, some of the perceived dangers in America's cities were considered to be harmful specifically to the cities' children.

Reformers in Lancaster's generation were the first to confront this uniquely modern crisis: could they offer all the children of their cities an education that would save them from the enticing clutches of the city streets? Though they trusted the old hierarchies that put them in charge, elites did not trust the old solutions. They did not believe that traditional arrangements could provide the answers for modern problems. In that much, at least, they were right.

At the time, cities such as New York, Philadelphia, and Boston were different from what they would soon become. As historian Thomas Bender has noted, in 1800 the six largest cities in the United States were mere "specks" in a mostly rural nation. At the time, those six cities had a total population of only 183,000 out of a national total of five million.[10] Yet the cities were growing fast. Between 1810 and 1830, for example, Albany grew from 10,762 residents to 24,209; Philadelphia, from 53,722 to 80,462; and Baltimore, from 46,555 to 80,620.[11] The numbers may have been fairly small, especially compared to the decades of truly explosive growth that followed, but elite reformers fretted about their "specks" as if they were malignant sores on the body politic. They did not have to be large to be worrisome.

American elites had long worried about the ruination of their republican countryside by the spread of urban problems.[12] Elites looked askance at cities as agglomerations of vice and violence, harboring clusters of the poor, the Irish, the criminal.[13] De Witt Clinton wasn't the only one worried about cities as sinister nurseries. If yeoman farms were the birthplaces of republican virtue, many elites saw the modern city as the place virtue went to die. Not all of the anxieties of urban elites were imaginary. Modern cities—even relatively small ones in the United States—really had acquired some unsavory elements. Streets occasionally really did become battlegrounds, with riots fueled by "bitter ethnic hatred."[14] Business owners complained that they were thronged with "crowds of idle boys and disorderly persons."[15] And by the 1820s, as historian Thomas Gilfoyle has uncovered, there were at least two hundred brothels in New York City alone.[16]

Among America's urban reformers, however, cities were also seen as the solution to their own modern problems. The right kind of education system was assumed to have the power to overcome urban poverty. As early as 1789, for instance, pundits were calling for a new kind of public education for cities as "the best way of preventing the existence of the poor."[17] By 1817, reformers could simultaneously condemn modern cities as "disgusting exhibitions of human depravity and wretchedness" while promising that "good instruction will secure the morals of the young."[18]

Lancasterian reformers shared these worries and these dreams. By the first two decades of the 1800s, they already believed that their cities were enduring unmanageable growth. In 1814, for instance, the founders of New York's Free School Society worried about "a large number of children" that could overwhelm the city's limited network of tuition-free charity schools, schools traditionally operated by Protestant churches. These "destitute" children were adrift, "wandering about the streets."[19] New York's philanthropists looked askance at the "great and increasing number of poor children."[20] Frozen out of school and church, the children would grow up without God or literacy, reformers assumed, without any hope for an upstanding civic life.

New York's elites were not the only ones to see crowds of children—simultaneously threatening and endangered—when they looked out their windows. It was a common lament in all of the cities of the United States. In Savannah, Georgia, a group of "several philanthropic Ladies" worried about the "large and increasing number of children" on the streets of their city.[21] In Baltimore, even opponents of public schooling assumed that their flourishing city needed some way to control "the growing numbers of disruptive elements in the population."[22] The elite reformers of the era cannot be blamed for not knowing the future. They were not aware that the growth of their cities would seem tame in retrospect, that the crowds of the 1800s, 1810s, and 1820s would seem scanty by the 1840s, let alone the 1870s. No matter what the future held, in the first decades of the 1800s urban elites had good reason to already be anxious. Even though the numbers of children in America's cities would soon grow enormously, they were already significant. Moreover, it was not the absolute number of children that mattered; it was the number of children from low-income families relative to the number of free-school options that caused high anxiety among urban reformers. In the first two decades of the 1800s, there were simply not enough spots available.

In making more schools available for those thronging hordes of urban children, Lancasterian reformers thought of themselves as the best friends of the poor, but their language betrayed their deep distrust of the people they promised to help. Joseph Lancaster, for example, called London's city children "miserable and almost friendless objects."[23] Likewise, Lancasterian reformers in Pennsylvania described low-income children in Philadelphia as "the ignorant and vicious multitudes."[24] Yet reformers imagined themselves as the only bulwark of protection for the children they insulted. They shared stories of the dangers that lurked for children who could not afford to attend school. Children were regularly exposed to woeful sights in the city's streets, what Mayor Clinton called the "dreadful examples of vice."[25]

Those examples of "vice," however, were far from the worst threat that lurked. In 1813, for example, a prominent New York court case brought to light the lurid and brutal story of thirteen-year-old Betty Whiteman. An adult trafficker on the prowl for more girls to staff her brothel held Whiteman down as she was raped. After that assault, young Whiteman was forced into a life of prostitution.[26]

As gruesome as Whiteman's story was, the city's elites feared that it was a sign of the times. Moreover, they knew that children in America's cities could do more than suffer grievous crimes; they could also commit them. Throughout the first decades of the 1800s, elites worried about increasing violence from youth gangs. Like the story of Betty Whiteman, a few high-profile cases stood out. In 1825, New York businessman Henry Lambert was murdered by a group of children, the "Spring Street Fencibles." According to reports, around 1:00 a.m. on June 3, the youths refused to clear out of the way of Lambert's carriage. Instead, they "blew cigar smoke in the gentlemen's faces, called them dandies, and tried to trip them." One punched Lambert in the stomach, a blow from which Lambert eventually died.[27]

No matter how rare these kinds of stories were—and they were both extremely unusual—they exacerbated elite anxieties. Sensational tales were common in the press, told and retold in the social circles in which reformers moved, in hushed and euphemistic terms perhaps, but the gruesome possibilities of crime were all too clear. There were simply too many children on the loose. Reformers worried about the terrible consequences of wild packs of near-feral children, both for the children themselves and for their city as a whole. It was a double-headed danger: without schools, children had nowhere healthy to go. And without a formal education, even a basic one in reading and writing, unemployable children could easily sink into criminality. Reformers were comfortable with their assumptions, namely that they were the ones who had to solve the problem and that free schools represented the solution. But those assumptions led them to a decidedly uncomfortable conclusion: it seemed that there was no way to provide free schools for all the children who needed them.

Schools for a New Nation

It's not that there weren't already plenty of schools in American cities. In the years just before and just after 1800, American cities had lots of schools. If families could afford it, they could hire private tutors for their children or send them to expensive boarding schools in the United States or Europe. For most families, those options were out of reach financially. However, there were many affordable options. The norm was what the leading historian of the era called "common pay schools," schools that charged a modest tuition, within the reach of most families.[28] For families that could not afford even those low rates, churches and charitable organizations offered some courses in basic literacy and math. At the turn of the century, elites in philanthropic organizations scrambled to create more, but they quickly discovered that their desperate efforts would not be enough.

It was not for lack of trying. In Philadelphia, a group of well-heeled white men came together in 1799 to found the Philadelphia Society for the Free Instruction of Indigent Boys. It was a ferociously dilettantish group. Each of the nine members contributed one dollar per month to fund a school. Membership was at least as much a mark of social prestige as of administrative savvy. At first, they opened a night school for a few dozen students. In 1801, they changed their name to the Philadelphia Society for the Establishment and Support of Charity Schools and expanded their efforts.[29]

In New York, a similar group of elites organized themselves in 1805 into the New York Free School Society. Originally, the leaders chose a more burdensome but informative name, "The Society for establishing a Free school in the city of New-York, for the education of such poor children as do not belong to or are not provided for by any religious society." The thirty-seven white male members, including New York mayor De Witt Clinton, were selected primarily for their willingness to fund the society's work or to lend their well-known names to fundraising tasks.[30]

Elite white men were not the only ones who tried to organize their way out of modern urban dilemmas. In New York, a group of white women began, in their words, "visiting the neglected abodes of the poor." What they found there shocked them. Like most reformers of the era, they assumed that the best single intervention they could make was to offer basic literacy instruction for girls. With the proper education, this "Female Association" hoped to save poor children from "their future helplessness and distress."[31]

African American elites also opened and supported schools for low-income Black children. In Philadelphia, for example, in 1804 African American leader Richard Allen formed the Society of Free People of Colour for Promoting the Instruction and School Education of Children of African Descent.[32] Black teachers, too, often waived tuition payments for poorer students who studied alongside paying students. For instance, even after the white-led Pennsylvania Abolition Society decided that "it is not practical at present to have black children properly taught by a black person," Black leaders in Philadelphia such as Absalom Jones continued to teach Black children on their own.[33]

In New York, African American elites allied with organizations such as the white-led Manumission Society, which opened the first "African Free School" in 1785. African Americans in New York began their own groups too, such as the New York African Society for Mutual Relief, founded in 1808.[34] These organizations were dedicated to providing schooling for all members of the African American community, free or enslaved, relatively affluent or poor.[35]

These organizations and others like them scrambled to scrape together enough money to operate schools that did not charge tuition. As ever, public money was difficult to secure. Some cities, most famously Boston, had a long history of government-funded schools. Those schools were open, in theory, to the general public. By 1651, eight communities in Massachusetts had established such schools.[36] In 1789, Massachusetts codified its traditional commitment to providing tax funding for schools, and the city of Boston passed a similar municipal law the same year. Boston's 1789 law established a school committee and devoted 20 percent of its annual budget to school funding.[37]

After the Revolution, several states inserted provisions for publicly funded schools into their new constitutions. Pennsylvania, for example, required schools to be established in each county, with teacher salaries paid out of public coffers.[38] Some states specified requirements for schools. New York State's 1795 School Act divided up state funds by county. Counties were charged with raising local money to match the state allocation. New York City was singled out in the 1795 law and charged with opening a "charity school" for all students, "whether the children taught in such charity school shall be the children of White parents or descended from Africans or Indians."[39] The laws in each city and state varied, but the principles were similar. Like Philadelphia's law of 1802, the idea was that government had an interest—a "public" interest—in funding schools for children unable to pay tuition.[40]

How successful were these laws? To this question at least, urban reformers knew the answer: never successful enough. It may have been legally required in some places, but in the first few years of the nineteenth century reformers could not figure out how to create enough seats for all the children who needed them. More precisely, they could not figure out how to pay for schools that did not charge tuition, or how to pay all the tuitions that poor families could not pay themselves. It is difficult to say with certainty exactly how many charity schools there were in cities at the time. For one thing, without any concern for future historians, people used a variety of terms to describe them. Reformers and philanthropists talked about "free" schools, "charity" schools, and "public" schools, often in the same breath. Nor did they draw bright lines between types of schools. In Philadelphia, for example, school teacher Arthur Donaldson operated a successful school for African American youth. He charged modest tuition, but he also appealed to both the city and the wealthy to help him serve families that could not afford it.[41] By any fair definition, Donaldson's privately run, tuition-charging school did not count as a "free" school, "charity" school, or "public" school, but some of his tuition-paying students likely had their fees paid by philanthropists, rather than by their parents.[42]

At the time, like Arthur Donaldson, reformers in America's cities combined funding from a variety of sources, muddying any clear count of the number of free schools. In Boston, for example, a group of sixty-seven Black citizens petitioned the city in 1800 to help pay the costs of their segregated school. Their bid was initially rejected, but in 1806 white city leaders grudgingly agreed to contribute $200 annually.[43]

These efforts contributed to the patchwork of tuition-free schools that existed in larger cities, but they only underlined how impossible it seemed to provide teachers for all the poor students who needed them. Without charging tuition, there did not seem to be enough money to keep enough schools afloat. Yet reformers kept trying. Despite imperfect historical records, we can draw some tentative conclusions about the numbers of charity schools in different cities. For one thing, even before the creation of separate charity schools, there was a long tradition of offering a few free seats to low-income students in pay schools.[44] As early as 1750, for example, Benjamin Franklin specified that his Philadelphia Academy should include a few charity spots.[45] The creation of separate charity schools, however, took longer. In New York, the Manumission Society opened a free school for Black children in 1785, followed by a second in 1794.[46] Similar free schools for African American children operated in Baltimore and Philadelphia by 1793.[47] For white children, historian Carl F. Kaestle estimated that there were at least six charity schools run by churches in New York City by 1796.[48] Before the Lancasterian school expansion in Philadelphia in 1818, there was one nondenominational charity school for white children, opened by reformers in 1801.[49] Quakers were more active in the City of Brotherly Love. In 1796, for example, Ann Parrish opened the Aimwell School. By 1799, Quakers operated at least fourteen free schools in Philadelphia.[50] Across the color line, reform organizations operated at least seven separate schools for African Americans in Philadelphia by 1805, including pay and free schools for both adults and children.[51]

Other cities had different traditions. In Boston, for example, by 1800 the city operated seven grammar schools, but in practice these were not accessible to the poorest citizens, though in theory all were welcome. Instead, until 1818 Boston's famous "public" schools required students to have a basic literacy education when they started at age seven, an accomplishment beyond the means of most low-income families. Though Boston's earliest public schools were legally open to all, in reality they served the male children of the city's white elites.[52] In New York, although the school law of 1795 had specifically authorized the opening of a "charity" school, there were not many nonchurch charity options before the Lancasterian revolution took off in 1806.[53] One exception was the free school operated for white girls by the Female Association, which opened in 1800.[54]

Until Lancasterian enthusiasm sparked a wave of new charity schools—a wave that peaked when Lancaster himself moved to the United States in

1818—philanthropists, churches, and governments simply could not square the circle. Without money from tuition, they could not figure out a way to pay for enough free schools.

An Educational Competition

For urban elites, the situation seemed desperate. In their minds, the case was clear: either they could provide enough free schools for all low-income children, or they could endure the crimes and attacks of the young. The problem, at least as reformers saw it, was not simply that unschooled young people would learn nothing at all. To the contrary, reformers feared that street children were getting far too much education, of the wrong sort. Reformers fretted that the patchy and inadequate charity school networks could not compete, educationally, with the lessons children learned on city streets.

As Philadelphia reformers warned in 1810, the alternative to free schools was not simply a lack of education but a choice between formal school education and "street education." As they assumed, "a street education is a dreadful one."[55] The assumption was a common one among reformers.[56] Lancaster himself had warned that children on the street would pick up a "pernicious and dangerous" education.[57] And street education had a decided advantage. In frank moments, reformers admitted that street lessons were infinitely more attractive to children than lessons in basic literacy. As De Witt Clinton put it, children left on their own would be drawn in by the "alluring forms" of crime.[58]

In the first decades of the 1800s, the desperation among American urban elites was palpable. It might have been less intense if elites saw themselves as merely offering optional aid, expending the munificence of disinterested benevolence, and providing a nice but not necessary service. It might have been different if elites felt they were dealing with an old problem, a problem for which they had traditional solutions. Instead, a deep anxiety filled the pages of philanthropic reports, an anxiety bred from a sense that providing schools for the poor was not merely a boon but a desperate and losing competition with a far more attractive type of education. Moreover, the rhetoric of elites betrayed their profound anxiety at the newness of their dilemma. Modern cities had grown wild, in malignant directions, offering new temptations without providing any new solutions. What would happen if poor children were left without schools? As Philadelphia reformers assumed by the 1820s, without "public schools," young children would be "wandering about the streets and wharves." Instead of learning to write, do math, pray, and prepare for legitimate work, the Philadelphians warned, children were "becoming adepts in the arts of begging, skillful in petty thefts, and familiar with obscene and profane language." When such children grew to adulthood, they would not lack an education. No, they would be well prepared for all-too-successful careers in the "highest grades of crime."[59]

In the imaginations of these reformers, the best response to a modern problem was a modern solution: universal schooling. For the poor, reformers assumed, education must be wrenched from the hands of prostitutes and thieves and placed under the control of elites like themselves. But schools were not the only answer. Modern publishing technology also offered new ways to communicate with endangered city kids. A surge of children's books warned children about the dangers of a street education. One 1810 book, *Cries of Philadelphia*—unapologetically plagiarized from an earlier New York edition, which was itself shamelessly copied from an earlier London edition—explained that some children had to make money on the streets. One example was the honest and upright girls who sold matches. The anonymous authors praised these "few little girls" who performed an "honest" and "useful" service. Yet the "match girls" lived lives of "distress," stalking frozen city streets in order to earn a few desperate pennies.[60] The Philadelphia edition added a warning for children about the dangers of "punch." Coming to the big city for the first time, children needed to know that some of the new things they would see would be perfectly safe. Oranges and lemons, for example, were healthy. Punch was different. Yes, it was made from fruit, but children must be wary of this "dangerous drink" that could get them drunk and turn them into mere "object[s] of pity."[61]

City streets could be dangerous for anybody. They could lure adults as much as children with punch and prostitution. However, when it came to children specifically, in the first years of the 1800s a new attitude had become more widespread. It is very difficult to trace the emergence of broad cultural attitudes about youth—at least in part because over time these attitudes can come to seem simply "natural"—but American reformers at the time were participating in a changing vision of the nature of childhood. On both sides of the Atlantic, as William J. Reese has argued, educational thinking was driven by a new romantic vision of what it meant to be young, an emerging "cult of childhood."[62] And, as historians have described, in the

Anglo-American world attitudes toward youth were changing in complicated ways. For one thing, young people in the colonies grew increasingly independent throughout the years surrounding the American Revolution. Old ideas about control and ownership of young people grew harder to maintain. Traditions of apprenticeship and indentured servitude no longer seemed to fit with children's modern rights. It was not simply that revolutionary attitudes bred new expectations of freedom for American youth, though those new attitudes certainly played their part. In total, the changes were far broader than that and occurred in fits and starts over a much longer period of time.[63]

In addition, these changes were not only in a single, simple direction. America's children were growing more independent, true, but they were also becoming something different, contrasting with earlier European traditions about the nature of youth. They were increasingly seen as needing a unique sort of custodial care. These complex ideas had been expressed most articulately by thinkers such as John Locke and Francis Hutcheson. Children, the new thinking went, were not just smaller, less experienced adults. Rather, childhood was a uniquely important time, a malleable time in which the young must be steered, formed, and directed, precisely because children needed to learn how to manage their modern independence.[64]

In the new United States, old ideas of control and ownership of children were giving way to modern notions of custodial care, of nurturing the young as they developed their ability to be truly independent. The social and legal implications were enormous. Even as late as 1811, for example, a two-year-old child in Pennsylvania was considered legally capable of signing her own legal forms.[65] By that time, however, it was far more common for Americans to view childhood as something different, something that required adult supervision. Most reformers came to assume with greater frequency that only adults could be held legally responsible for their decisions. They also came to assume that children needed to learn how to handle their eventual responsibilities. Whatever guidance children received would determine their adult futures, whether that future held legal employment and upright citizenship or plundering, thieving, and prostitution.

The reformers who embraced Joseph Lancaster's ideas were certainly people of their time. They assumed that children in their growing cities were particularly susceptible to the influence of education, whether that was school education or the education they could receive in the streets. In children's uniquely impressionable state, reformers thought, the lessons they learned would shape the rest of their lives. If they fell for the allurements of crime, they would learn to be criminals. If they tasted the delights of punch, they would become drunkards. If, on the other hand, they could be educated in a network of schools, if they could be taught to read and pray properly, they would learn valuable economic and social skills. More importantly, as one scholar put it, elites at the time assumed that a successful formal education could make children "safe from serfdom, pauperism, and slavery."[66] The stakes were enormously high. That was why, as historian Benjamin Justice has noted, questions of schooling and formal education became a "central preoccupation of intellectuals" at the turn of the nineteenth century.[67]

Those intellectuals felt frustrated. They had already done so much, only to find their efforts inadequate. They had formed benevolent organizations and had recruited local elites as subscribers. They had solicited funds from governments and philanthropists alike. They had passed laws, opened schools, made speeches. Yet it was not enough. They could not create enough tuition-free schools to accommodate the children who needed them. Every day, they feared, the streets of their modern cities were chewing up the innocent young and spitting out packs of thieves, prostitutes, and murderers. What they needed was something dramatic, something new. They needed a modern solution to the modern problems of urban life. Like their elite counterparts in London, when they heard of Joseph Lancaster's new kind of school, they rejoiced. They rushed to read his books—or at least read about them—and implement his system. Lancaster's promises fulfilled all the dreams of American reformers, and reformers swallowed them whole. In 1818, leaders in New York invited Lancaster to the United States to help spread and improve their networks of modern new schools. The timing was perfect. Lancaster had long since worn out his welcome in his native city, so he jumped at the chance.

3
Mr. Lancaster's System

Even back before Lancaster fled to New York, in the first bloom of his British success, some people asked difficult questions. Writing from a town about a hundred miles from London, one ardent Lancasterian told Lancaster in 1810 that he and "some persons in this place" shared the dream. They had read Lancaster's manual describing his wondrous system—the very latest edition having rolled off Lancaster's press in London. They had followed up and ordered "a complete set of lessons" from Borough Road. They wanted to open a new, modern Lancasterian school in their town to educate three hundred boys. They had faith that Lancaster's system could bring a glorious new day to their town, that it could deliver universal basic education at a price the town could afford. But some town leaders still expressed doubts. They wondered if the system really worked as described, or if it was "only theoretical."[1]

They were right to wonder. Lancaster's greatest successes came not in his schoolrooms but in his imagination. His endless stream of manuals and brochures described his system in painstaking detail. On paper, the system was always perfect and always achieving greater heights of perfection. The same words kept cropping up: "scientific," "efficient," "perfected," "economical," and "modern." Lancaster promised a complete prepackaged educational success, one that could be implemented anywhere by anyone. The system as promised never really matched the reality of Lancasterian schools, but the promise itself was what mattered at first. Before we get to the resoundingly anticlimactic story of Lancaster's arrival in the United States, we need to look at what his American hosts thought Lancaster represented: the promise of Lancaster's modern, transformational system.

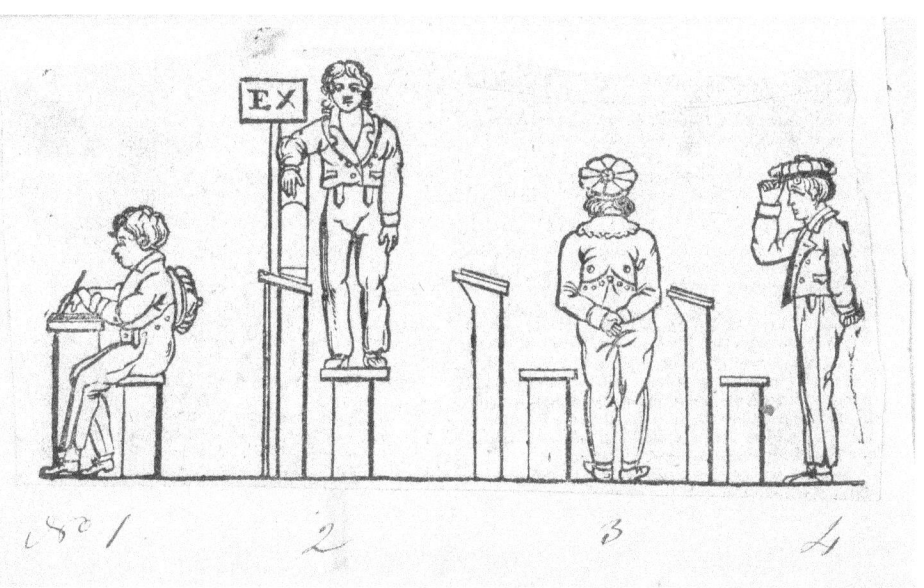

Lancaster promised a system of perfect behavior. From his notebooks. Courtesy of the American Antiquarian Society.

That system promised ultimate, unflappable classroom order. It assigned every student and teacher a role in the classroom. Minute by minute it charted exactly who would say what, when they would say it, and how everyone would respond. It laid out in blueprint-like detail the new technological gadgets that allowed such efficiency and precision. It explained the marvelous way students would embrace their assigned procedures, without any need for the rod or ferule. Perhaps most intoxicating, on paper the system required very little money to start and offered revolutionary results.

Joseph Lancaster relished describing the actions of his "theoretical" students. In one early notebook, for example, he sketched out the activities of his students in meticulous detail. In his imagination, his system eliminated any possibility of misbehavior or mistake. He described student one, who was learning to write by drawing out his letters on an inexpensive sand table instead of using paper and pencil. Student two—a monitor—was using another piece of Lancasterian technology, the "Ex" sign. By displaying this sign, the monitor was communicating with perfect efficiency that he had examined his group of students "and waits further orders." Student three was ready to enter his seat for the day. Like all of Lancaster's theoretical students,

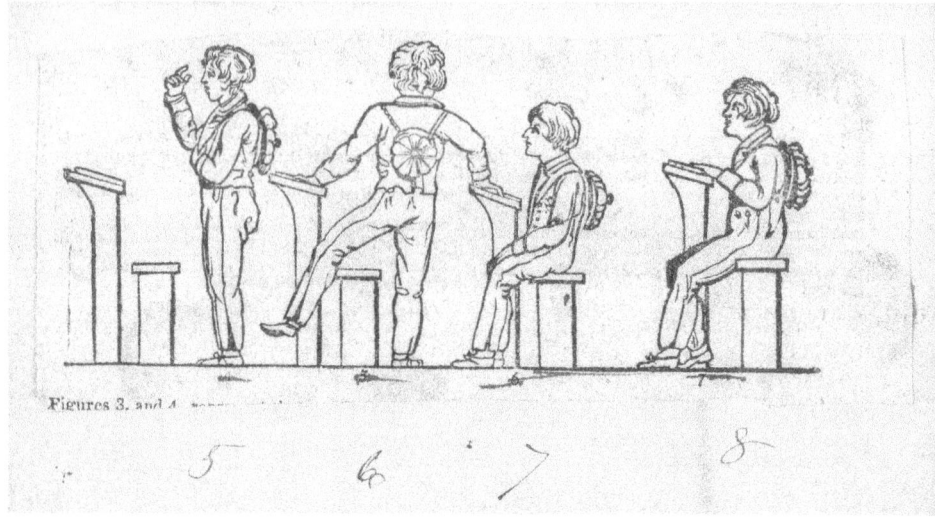

Theoretical students knew exactly what to do. From Lancaster's notebooks. Courtesy of the American Antiquarian Society.

student three knew at all times exactly what he was supposed to do. He entered the long bench as all students did, "with their hands behind them which position prevents all rudeness and disorder." Student four awaited a command from the chief monitor to remove his hat. As Lancaster fantasized, when the student hears the command, his hat will be "instantaneously taken off the whole school moving as if but one hand was moved by the will of the monitor who commands."[2]

In the earliest editions of his manuals, Lancaster offered a vision of a perfected system like the one sketched out in this notebook, with all educational problems anticipated and prevented. Students, monitors, and teachers all moved with precision throughout an intricately choreographed learning experience, every moment calculated to maximize education and minimize mischief. Lancaster's descriptions tell of students waiting breathlessly for their next command, seeking only and always to implement orders from above.

When students like number five heard the command "Sling Hats," they instantly took off their hats and let them dangle on strings around their necks. That way, no time was wasted in jostling for hats at the beginning or end of the day. Student six and the rest of the student body, meanwhile, had just heard the word "In" and "instantly entered their seats." As soon as they were seated, Lancaster's theoretical students heard another order, "Hands Down," and they sat patiently waiting with their hands in their laps, like student seven. As soon as they heard the word "Prepare," all the students moved their hands into position on their desks, like student eight. They were not yet to clean their slates, but they prepared their hands for that next maneuver.

Every moment and every activity were accounted for. There was no possibility of mistake; every monitor knew just as well as every student what came next. When the pupils heard, like student sixteen, to "Show Pencils," then of course "every pencil is immediately shown." With ease, the monitor scooped up the pencils and put them away. When the "Out" command was given, students (like student seventeen) left their benches and (like student eighteen) trooped off to the next activity.

It was beautiful to behold, even if Lancaster only beheld it in his imagination. At first, the fact that such lockstep perfection could obviously only take place with "theoretical" students was not much of an obstacle to Lancasterian enthusiasm. Ardent Lancasterians could go a long way on imagination alone, on their own fantasies about a perfected system for theoretical schooling. As the years went on, Lancaster amended some parts of his system to address the problems that cropped up with real-life Lancasterian schools. Lancaster's followers offered their own tweaks and improvements to the system as well. Working out the details of the system became a sort of parlor game, with Lancaster and other reformers offering endless improvements and elaborations. The one thing that never changed was the Lancasterian fascination with the details of the system. Educational problems could always be worked out in advance with the right combination of technology and methods.

For the first generation of Lancasterian reformers, the various editions of manuals and instruction booklets were the heart and soul of Lancaster's promise. For years, when they witnessed the widening gaps between theory and practice, they believed Lancaster's assurances that such growing pains were being worked out, that the system was being continually brought into an ever-more-perfect state. Among historians, too, these manuals and elaborate descriptions of an imaginary system have often been confused with school realities. It is easy to see why. The manuals were published in such

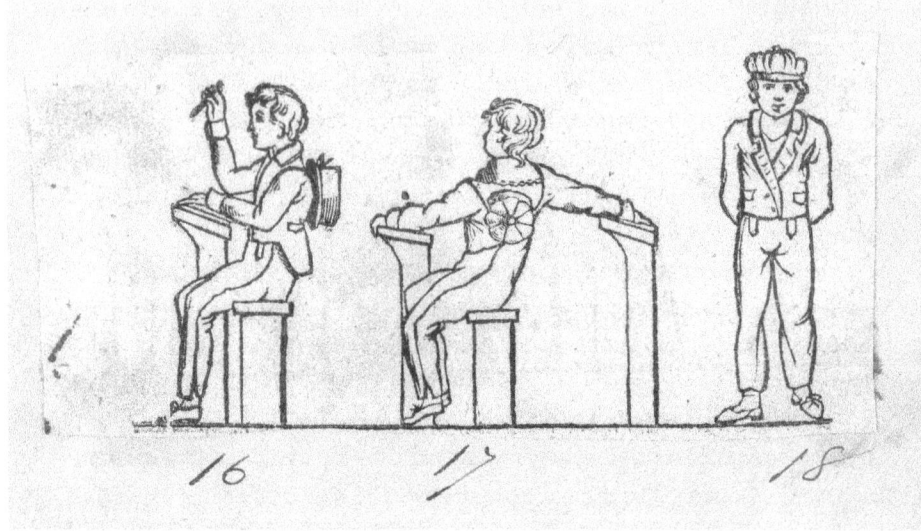

Lancaster imagined students moving in perfect synchronicity. From his notebooks. Courtesy of the American Antiquarian Society.

abundance that they fill archives and libraries. They seem to explain in satisfying detail what went on in Lancasterian schools. More than that, they explicitly claim to describe real scenes from real schools. They didn't, of course, and the gap between promise and reality conceals the true importance of the Lancasterian reform movement. The movement's long-term impact did not come about because of the detailed perfection of its plans and prescriptions. Those never worked as promised. However, the promise of perfect educational progress led to long-lasting changes; it led city leaders to think differently about their cities, their schools, and their responsibilities.

In chapters to come, we will see how the Lancasterian dream came true—sort of—in two prominent privately funded schools, as well as how the all-too-predictable crash of inflated Lancasterian expectations everywhere else led to the establishment of modern urban public school systems. This chapter examines the dream itself. The endless pamphlets that describe Lancaster's system may have been only theoretical, describing an imaginary system doomed to failure, yet their far-fetched precision gave reformers the confidence to overextend themselves and promise universal education for their cities. In the end, this confidence mattered most, not the details of the plans. And when it came to confidence, no one could beat Joseph Lancaster.

A Place for Everything

The pages of Lancaster's manuals reeked of confidence. He had published his first description of his school in 1803, with the typically long nineteenth-century title *Improvements in Education, as It Respects the Industrious Classes of the Community, Containing among Other Important Particulars, an Account of One Thousand Poor Children, Borough Road Southwark; and of the New System*. The publication proved popular enough that Lancaster reprinted it twice by 1805, with the third edition attracting worldwide attention. In 1807 the New York Free School Society reprinted Lancaster's book in an American edition. The New Yorkers cut some of the detailed financial accounts of the London edition and added a new preface about the history of their own organization, but they left the body of the book unchanged. In 1810, Lancaster and the Royal Lancasterian Society published a new manual, now titled *The British System of Education*. A US edition was printed in Georgetown in 1812. After they separated legally from Lancaster, the British and Foreign School Society published a Lancaster-free Lancasterian *Manual* in 1816. In 1817 and 1820, respectively, publishers in Philadelphia and New York printed their own editions of the 1816 *Manual*, updated with some minor changes. In Philadelphia, the title became *Manual of the System of Teaching Reading, Writing, Arithmetic, and Needle-Work, in the Elementary Schools of the British and Foreign School Society*. The New York edition tweaked the title slightly, calling it the *Manual of the Lancasterian System*. There was a cascade of editions and versions. In 1820, for example, William Tweed Dale of Albany, New York, published his *Manual of the Albany Lancaster School*. In Boston, Lancasterian teacher William B. Fowle published his *Manual of Mutual Instruction* in 1826. The next year, J. L. Rhees published a "pocket" edition in Philadelphia.

All these manuals, guidebooks, and instruction booklets traced the evolution of Lancaster's system. Some of the changes were minor, but some were more significant. In later editions, for example, Lancaster and the Lancasterians eliminated the shocking punishments that were such a popular part of his first editions. No matter what changed, one thing remained the same in every edition: they all chased after the dream of always-improving perfection. The full title of the 1827 manual from Philadelphia, for instance, was *A Pocket Manual of the Lancasterian System of Education in Its Most Improved State*. The system was always perfect, and it was always being perfected.

That was the promise of every edition: these books would lay out the very latest system of rules, roles, procedures, and technology that would make a Lancasterian school work.

Lancaster himself started with endless lists of rules for his students. There were general rules, rules for students, and rules for monitors. There were new rules, amended rules, and clarified rules. In his early notebooks, the lists seemed haphazard, with some rules addressing important administrative questions and others focusing on Lancaster's purely idiosyncratic concerns. All students, for example, were required to attend regularly. More than three weeks' absence could lead to expulsion. Yet just as important, apparently, was Lancaster's hat rule. Every student was absolutely required to add a string loop to their hat or cap. At the specified time, students would sling their hats off their heads, with the string allowing the hat to dangle around students' necks.[3]

Sometimes, one rule contradicted another. For instance, rule 1 on Lancaster's "rules for admission" was that everything would be free for students. Yet rule 7 was that parents should give money for slate pencils. Rule 8 specified that parents had to pay half the replacement costs if a student broke a writing slate. On this list, Lancaster did not hesitate to prescribe proper lifestyles for his students outside of school. Students were required to attend church of some sort, though the denomination was up to them and their families. Finally, inside of school, students were prohibited from having knives, marbles, or spinning tops.[4]

Lancaster also sketched out student rules. Students should arrive at school at nine in the morning and return after lunch at two in the afternoon. They must wash their hands, face, hair, and clothes and clean their shoes before leaving home. They were to be especially reverent when reading the Bible aloud, though otherwise silent in school. If they had to speak, they were to speak in whispers. As they came and went, they must do so "in a quiet and orderly manner." Obedience to the monitors was essential.[5]

In addition to these school guidelines, Lancaster required that students follow his "General Rules for Conduct." Unlike his other lists specifically about school behavior and procedures, this list offered broader guidelines for life. Students were enjoined to "study cleanliness," as well as to "study kindness and love to all." They should "avoid quarreling" and steer clear of "quarrelsome companions and Playfellows." Students should also "behave in a civil manner to every one rich and poor." That meant never using "bad words, wicked language, swearing or ill names." All "nick names" were forbidden. One can almost picture Lancaster composing this list, adding to it regularly. For instance, rule 8 of this list repeated the advice to "avoid all bad company." Then, it added the advice to avoid "running after crowds when bad people abuse each other, or fight, and idle people stay to see them." Seemingly as an afterthought, this list demanded that students behave well in church and be obedient to parents at home.[6]

Lancaster also made lists for his monitors. On paper, they had plenty of guidance about what they should do. Lancaster assigned different roles to different types of monitors, all supervised by a "principal monitor." These principal monitors were responsible for detailed duties such as ringing the opening and closing bells at 9:00 a.m. and 2:00 p.m., as well as general tasks such as limiting "loitering or confabulation" among both students and other monitors. There was nothing too small to escape the purview of principal monitors. They had to be sure they had a replacement for themselves, in case of illness. They had to supervise all academic exercises and student behavior. They would show the school to visitors and supervise student exhibitions. They transitioned the students from each exercise to the next. They had to train each monitor and keep track of school equipment.[7]

The earliest editions of Lancaster's guidebooks tended to focus on curriculum and philosophy, but in later editions the manuals grew far more specific about day-to-day procedures. The 1817 Philadelphia edition of the *Manual of the System*, for example, laid out a detailed explanation of how a Lancasterian school must operate. For reading and writing lessons students should separate into eight groups. The first group would learn the alphabet; the second group, words and syllables of two letters. Then, the third and fourth groups tackled three-letter and four-letter words. In the fifth group, students would read and write passages made up entirely of one-syllable words, advancing in the sixth group to passages made up of two-syllable words. The seventh group would read from religious tracts, and the top group would read passages from the Bible and elementary primers.[8]

Writing practice progressed through a series of writing media. The first group of students wrote their letters on sand tables. This allowed schools to avoid the expense of paper and ink for the youngest students. Indeed, only advanced students wrote with paper and ink. Learners first used sand and then slates to practice their writing. As in all things, the manuals gave detailed descriptions. For the first class of students, the monitor would begin

How a reading circle was supposed to look. From *Manual of the System of Teaching Reading, Writing, Arithmetic, and Needle-Work, in the Elementary Schools of the British and Foreign School Society*, 1st American ed. (Philadelphia: Philadelphia Society for the Establishment and Support of Charity Schools, published by Benjamin Warner, printed by William Fry, 1817), 16. Courtesy of the Library Company of Philadelphia.

by saying, "Prepare." The students were to look at a letter posted on a board before them. They were to place their right hand—always the right hand—on their sand table, forefinger out. Their left hand was to remain on their left knee. The monitor was to say, "Make the letter A." The students would do so. Then, the monitor declared, "Hands down," and students were to put their hands on their knees.[9]

The manuals included similarly detailed descriptions of reading instruction. Each group of students would leave its bench and move to the walls of the schoolroom, where the floor was marked with semicircles. Students would stand with their toes on the line of the semicircle, their hands clasped uniformly behind their backs. Large reading boards were placed along the wall, so that students could share texts instead of buying expensive books. The students in each group were ranked, and the top-ranked student—who was allowed to wear the "first boy" or "first girl" badge—always started first. She or he read the lesson on the wall, carefully observed by the monitor. If she made no mistake, she retained her spot. If she made a mistake, the monitor stopped her at once and instructed the next-ranked student to read. Whichever student first read the passage without error moved to the first spot and wore the "first boy/girl" badge.[10]

Mathematics was taught along similar lines. The students were broken into ten classes, moving from the simplest numbers in the first class through addition, subtraction, multiplication, and division of ever-increasing complexity. The top class learned higher rules of arithmetic, such as "reduction, rule-of-three, practice, &c."[11] Students would be subject to quizzing by the monitors, called "interrogation." As with reading and writing practice, students who answered all arithmetic questions correctly moved up to the status of "First."[12]

The manuals had separate sections for girls' schools. The methods were generally the same, with one big exception: in addition to reading, writing, and arithmetic, girls were broken into twelve classes to learn to sew. The first class hemmed. The second did sewing and felling. The third drew threads and stitched. They would later learn more advanced techniques, including darning and "tucking and whipping."[13]

Page after page, the manuals described with reassuring precision how a Lancasterian school would operate. Over the years, Lancasterian enthusiasts published their own manuals, including, as one Albany teacher put it, "a number of alterations [that] have been successfully introduced."[14] In Albany, the reading circles had required a slight change. When the "first" student was reading, it was not only the monitor who pointed out mistakes; any student in the semicircle could do so. Whenever a reader was called out for a mistake, the next student had an opportunity to read aloud.[15]

From Boston, Lancasterian teacher William Bentley Fowle offered his own perfected system. When teaching grammar, for example, Fowle offered an elaborate list of examples. To teach the difference between the "agent" and "object" in a sentence, Fowle offered a list of sentences to use:

Men strike boys.	Worms eat animals.
Boys strike dogs.	Animals drink water.
Dogs kill cats.	Water wets land.
Cats kill rats.	Land bears flowers.
Rats gnaw cheese.	Flowers perfume air.
Cheese breeds worms.	Air gives life.[16]

Like earlier manuals, Fowle left nothing to teachers' imaginations. He described precisely how monitors would use his list to teach grammar properly. The monitor, Fowle explained, first showed students that nouns did not change, whether they were agents or objects. "Boys" were "boys," whether they were striking dogs or being struck by men. "Cheese" was "cheese," whether it was breeding worms or being gnawed by rats. Fowle laid out how monitors should teach this concept. Monitors were to read a sentence, such as "Men strike boys." Then, they would ask students, "Who strike boys?" Monitors would then vary their question and ask, "What do men strike?" Fowle's manual continued the Lancasterian tradition of laying out endless descriptions of minute-by-minute guidance for monitorial teaching.[17]

Indeed, as Fowle tried to prove, a Lancasterian school could be run on a tight, preordained schedule. In his own 1826 *Manual*, Fowle explained how he operated his "improved" Boston Lancasterian classroom. At precisely 9:00 a.m., the teacher was to ring "the little *bell*." Every student would immediately take their seat, and the teacher would call the roll.[18] After fifteen minutes, the teacher would "order monitors of reading to their stations," followed by their assigned groups of students who would take their spots on the reading circles "in perfect silence, with hands behind." The teacher was to circulate around the entire schoolroom as the different reading groups proceeded, "keeping a vigilant eye upon the whole school."[19] At 9:55, the teacher would ring the bell to signal a stop and would "require all to do so *instantly*, even if a word be half pronounced."[20]

On and on, in five-minute intervals, Fowle's manual explained exactly how a successful Lancasterian school would operate. The details were new, but the fascination with detail had always been central to every edition of Lancasterian manual. It was no accident that every manual featured page after page of mind-numbingly specific procedures. It was no accident that the lists kept growing in every edition, with rules and roles made more elaborate and more specific. That specificity was precisely the attraction of Lancaster's system. The confidence with which Lancaster and his followers described their theoretical schools seemed convincing. The descriptions of students marching in quick lockstep was something that reformers at the time found beautiful to behold. And Lancaster promised that his system included a new, modern way to make sure students did so. Unlike traditional schools that relied on corporal punishment, Lancaster insisted he could spark enthusiastic obedience among students with an elaborate system of rewards and public humiliations. Just like the procedures, those systems of discipline evolved over the years, but the central premise remained the same.

The Emulation Game

For one thing, discipline in a Lancasterian school was never supposed to rely on corporal punishment. As Lancaster wrote in 1810 with his usual dramatic style, "The sinking empire of the rod is tottering daily to ruin, and many and bitter are the lamentations of its partizans [sic]."[21] On this one point, Lancasterians all agreed. As Albany's Lancasterian leader William Tweed Dale wrote ten years later, corporal punishment was always self-defeating; it "has a great tendency to harden the offender, and to irritate the mind of him who administers the chastisement."[22] From Boston, William B. Fowle wrote in 1826 that corporal punishment could indeed make students obey, but only "with a spirit full of revenge, anger, and other bad passions."[23]

Other elements of discipline and punishment in the Lancasterian system changed dramatically over time. In his first years of teaching, Lancaster advocated an elaborate system of rewards backed by a catalog of calculated public humiliations. He promised that most students would respond wonderfully to positive feedback. He developed a system of tickets, prizes, and titles that he thought would spark a healthy spirit of "emulation" among students.[24] Students would vie with one another to improve in both academics and behavior. Lancaster was fond of telling the story of two tough boys who had reputations as trouble makers. Instead of whipping them, Lancaster encouraged them to challenge one another—who could be a better student? In Lancaster's telling, this simple trick transformed his classroom and his students' lives.[25]

Like so many of Lancaster's plans, his idea of "emulation" was not original. At the turn of the nineteenth century, as historian J. M. Opal has noted, urging students to emulate superior behavior was a popular goal among teachers and educational thinkers. It was more than just a way to overcome long traditions of corporal punishment; it captured a new sense of the goals of education, a new vision of schooling for a modern enlightened age, a kind of "creative contention between an individual and a goal, a standard, or an other individual."[26]

In Lancaster's telling, he had discovered this widely held idea on his own. To be fair, his version of "emulation" was decidedly different from that of many of his contemporaries, but only because it was far less ambitious. For Lancaster, urging students to emulate better behavior was only one of many ways to control students without physical violence. In his early manuals, he laid out a system of escalating punishments. First, monitors would distribute warning tickets, tickets that students would be required to show the adult teacher. When a student accumulated a number of warnings—the exact number was not specified in early editions of Lancaster's guidebooks—the teacher could impose various punishments. Students could be forced to wear a log around their necks describing their repeated offenses. It wasn't meant to be physically painful. As Lancaster clarified, "The neck is *not pinched or closely confined*" by the log.[27] The point, rather, was the embarrassment the student would feel.

Lancaster promised that his punishments would fit the crimes. If a student habitually wandered around the classroom at inappropriate times, for example, he could be forced to wear wooden shackles around his legs, then have one arm tied behind his back, then have both arms tied behind his back if necessary. Multiple students could be yoked together in this fashion in a "caravan," shackled together ankle to ankle and made to parade backward around the outside of the classroom, with a monitor preceding them and announcing their misbehavior in a loud voice.[28] If a male student arrived at school dirty or untidy, Lancaster recommended having a female student wash him in front of the entire school. After the wash, the girl was to gently slap the boy's face, not to cause pain, but only to drive home the point that an unwashed face resulted in this kind of social agony. In Lancaster's telling, it worked. As he put it, "*One punishment* of this kind has kept the boys faces clean for two years."[29]

Lancaster's list went on and on. Students might have labels attached to their coats, publicizing their misdeeds. They might be forced to wear a cap made of tin or paper, again with a public description of the student's faults. Lancaster liked to force students to wear a special coat—a "fool's coat"—with three long "tails" on which bad behavior was described. Most dramatic of all—what Lancaster himself called the "most terrible that can be inflicted on boys of sense and abilities"—was a sack, basket, coop, or cage suspended above the main schoolroom. Repeat offenders would be forced into the basket, where they would dangle. Other students would be encouraged to ridicule them, to "smile at the birds in the cage."[30]

Taken together, Lancaster argued, these humiliations were key to the smooth running of his system. Instead of an old-fashioned teacher who ruled by physical intimidation, the Lancasterian teacher must stand aloof, to act as "a silent by-stander and inspector." Individual punishments and rewards might vary, but Lancaster insisted that students would respond with remarkable alacrity to his system. "When the pupils," Lancaster concluded, "understand how to act and learn on this system, *the system*, not the master's vague, discretionary, uncertain judgment, will be in practice."[31]

By the time Lancaster moved to the United States, he and his followers had quietly abandoned the most appalling punishments from his system. For one thing, as we will explore in chapter 6, African American parents absolutely refused to allow their children to be shackled for any reason. In practice, the goal of humiliating students did not disappear, but in theory it mostly did. In American editions, Lancasterian manuals after 1817 shifted to a simpler system of merits and demerits. The Philadelphia *Manual* of 1817, for instance, vaguely encouraged adult teachers to "govern by love rather than by fear."[32]

Monitors in the Philadelphia system would be provided with a set of reward tickets and wooden disgrace marks. At the end of every week, students could trade in their reward tickets for prizes such as books, toys, and clothes. The school week would end with a parade, students marching around the outside of the schoolroom holding their prizes above their heads and the adult teacher praising them with a loud "*eulogium.*"[33]

On the other hand, if monitors noted a student playing, being idle, talking, or coming to school dirty, they would hang a demerit badge around that student's neck. These wooden badges were to be six inches long, three inches across, and a quarter of an inch thick.[34] Only a truly "incorrigible" student would be sent to the front of the room to see the teacher, though no specific additional punishments were described.[35]

New York's Lancasterians tried to hone this system of merits and demerits. In 1818, a committee of the Free School Society came up with an extensive clarification of the ticket system. Each merit ticket would, in theory, be worth one-eighth of a cent. Low-ranking monitors, such as the "Assistant Monitor of Reading," would earn four merit tickets each day, just for showing up. "Draft Monitors" were to receive one ticket per writing exercise. The New Yorkers assigned similarly specific values for a variety of monitorial tasks, such as "Assistant Writing Monitor" (four tickets), "Lesson fixer" (one), "Printing stick fixer" (one), "Door Keeper" (one), "Street Monitor" (one), "sweeper" (three), and even for the "Dictator" (two—for dictating a writing lesson).[36]

The committee showed its Lancasterian enthusiasm by laying out an elaborate system by which theoretical students might move up the ranks of the monitors. Any monitor might nominate a student to become a monitor. After an examination, if that student was promoted, the nominator would receive twelve tickets, as would the new monitor. However, if the student did not pass the teacher's oral examination, the nominator would lose six tickets. On the other hand, if the adult teacher noticed a sharp student who should have been promoted but was never nominated, the head monitor—in New York he was called the "Monitor General"—would be penalized twelve tickets.[37]

The committee's chart laid out specific penalties as well. A student could lose four tickets for "Talking, Playing, Inattention, [or being] Out of seats." They could lose four more for "Being disobedient or saucy to the Monitor." It is easy to imagine that the members of this committee might have visited one of the free schools, because they specified a four-ticket penalty for "Staring at persons who may come into the room." Monitors charged with neglecting their duty lost six. Students throwing stones lost ten. Dirty hands or face cost four. A first truancy was charged twenty tickets; a second, forty. Fighting was big—twenty tickets. Lying, stealing, or cheating were even bigger: fifty. Scratching or cutting the desks cost twenty. And what if a misbehaving student could not afford the fine, that is, if he or she had not accumulated an adequate endowment of merit tickets? In New York's theoretical system, the teacher would "immediately and publicly, expel said boys."[38]

Like Lancaster's earliest manuals, these emendations and elaborations were mostly theoretical. The New York committee had big plans for their list. They asked the Free School Society to publish two hundred copies. They hoped to distribute the list to parents and members of the free school committee. Their intention, as always in the world of Lancasterian reformers, was to eliminate problems by laying out a perfected system. It never really worked out that way, in part because the Free School Society never published the copies, but like every other element of the Lancasterian dream, every new articulation of school discipline relied on a modern-sounding set of new technology, from "telegraphs" to tickets.

A Modern Miracle

The first and most important piece of Lancasterian technology was the schoolroom itself. Like other education reformers before him and after, Lancaster never doubted that proper education required the proper architecture.[39] Instead of using rooms in existing houses or buildings, Lancaster dreamed of teaching in large, purpose-built schoolrooms engineered to his specifications. The ideal Lancasterian school building had one large, open room, with an elevated platform at one end for the adult teacher's desk and a rising set of long desks for students. The outer walls of the room would be lined with semicircles for the various reading groups.

Lancaster liked to specify more than just the basic layout of a proper schoolroom. He insisted on specificity, like the parts fashioned for complex

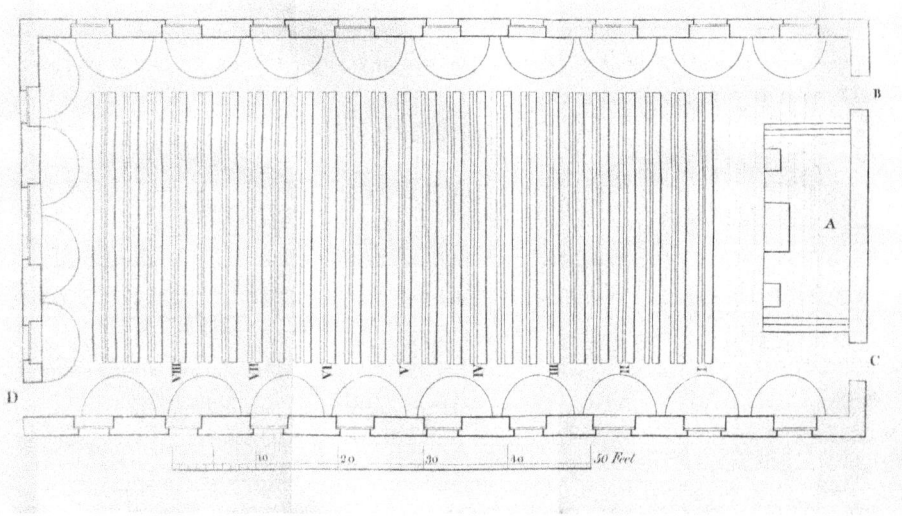

Lancasterian manuals were full of architectural plans for the perfect schoolroom. From *Manual of the System of Teaching Reading, Writing, Arithmetic, and Needle-Work, in the Elementary Schools of the British and Foreign School Society*, 1st American ed. (Philadelphia: Philadelphia Society for the Establishment and Support of Charity Schools, published by Benjamin Warner, printed by William Fry, 1817), pullout between 1 and 2. Courtesy of the Library Company of Philadelphia.

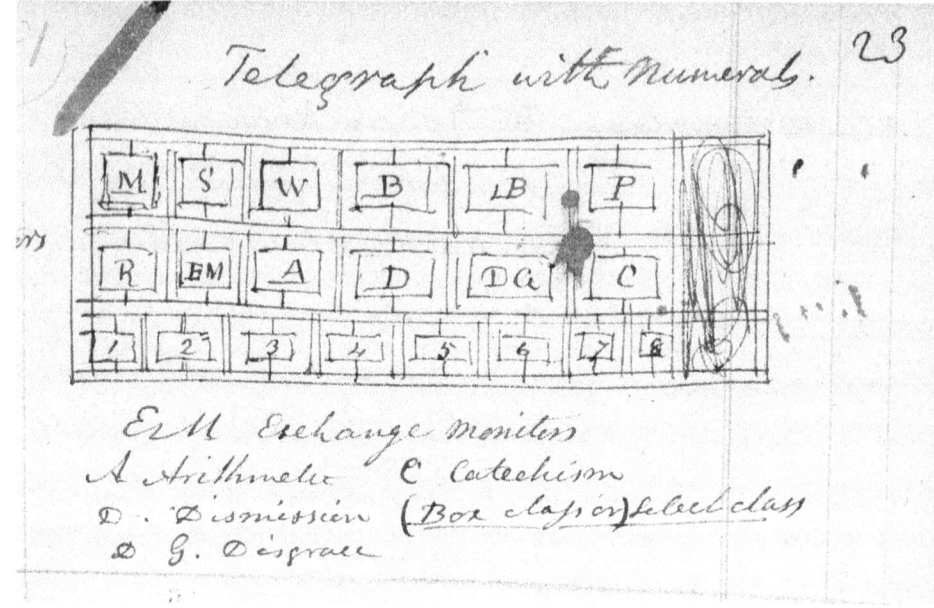

Lancaster enjoyed sketching plans for new and improved machines. Shown here is a sketch of his telegraph from one of his notebooks. Courtesy of the American Antiquarian Society.

machinery. School desks should have rounded corners instead of sharp ones, so that students would not hurt themselves as they entered and exited their long benches.[40] Heating systems ought to be warmed by "underground flues" instead of central stoves. This would prevent students from leaving their seats "to go to the fire" to get warm.[41]

In later editions, Lancaster and his admirers piled on details about their architectural requirements. By 1817, Lancaster recommended specific heights for the windows (at least seven feet above the floor), specific ventilation systems (using a network of "tubes" embedded in the ceiling), and even specific manufacturers of heating stoves ("the stoves may be had of R. Howden, of Oldstreet Road, London, an ingenious mechanic, who has obtained a patent for his invention").[42] The edition of Lancaster's *Manual* published by the New York Free School Society in 1820 included a handy chart for the recommended dimensions of variously sized schools. A school with five hundred students, for example, must be ninety-seven feet long and forty-two feet wide. The platform for the adult teacher's desk would be ten feet long, the desks ranging back to the end of the room three feet wide. There would be twenty-five desks total, with room in between.[43]

Boston's William B. Fowle elaborated his architectural preferences for the perfect Lancasterian schoolroom. Certainly, Fowle noted, the system could work in any room, but "its advantages cannot be so fully appreciated as when the room is more conveniently arranged."[44] It was more convenient, for example, to have the reading circles separated by "about eighteen inches," so that students would not touch one another. The circles should be four feet in radius, leaving two extra feet in each aisle for easy walking. Unlike Lancaster's original plan, Fowle advocated a "semicircular" desk for the adult teacher, ideally with "two circular steps around it" so that students could surround the desk for their examinations.[45] Like all Lancasterians, Fowle believed that the schoolroom was the most important piece of educational technology. It should be filled with helpful tools such as a "long board painted black" with lines and sample letters written on it. If this board were prominently displayed, Fowle explained, every "child may always have a copy to appeal to, when in doubt about the form of a letter."[46]

The room was important, but Lancaster and the Lancasterians also filled their ideal classrooms with modern-sounding lists of machines. For instance, Lancaster devised a "telegraph" machine to communicate within the large open room. In essence, a Lancasterian telegraph was an elevated sign, made up of cards with letters and numbers. Each card could be rotated to be hidden or revealed. By displaying a certain letter, such as "W," the teacher could tell monitors it was time to move to writing instruction. By displaying their own cards, such as "Ex," monitors could alert the teacher that their students were ready to be examined.[47]

Lancaster took credit for a number of fairly obvious teaching tools. For example, his manuals called for large placards to teach reading instead of individual books. That way, the placards could be displayed for a group of students to read.[48] Similarly, Lancaster praised his "new mode" of keeping attendance. Instead of calling names from a long roster, Lancaster assigned each pupil a number. Monitors could check the numbers to check attendance. How this system would save time or effort was not clear, but Lancaster described the method as a modern advance over old methods.[49]

Over time, Lancasterians added new technology to their manuals. In New York, for example, reformers in 1820 offered their version of Lancaster's "Alphabet Wheel." This large circle would allow teachers and monitors to

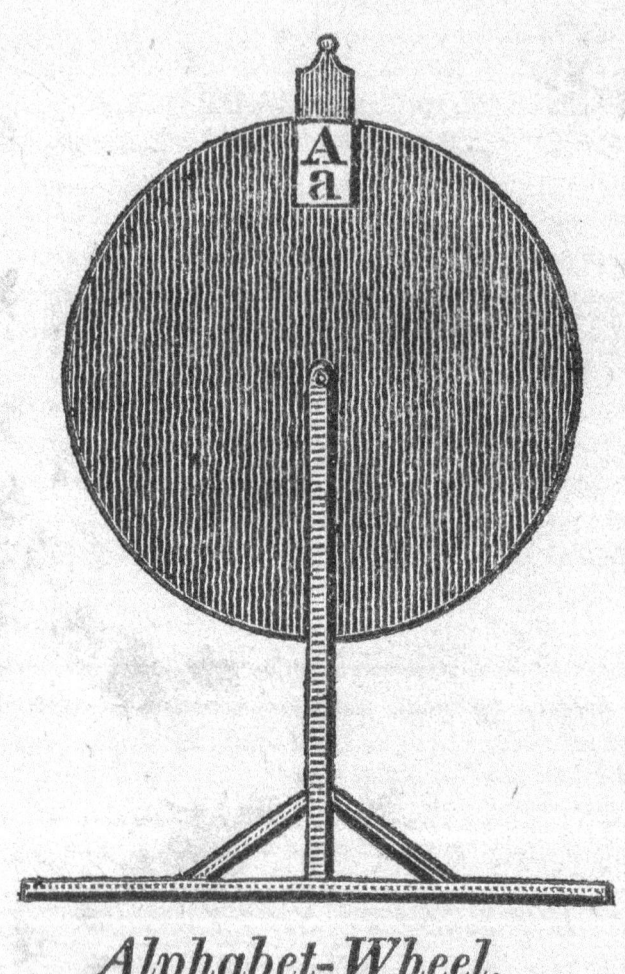

The New York Alphabet-Wheel, one piece of Lancasterian technology that was supposed to transform learning. From *Manual of the Lancasterian System of Teaching Reading, Writing, Arithmetic, and Needle-Work, as Practised in the Schools of the Free-School Society of New-York* (New York: Free-School Society, Samuel Wood & Sons, 1820), 9. Courtesy of the American Antiquarian Society.

display one letter at a time for students to copy. Ideally, according to reformers, the letters would go not in alphabetical order but in order of appearance. Letters such as "M" and "W" should be grouped together so that students could see the similarities.[50]

Other Lancasterians waxed even more technological. In Albany, for example, William Tweed Dale used an elaborate "pendulum" system to communicate with his students. In theory, at least, the pendulum would eliminate the need for teachers or monitors to keep track of student movements throughout the school day. As Dale described it, the pendulum would be a weight on a long cord suspended over the entry stairs of the classroom. If the pendulum was still, students were permitted to exit the classroom, presumably to visit the bathroom. When a student exited the classroom, she or he would pull the pendulum back fourteen inches and release. How would they know they were pulling it back exactly fourteen inches? Because they were issued a special fourteen-inch-long "permit" card to perfect the maneuver. They would be allowed out of the classroom for as long as the pendulum was swinging. When the student returned, they would stop the pendulum's swing. If other students observed the pendulum in motion, they would know they would have to wait their turn to go to the bathroom.[51]

In the imagination of Lancaster and his followers, these technological advances would eliminate much of the unnecessary inefficiencies of traditional classrooms. None of Lancaster's extravagantly imagined technologies ever really achieved their promised goals. But that didn't stop Lancasterians from dreaming. Some of those dreams never saw the light of day. In New York in 1825, for example, Lancasterian teacher John Griscom pleaded for funding to commission a set of "transparent paintings" to help teach children. If only he could get financial "encouragement," Griscom wrote, he would develop a set of "well chosen pictures" that he could project on the walls of his schoolroom.[52]

Griscom never got his encouragement, presumably because the supporters of Lancasterian schools never wanted to spend much money. Even as Lancaster and his followers described their elaborate technological solutions, they always claimed that their schools could be run cheaply. Just as with the rest of the Lancasterian system, promises of low-cost schools never came true, but that did not stop Lancaster from making ever-grander promises about ever-cheaper schools.

The Cheap Education of Youth

From the very beginning, one of the most alluring promises of Lancaster's system was that it would provide low-cost education, or, as Lancaster described it in 1801, a "School for the Cheap Education of Youth."[53] Of course, as we have seen, the budget of Lancaster's Borough Road School was always bolstered by off-the-books borrowing and Lancaster's catastrophic accounting practices. And as we will see in chapter 7, a few Lancasterian schools did manage to thrive in the United States, but only because they had the luxury of adequate budgets. Lancaster's American admirers did not learn that lesson until it was far too late. They took his word that the system would solve their fundamental financial problems. Before Lancaster's system came along, many city leaders could not figure out how to pay for charity schools that did not charge tuition fees. On paper, at least, Lancaster offered a way to achieve universal education on the cheap.

The Lancasterian system basically promised to cut costs by eliminating teacher salaries. As Lancaster bragged in an early manual, his biggest breakthrough was to eliminate all but one teacher's salary. Traditional schooling required a paid adult teacher to teach students directly. In the old way of doing things, one salaried teacher could only handle, at most, a hundred students or so. Lancaster's financial breakthrough, he explained, was tied to the revolutionary efficiency of his system. Once it was up and running, the argument went, one teacher could easily supervise hundreds, even a thousand students. The cost per student would drop dramatically. As he crowed, "This has been done by the author, and never was done till he did it."[54]

Lancaster's schools were supposed to cut costs in a truly revolutionary way. The New York Free School Society reported in 1807 that the academic progress of their students met even their "most sanguine expectations" at only a tenth of the cost of traditional charity schooling.[55] Others echoed the ten-to-one promise. For instance, as one entranced observer of Albany's Lancasterian school explained, Lancaster's methods made learning "delightsome," and they did so "on a plan in a tenfold degree cheaper than was ever before discovered."[56]

The cheapness relied on numbers. If enough students showed up, per-pupil costs would be lowered dramatically. As Lancaster's first British supporters had learned, real students did not always enroll, and smaller schools were not as cheap to run. As one Londoner warned his American counterparts, "a lesser number will not yield an economical result."[57] In early years, American Lancasterians were so enraptured by promises of vast savings that they did not heed the warning. Instead, they based their calculations on theoretical attendance and trumpeted the theoretical results. As the teacher of Albany's school promised, if his school enrolled five hundred children, it would cost only eighty cents to educate each student per quarter.[58] His school, however, never actually achieved such high attendance. In 1814 it peaked at about four hundred students.[59] The high hopes of Albany's Lancasterians were never realized. By 1826, though their school still theoretically enrolled 401 students, actual daily attendance hovered between 300 and 350.[60]

In the 1810s, American optimism outpaced any worries. Reformers assumed that students would show up and that per-student costs would plummet. And those imaginary plunging costs often became the bait with which reformers enticed public support. For example, in 1817 Philadelphia's Roberts Vaux promised financial miracles. Using their old system, Vaux explained to Pennsylvania lawmakers, the Philadelphia public schools spent $22,729.68 annually to educate only about two thousand students. Worst of all, of those two thousand officially enrolled students, most did not even attend. The new system, "the system of Lancaster," might not be ten times cheaper, but it would slash costs from almost twelve dollars to only three dollars per student per year.[61]

Unfortunately for Vaux and other Lancasterians, the financial promise of Lancaster's system was just as ephemeral as the rest. Yet the promise of radically lower costs was the single most important factor in launching the Lancasterian revolution in the United States. In Philadelphia, for example, county commissioners' support for Lancasterian methods ultimately came down to the financial bottom line. The commissioners might have hoped that the system would lead to better learning, but they only endorsed the plan when Vaux explained the presumed financial benefits. When the commissioners learned that the system would cut per-pupil costs in half or even more, they "immediately accepted" Vaux's Lancasterian proposal.[62]

As with the rest of Lancaster's system, his financial promises rested on a dense web of deception. Nevertheless, it seemed convincing enough to assure hardheaded politicians. The system, they were told, was cheaper because it was vastly more efficient. It slashed costs with its perfected combination of technology, procedures, and discipline. Best of all, because of its scientific perfection, it could work anywhere and be implemented by anyone willing to follow Lancaster's elaborate specifications. Not only would there be no problems, enthusiasts assured their audiences, but there simply *could* be none, thanks to the precision of Lancaster's theoretical system.

Those Who Can't Do

From the very beginning, Lancaster insisted that his perfect plan could be carried out anywhere, by anyone. As he wrote in the early editions of his guidebook, any child could teach any subject, "ALTHOUGH HE KNOWS NOTHING ABOUT IT."[63] If only a school followed Lancaster's rambling directions, there was no need for talent, expertise, or ingenuity. A teacher needed only to receive basic training in Lancaster's methods. The rest would be as simple as following a recipe.

For many American audiences, the promise of a teacher-proof system was alluring. Among reformers, lamentations were common about the terrible state of traditional teaching. In the preface to the 1817 Philadelphia edition of the *Manual*, for example, traditional teachers were derided as "not qualified to teach." Such improperly prepared teachers, the Philadelphians asserted, "do real injury."[64] In 1822, a committee of Pennsylvania legislators agreed. Too many traditional teachers, they wrote, showed "gross negligence or incapacity." Under the traditional system, bad teachers often could "defeat the object of public bounty and render the whole system useless." Lancaster's modern system promised to eliminate that danger.[65]

Lancasterian manuals offered everything anyone would need to run the system perfectly. At least, they claimed to do so. For instance, aspiring Lancasterian teachers could use the off-the-rack forms provided in the manuals to keep track of attendance, student achievement, and even student religious observance. Teachers could read the scripts provided to give word-for-word Lancasterian instruction. One manual, for example, offered a long script, an "Address to the monitors." It went on for several pages, offering the exact words for the lone adult Lancasterian teacher to speak to his or her monitors.[66] To teach a few famous words in Latin, for instance, the teacher would read the following script:

> MONITORS,—I wish to speak a little to you. I have often done so, but it seems that every day would require me to say something new; or at least, remind you that, what you have often heard, you ought to hear anew. I believe that you never have had a lesson in latin [sic] from me, I am now going to teach you a

short one in this language: and, if you should never be taught another in it, I do hope, that you will improve, by this one. It is very short, only two words; and these are "tempus. fugit." You will say, "what is the meaning of these words?" If you will promise me, that you will endeavor to mind them, I will tell you. Hold up your hands if you are resolved.[67]

In theory, these Lancasterian instructions offered a complete, prepackaged educational success. Teachers following Lancasterian directions would know what to do and say at every minute of every day. At 10:30, for instance, they would send their classes off to reading by "ring[ing] the bell for writing to cease. Give the word 'ready!—rise!—walk!' and then let them file off to their seats."[68]

The guidebooks offered assurance about the roles of the monitors as well. Every monitor, no matter how unintelligent or poorly prepared, would be able to fulfill his assigned task. As Lancaster told audiences, his system worked perfectly because it took away any need for "discretion and judgement" among its child-monitors.[69] They simply needed to follow directions. As one Lancasterian explained, in a Lancasterian school "as little as possible may be left to the judgement of the monitors."[70]

The goal was everywhere the same. In the Lancasterian system, there should be no room for a poorly trained or lazy teacher to gum up the works. The adult teacher would have an easy-to-follow guide. The monitors would have ample direction. The students would always know exactly what to do. The perfection of the system resulted from its perfectly exportable, replicable character. It did not depend on the charisma or wisdom of any individual teacher. Instead, it invested all its confidence in its own perfect guidance.

The enthusiasm of the Lancasterian movement, in large part, was a literary one. Reformers in US cities read the scientific-sounding descriptions of perfect educational order in Lancaster's guidebooks and manuals. They imagined the modern disciplinary system, laid out in such painstaking detail in the various editions. They thrilled to the technological modernity sketched in the pages of every new manual, a catalog of cutting-edge machines that would bring the latest wonders of the nineteenth century to shake up the ancient, antiquated patterns of traditional schoolrooms, in which dry teaching and corporal punishment were common. And, perhaps most of all, they relished the fact that the new system would provide such radically improved education at such a radically reduced cost.

None of these promises ever bore fruit. The purpose-built classrooms were often beyond the means of most schools. Even model schools—schools fitted out in accordance with the scriptures—found it impractical and cumbersome. The procedures were not as simple as promised. Students did not like public humiliation any better than they had liked corporal punishment. And Lancaster's schools never achieved the cost savings they promised.

Indeed, from the distance of two centuries, the claims of the Lancasterian system seem so outrageous, so obviously simplistic, that it can be difficult to understand how Lancaster's contemporaries accepted them so readily. In their defense, reformers and educators asked for proof and evidence, but they did not press too hard. Partly, their scanty skepticism resulted from their own sense of themselves as the first generation of truly modern, truly scientific thinkers. They understood that Lancaster's promises were difficult to believe, but they assumed that their age was one of dramatic change, an age that could bring unbelievable advances.

4
A Numbers Game

The numbers never matched. The hordes of students crammed cheerfully into the imaginary Lancasterian schools of reformers' plans never matched the much smaller numbers of students who actually showed up. Unfortunately for Lancasterian reformers, the numbers were always the thing. Lancaster promised that endless mobs of unwashed youth could be tamed and managed by his world-changing system. When reformers opened their schools, they found themselves wrestling with a problem that had no answer in all of Lancaster's manuals—namely, what should they do when the hordes did not show up?

Before examining the crash in enrollment in the early 1820s, this chapter will tackle another central question: if Lancaster's promises were so far removed from reality, why did thoughtful reformers ever believe them? Why did so many savvy urban politicians not realize that Lancaster's numbers were all imaginary—that his bottom line was not really the bottom, but floated precariously instead on pockets of false assumptions and wishful thinking?

As we'll see, leaders such as New York's De Witt Clinton did more than just believe Lancaster's claims; they actually thought they had seen them in action. In 1810, for example, Clinton attested that he had witnessed "one great assembly of a thousand children, under the eye of a single teacher, marching with unexampled rapidity, and with perfect discipline, to the goal of knowledge."[1] If Clinton had seen such a thing, it was only in his mind's eye, in the dream spun for him by Lancaster and his promise of perfect modern schooling. At the time Clinton made his claim, neither of New York's two Lancasterian schools taught more than a couple hundred children. In

England, the largest Lancasterian school never enrolled more than seven hundred children, and even there far fewer students actually showed up on any given school day. The average English Lancasterian school taught about two hundred students at a time.[2] The idea of a thousand children likely came to Clinton from the extravagant title of Lancaster's early guidebooks, in which Lancaster claimed to give "*an Account of the Institution for the Education of One Thousand Poor Children.*"[3] Such a school never existed in real life, but it became a common part of the Lancasterian vision.

Yet Clinton's collaborators never objected to the extravagance or exaggeration embedded in Clinton's claims. Like so many of his contemporaries, Clinton seemed truly to believe in his vision, though it was in fact only a dream. Clinton's dream relied on hope, not hard evidence. With imagination as its foundation, Clinton's vision had no limits. Lancasterian reform, as Clinton viewed it, was more than just a new way to organize classrooms. It was a dream of a new day for cities, of a new modernity that solved problems that had bedeviled humanity since time immemorial. As Clinton put it, "I consider [Lancaster's] system as creating a new aera [sic] in education, as a blessing sent down from Heaven to redeem the poor and distressed of this world from the power and dominion of ignorance."[4]

Like Clinton, urban reformers in the United States fell in love with a promise, not a workable plan. Lancaster's system seemed feasible in outline. As we have learned, Lancaster's books and pamphlets laid out the theoretical arrangement of a school in painstaking detail. That detail, however, was deceptive. It described a modern school humming along with an industrial productive whir. As Clinton put it, Lancaster's system brought to urban education what the most "finished machines" brought to modern factories.[5] Yet Clinton and other Lancasterians did not notice in their first flush of enthusiasm that children and teachers were something other than cogs and gears. Because American reformers assumed that science and systems could solve any modern problem, they did not question the shoddy evidence that Lancaster provided. They did not push Lancaster's early backers in London for more details about their experiences. They did not demand the Londoners' reasons for legally separating themselves from Lancaster's whirlwind of debt and abuse. Instead, American reformers swapped heartening rumors and encouraged one another to believe them. They played a desperate numbers game, hoping that Lancaster's system could provide the schools they needed to contain all the children thronging their city streets.

To a large degree, the deluded enthusiasm for Lancaster's system was due not to Lancaster, or even to the system itself, but to the ways urban reformers at the time thought about their modern world. They saw modern factories go up in Lowell and New Lanark, factories that revolutionized production and social relations. They dug modern canal systems that revolutionized agriculture and transportation. They assumed that science, technology, and modern systematic thinking could revolutionize their world, solving problems that had stumped the ancients. It was reformers' assumptions, as much as Lancaster's bluster, that led them to invest wholeheartedly in a half-baked plan. By the early 1820s, American reformers had built a network of Lancasterian schools, built on the shaky foundation of Lancaster's sketches and promises. Fired up by Lancaster's hazy vision, they expanded the meager network of urban charity schools that existed when Lancaster arrived in New York in 1818. They invested time, money, and prestige in Lancaster's fantasies because they assumed he was the savior they had been expecting.

Delightful Train of Success

When Lancaster first arrived in New York City, he was greeted by De Witt Clinton, who had by that time assumed the governor's seat. As New York City's mayor off and on between 1803 and 1815, Clinton had played a leading role in bringing Lancasterian methods to the city's charity schools. As governor since 1817, Clinton gave Lancaster a hero's welcome, arranging for a lecture in New York City and then a luxurious cruise up the Hudson River to the state capital in Albany. There, Lancaster spoke to the state legislature, glorying in their ovation.[6]

After his bruising experiences in London, it must have been a balm to Lancaster's blistered ego to receive once again the flattering attention of the rich and powerful. He relished Governor Clinton's "very attentive" attitude during their time together.[7] When Lancaster traveled to the nation's capital in January 1819, President James Monroe received him, Lancaster bragged, "with honest simplicity."[8] Congress invited Lancaster to deliver a lecture about his education ideas, and afterward Lancaster savored the "elegant compliment" paid to him by Speaker of the House Henry Clay, who told Lancaster that Congress had never heard a better talk. At least, that's how Lancaster reported the encounter to Roberts Vaux.[9] Maybe most satisfying to Lancaster, the French ambassador to the United States invited him to dinner and—as Lancaster told anyone who would listen—praised Lancaster as a "man of taste," genius, and modern systematic thinking.[10]

To Lancaster, these diplomatic compliments were not merely protocol; they were proof that he was in fact something beyond the average, that this striving son of a Quaker chair-maker was destined for something beyond merely scraping out a living. For Lancaster, fresh from the humiliations of his London debacle, American adoration was proof that his famous system of education reform merited the adulation of the world's leaders. It was proof that he had been right all along, no matter what everybody else said—his failures in London had not been his fault, but merely the machinations of a sinister cabal of shortsighted detractors.

The kind of praise heaped on Lancaster by his American devotees was enough to turn anyone's head. Writing from Albany, New York, for example, one admirer wrote that Lancaster deserved a unique place in world history. As this fan put it, "no one man, either ancient or modern, has afforded to the world more important benefits, than have been bestowed by JOSEPH LANCASTER."[11]

Beyond such praise, some Lancasterian schools in the United States did appear to be thriving. As Lancaster arrived in New York, for example, the city's Free School Society opened its third school based on Lancasterian methods. As Lancaster relished the compliments of governors, presidents, and ambassadors, the Free School Society found that the "reputation of Lancasterian schools" in New York City made their schools wildly popular.[12]

In Albany, too, the local Lancaster School Society invited Lancaster to visit their thriving school. As the group's vice president told him, their school was "young, but flourishing and full blossoming." Such evidence of success—no matter how temporary and illusory it proved—must have reassured Lancaster and other American reformers who had embraced the faith. Lancaster enjoyed the compliments of his Albany host, who called him "one of those rare benefactors of Mankind whose services merit such peculiar public acknowledgements, as cannot be withheld without incurring the justly deserved imputation of public ingratitude."[13]

Up and down the Eastern Seaboard, Lancaster received similar praise and reports of success at Lancasterian schools. He seemed to have found once again the success he had ruined so embarrassingly in Britain. As he wrote to one Philadelphia supporter at the end of his first year in America, his time there had been "a delightful train of success."[14]

Dark Clouds

Joseph Lancaster was not one to question his own delightful success, but if he had, he would have seen ominous signs looming. If someone with a more critical eye were to read his mail, they might have noticed a trend. Many of the letters praised Lancaster and his system but qualified their promises to open Lancasterian schools. Much of the admiration for Lancaster's system was still only theoretical, never quite overcoming real-world obstacles. Writing from Boston, for instance, one admirer flattered Lancaster with talk of the "modern and improved plan—in the introduction of which you have taken so original and distinguished a part." The Bostonian would love to open a Lancasterian school, he told Lancaster, but unfortunately he was suffering in health and could not devote his energy to the project.[15]

Similarly, a correspondent from Wilmington, Delaware, admired Lancaster's system but said he could not interest enough students.[16] A writer from Warminster, Virginia, told Lancaster of his "high respect" for Lancaster's wonderful "system" but doubted that it would work in Virginia, which lacked enough cities to provide more than about thirty students for any school.[17] From Concord, New Hampshire, an admirer begged Lancaster to come to their city to explain his system. If Lancaster could make the trip, the Granite Stater promised that "many of our most respectable Townsmen" would be sure to attend—at least the fan thought they might.[18] Even from far outside America's cities, Lancaster received flattering attention. One roughly literate frontier admirer wrote to Lancaster. He had read Lancaster's "valluable improvement in lerning" in a rare copy of Lancaster's book that had "bin takin down the Ohio" River. If only Lancaster could send more copies, this backwoods patriarch hoped that his children—one of whom was a teacher—could "reape some of the bennifits of yore improvments."[19]

Careful readers of Lancaster's plans smelled a rat. In his role as secretary of war, crusty proslavery South Carolinian John C. Calhoun deflated Lancaster's presumptions. In his perambulations among Washington's leaders, Lancaster buttonholed Calhoun and needled him to support Lancaster's dreams of a network of Lancasterian schools for indigenous children. An endorsement from such a prominent politician would go a long way toward making the plan a reality. Calhoun put Lancaster off again and again. When Calhoun finally agreed to read Lancaster's proposals, he rejected them out of hand. As Calhoun curtly informed Lancaster, there was no evidence that the plan would work. In the end, Calhoun brusquely refused to endorse the project.[20]

Calhoun was not the only skeptical one. Lancaster's family and closest supporters knew that he was interested in something besides the public good. In his letters home to his wife and daughter, for example, Lancaster focused on the bottom line. As he told his wife, a speech in Albany in September 1818 might not have convinced anyone in the audience, but it brought in sixty-nine dollars.[21] In January 1819, two speeches in Wilmington, Delaware, netted him a cool $125.[22] In his private ramblings, Lancaster did not express much interest in the effect his ideas might have on the poor. Instead, he only detailed the size of his audiences and the amount of money they were willing to spend to hear his ideas.[23]

At the time, there was no way the general public could know such things about Lancaster's private ambitions. Like Secretary Calhoun, however, they might have looked a little more closely at Lancaster's public claims. If they had, they would have tempered their early enthusiasm. In 1819, for instance, Lancaster pulled an old trick out of his London playbook and dusted it off for his American audience. He offered a new publication explaining his wondrous "Lancasterian System." He listed the famous Americans who had subscribed for dozens of copies, including Speaker of the House Henry Clay, Congressman Burwell Bassett, future president John Quincy Adams, and New York governor De Witt Clinton. A subscription of one dollar would earn the subscriber two copies of the short book and would pay for two additional copies to be sent out for free to influential Americans. Once Lancaster received $500, he would begin printing. As he had done in the past, Lancaster asked for the money up front. As he had also done in the past, Lancaster never followed through with the publication.[24]

Certainly, not every American reformer fell in love with Lancaster and his plan. Like Secretary Calhoun, some reviewers were unimpressed. Writing from Washington, DC, in early 1819, one member of one of Lancaster's audiences thought he lacked "dignity" or even a carefully thought-out plan. Yes, it had "become fashionable" to endorse Lancaster's system as an educational panacea, this audience member sniffed, but it was "a little overrated."[25]

In the first year or so of Lancaster's sojourn in the United States, however, such voices were in the minority. Like Lancaster himself, most of the prominent education reformers waxed rhapsodic about the promises of Lancaster's system. The system itself promised to answer every educational question in advance. Its ardent supporters bought into its promises without giving them a very close examination. Many Lancasterians realized their mistake only after they had committed to providing a free education to all the children of their cities.

For some of them, their rash investment in Lancaster's empty promises is excusable. They simply did not know the future and did not look too closely at Lancaster's claims. For others, though, their lack of critical examination of Lancaster's schemes is more difficult to understand. In Philadelphia, Roberts Vaux could have heeded the many warning signs. Vaux couldn't be blamed for not knowing about the charges of physical and sexual abuse leveled at Lancaster by his students in London—as we've seen, the London committee covered up those charges—but he certainly had an overly sanguine attitude about Lancaster's personality and promises. After all, Lancaster told Vaux repeatedly about what really mattered to him: bigger audiences and bigger paydays.[26] Plus, Lancaster's former supporters in London had warned Vaux directly about Lancaster's impossible personality. Just as Lancaster was landing in New York City, one member of London's Royal Lancasterian Society warned Vaux that Lancaster "will give you some trouble without extreme caution." Still bruised from his fight with Lancaster a few years earlier, the London reformer warned Vaux in no uncertain terms: "you have frequently heard from me and others . . . he always rides a high horse that will neither drive or lead."[27]

Behind the Curtain

The first generation of American Lancasterians certainly voiced some skepticism of the elaborate promises they heard. In the end, though, they allowed themselves to be satisfied with assurances. They listened to confident-sounding testimonials without insisting on greater evidence of effectiveness.

In his earliest published manuals, for example, Lancaster himself assured readers that his system had been proven in London.[28] He did not offer any details, but rather assured readers that the evidence had been definitively established. Early supporters, such as William Allen, a member of London's Royal Lancasterian Society and one of the most prominent antislavery Quakers in London, offered a firsthand report of his visit to Lancaster's Borough Road School in 1808. "I can never forget," Allen described, "the impression which the scene made upon me." He had had some doubts, but when he saw "a thousand children collected from the streets," all learning in perfect lockstep order, he could not help but believe in the system.[29] Like De Witt Clinton, Allen had not actually seen a thousand children. At the time, the Borough Road School typically welcomed, at most, a couple hundred students per day. But Allen had been told it was a thousand, and that is what he assumed he saw.

Even more damaging to Allen's testimony, unlike a few of the London Lancasterians, Allen did not know at the time that Lancaster was paying for his marvelous school by burying himself in off-the-books debt or that Lancaster habitually abused his monitors for pleasure. It only became clear later that Lancaster's early successes at his Borough Road School were paid for by vast unregulated debt and driven by fear. When Allen visited the school in 1808, none of those shady financial dealings were evident. He saw a school teaching hundreds at great cost, but he thought he saw a school teaching thousands cheaply. Just a few years later, Allen and his London allies realized the disparity.

American reformers read reports like Allen's without knowing the financial background or the depressing, abusive denouement. Americans did not learn the full, ugly story of Lancaster's career in London until much later. They did not know that William Allen and his friends in the Royal Lancasterian Society repeatedly paid off Lancaster's debts and covered up his abuses. They assumed that Lancaster's financial promises were true, that his system worked as planned. When they reassured a skeptical public about Lancaster's glorious system, they were not intentionally lying, but they were themselves deceived. From Philadelphia, for example, reformers promised that the advantages of the system were "not the suggestions of enthusiasm." When they wrote their report in 1817, they insisted, "The System has been established in England long enough to develope [sic] all the advantages ascribed to it."[30]

At the peak of Lancasterian enthusiasm in the United States—roughly between 1815 and 1825—American reformers regarded themselves as hardnosed realists, not lofty dreamers. Among themselves, they shared evidence and examples that purported to prove the transformative power of the system. In New York, the trustees of the Free School Society demanded detailed reports from their teachers. In 1817, for example, the teacher at School Number One reported that he currently enrolled 489 boys. When they entered, eighty-nine of them were entirely "ignorant of the Alphabet," sixty-one of them could spell a little, sixty-five could read in a primer, and only ten could read the Bible. After spending time in his school, the teacher reported that fifty-five had moved up from reading only individual letters of the alphabet to reading short texts. Fifty-two had improved from reading short texts to longer selections from their primer. Nineteen had begun writing on slates; fifty had advanced to writing on paper. A full dozen had progressed to reading the Bible.[31] Those numbers sounded good, but trustees asked no follow-up questions. They did not wonder how long individual students had spent in the school. They did not seek out comparisons from other types of schools. They looked for reassurances, not real proof.

Elites also relished other kinds of evidence of effectiveness. In Philadelphia, for example, school board leader Roberts Vaux saved a thank-you letter from a student in one of the city's Lancasterian schools. As the student wrote in beautiful, polished handwriting, "Be pleased to accept from a pupil of the Lombard St. School a small return for your kindness and attention in promoting the best interest of the Public's charge."[32] By the time the student expressed his gratitude in 1827, Vaux and other Philadelphians had begun to doubt the system's promises. Yet Vaux still clung to notions about the effectiveness of the system. Like other early fans of Lancaster's system, such as the leaders of New York's Free School Society, Vaux wanted proof and evidence. And like enthusiasts around the world, Vaux had received only vague warnings about Lancaster's character, not thorough descriptions of his crimes and lapses.[33] Without the full story or anything to compare it to, reformers in New York, Philadelphia, and other cities tended to accept whatever proof they could find. They tended to confirm their hopes that Lancaster's system would work instead of testing its elaborate promises.

The general public also received its fair share of assurances. As one writer to the editor of a popular monthly magazine attested, he had visited the annual examination of the Lancasterian African Free School in New York. The "Lancasterian system," this writer explained, needed no more proof than such a visit. In his trip, "I saw enough to convince the most sceptical."[34]

At the time, as William J. Reese has demonstrated, the American public still considered public exhibitions one of the hallmarks of proper schooling. Though contemporary critics sometimes blamed exhibitions as a waste of precious classroom time, parents and community members still often viewed traditional school exhibitions as the fairest measure of any school.[35]

In addition to elaborate public performances, the segregated New York

Students at the African Free School showed off their talents for their parents and community. *Contempt*, by M. Burns, drawn December 2, 1812. From the records of the New-York African Free School, vol. 4, 44. Courtesy of the New-York Historical Society.

school also published examples from its annual public examinations. The general public could view students' work in mathematics, poetry, rhetoric, or art. New York's Black Lancasterians used student essays as evidence that Lancaster's system worked. They hoped that student accomplishments would justify their faith and funding. As one student essay explained, "Our schools . . . continue to be conducted on the Lancasterian system, and the improvement of scholars is such, as to be satisfactory to the trustees, and all visiters [sic] who come to the school."[36] Black reformers knew that their evidence would be treated with skepticism, even hostility, by a profoundly racist white society. As twelve-year-old student George Allen wrote, he had made great academic progress in 1827. His school had been "frequently visited by gentlemen from the South and other parts of the country." Time and time again, this student and his fellows were asked to show off what they had learned. At every exhibition, Allen wrote, visitors "always expressed themselves highly gratified with our performances." In case white visitors might doubt the academic achievement on display, the school's leaders added a note: the essay was "the genuine, unaided production of George R. Allen, a very black boy of pure African descent, who is now between 12 and 13 years old, and was born in this city."[37]

The proof of Lancaster's system, reformers thought, could be found in the achievements of students like Allen. White and Black, boy and girl, European and American—all represented proof of Lancasterian excellence. As one Irish Lancasterian acknowledged, the burden of proof lay with the reformers. After all, the claims of the system were extravagant: they promised schools for thousands of poor children with minimal expense, they promised to turn dangerous youthful criminals into productive youthful citizens, and they guaranteed unbelievably rapid academic progress for all. They promised to finally win a numbers game that had long seemed unwinnable. As the Irish enthusiast admitted in the pages of the *Belfast Chronicle*, such claims were so outlandish "as almost to border on the incredible!!!"[38]

An Age of Systems

Incredible, indeed. In historical perspective, the trajectory of Lancasterian enthusiasm seems difficult to explain. Like De Witt Clinton, urban leaders in the United States convinced themselves that they had witnessed something they had not, that they were standing on the cusp of a bold new modern age, an age in which Lancasterian schools would wipe away the ancient scourges of poverty and crime. They believed they had seen the system working in all its glory, when in fact they had only heard exaggerated promises.

How could so many otherwise reasonable people fall for Lancaster's in-

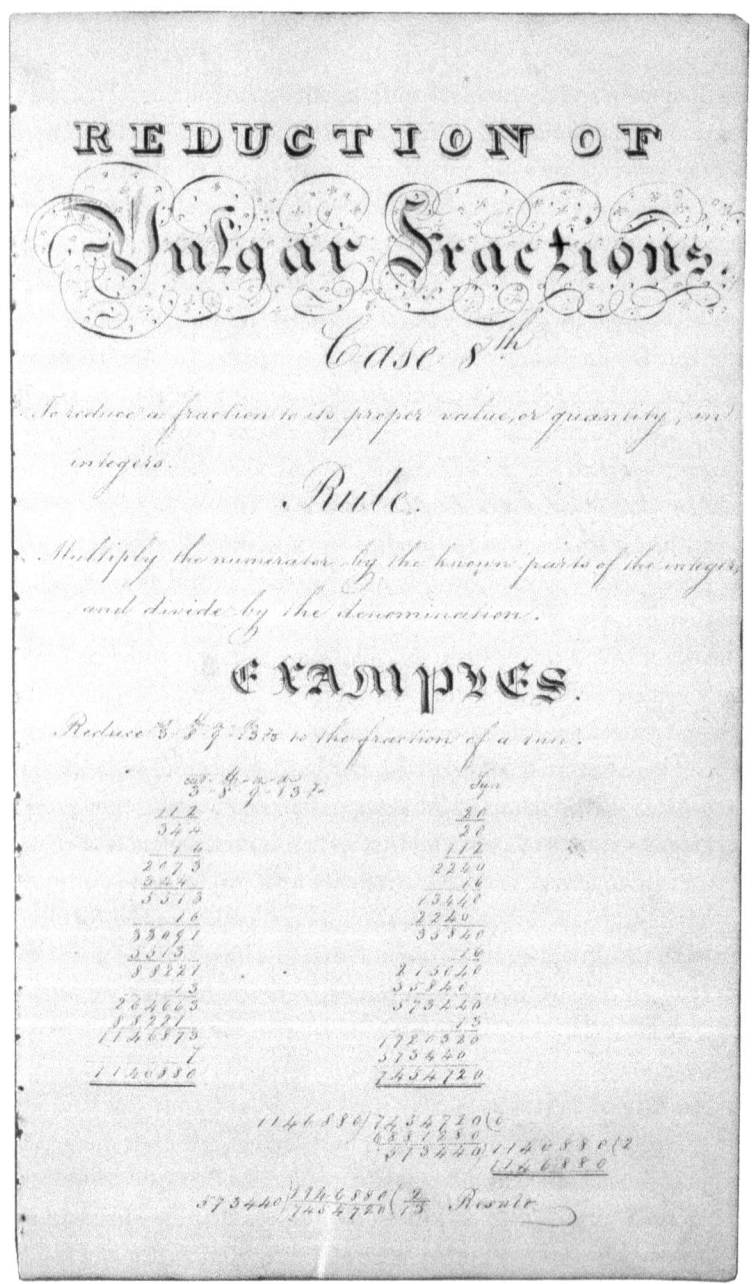

Exhibitions of student work were meant to reassure skeptics about Lancasterian methods. "Reduction of Vulgar Fractions," Andrew R. Smith, penmanship and drawing studies, 1816–1826. New-York African Free School records, 1817–1832, New-York Historical Society. Courtesy of the New-York Historical Society.

flated claims in the 1810s and 1820s? Reformers at the time did not simply take Lancaster's word for it. As we've seen, Lancasterians provided evidence of a sort. Over and over, however, the evidence was only convincing because Lancasterians were so thoroughly prepared to believe it. Urban reformers at the time fell for Lancaster's misleadingly detailed descriptions because they believed in advance that a modern scientific solution must exist. Reformers assumed they lived in a special time in world history, a time in which formerly intractable human problems disappeared thanks to revolutionary advances in technology and social organization.

Writing from the law school that would become part of the University of Maryland, one Lancaster enthusiast prefaced his review of Lancaster's system by noting that the new nineteenth century was an "age of contradictions and extremes." It was an age of "numerous systems," some of which were "calculated in the highest degree to exalt the mind and ennoble the character of man." Lancaster's "admirable system of practical education," he wrote, was merely the most "excellent" of all these modern systems.[39] Similarly, New York's Lancasterians noted that "the age in which we live" was full of marvels, and the "monitorial method is among the greatest."[40] In Philadelphia, one working-class writer proclaimed his faith that modern education systems would soon eliminate "the whole dark and undigested mass of ignorance, superstition, intolerance and vice." Such evils were on the verge of healthy extinction, "never to torment mankind again." Just as the past few years had witnessed "vast improvement in physical and moral science," this working-class pundit believed, a new system could do the same for the presumed science of education.[41]

In an age of faith in world-changing systems, Lancaster's inflated rhetoric fit right in. One of Lancaster's most prominent American supporters, for example, had his own famous system. Congressman Henry Clay of Kentucky, the powerful Speaker of the House who greeted Lancaster on his arrival in Washington, DC, had created the "American System" of infrastructure improvements and economic reform. Just as Lancaster's system promised for education, Clay's system promised to revolutionize society, replace stagnation with progress, and eliminate class conflict.[42] Similarly, Lancaster's Scottish friend Robert Owen came to America with vast promises of systems and improvements. In 1825, Owen started the new intentional community of New Harmony, Indiana. His new town, he explained, would "introduce an entire new system of society; to change it from an ignorant, selfish system to an enlightened social system."[43]

It was an age of enthusiasm that thought of itself as an age of systems. Many intellectuals and reformers believed that the field of education must certainly be capable of revolutionary systematic improvement, just as were agriculture, industry, and transportation. Right before the turn of the century the American Philosophical Society sponsored an essay contest searching for just such a system, always assuming that it must exist. Entrants were prompted to contribute "an essay on a system of liberal education . . . best calculated to promote the general welfare of the United States."[44] As one leading historian explained, reformers of the era shared "an understanding of education as being systematic, scientific, simple, and above all, useful."[45]

City reformers assumed they would find their systems in the modern city itself. In the early decades of the 1800s, Americans of all backgrounds took for granted that cities were the birthplaces of the new, the place to go to find new trends—to "revel," in the words of one historian, "in urban novelty."[46] And of the cities of the world, London stood out. As Philadelphia's Benjamin Rush wrote his son in 1810, "That great city is the epitome of the whole world."[47] When American reformers found problems in their cities, they looked to bigger cities for solutions, and London was the obvious place to start. "Commerce looked to London; so did schoolmasters," as another historian aptly explained.[48] There was simply no doubt in reformers' minds that cities like London—the "epicenters of modernity"—were the proper place to find modern answers for modern problems.[49] Those assumptions, as well as the blithe confidence with which reformers made them, made it impossible for elites to see where their true answers would come from.

Those realizations would come later, at great cost. When Lancaster stormed onto the public stage, both British and American audiences were well prepared to believe his extraordinary claims. They did not much question the idea that they could solve their problems cheaply, thanks to the modern magic brewed in cities like London.

Part of the reason so many otherwise-reasonable Americans caught Lancaster fever was that they thought of transformational systems as a predictable benefit of their modern scientific age. It was easy for them to believe in revolutionary new discoveries, discoveries with the potential to change the world. Reformers often spoke of Lancaster in such terms, as a lucky discoverer of the system. One member of Parliament, for example, described modern educational systems as "the discovery of a Mr. LANCASTER."[50] He was not the only one to think of Lancaster as a discoverer of modern magic. While still at his innovative factory in New Lanark, Scotland, Robert Owen praised Lancasterian education as "the most really useful and valuable discovery, that has been made for centuries past."[51]

Reformers also talked about Lancaster's system as if it were a technological breakthrough, yet another mechanical marvel of the modern age. For instance, De Witt Clinton described the system as achieving "in education what the most finished machines for abridging labour and expence are in the mechanic arts."[52] Other Lancasterians used similar language. One fan wrote to Lancaster in 1811 and praised his "true mechanical and unerring system."[53] Another Lancasterian lauded a school where "all moves on like a powerful engine, every wheel of which sets some other wheel in motion."[54] Modern machines were proving every day the benefits of world-changing technology. Why couldn't a school machine do something similar?

Lancaster's system, many supporters assumed, merely extended the incredible benefits of modern technology and modern science to the field of education. Indeed, Lancasterians harped on the scientific nature of Lancaster's system as proof of its revolutionary significance. As Lancaster wrote to President Monroe, his system allowed schools to take their place "in the circle of sciences" that had abolished so many ancient curses.[55] In an age of advances, an age of machines, an age of scientific revolution, Lancaster promised that his system had carried education reform to "scientific perfection."[56]

It is tempting to dismiss reformers' enthusiasm as mere excess. At the time, however, other modern marvels were proving their worth. For example, though De Witt Clinton was wrong in the end about Lancasterian reform, he was on the right track about other world-changing technologies. Most dramatically, Clinton made similarly expansive claims for the Erie Canal project. While his New York rivals mocked his "big ditch," Clinton waxed positively Lancasterian about the promise of the canal. He called the canal "a work more stupendous, more magnificent, and more beneficial than has hitherto been achieved by the human race."[57]

In his support of Lancasterian schooling, Clinton's enthusiasm was misplaced. But when it came to the canal, it was not. The canal really did change the world. As Nathaniel Hawthorne effused, when it came to building the canal, De Witt Clinton was nothing less than "an enchanter, who had waved his magic wand from the Hudson to Lake Erie."[58] The canal allowed new ways of tackling ancient problems. It seemed to shrink the distance from the Great Lakes to the Atlantic; it turned weeks of transport into days. With systematic organization, hard work, investment, and modern technology, New Yorkers had truly overcome fundamental challenges of space and time. Clinton's enthusiasm had proven well-founded; the modern world of technology and systems had changed everything. Clinton had not seen the actual canal in advance, but what he saw in his mind's eye became reality.

He thought that Lancaster's system would do the same thing for schools.

The Horde That Wasn't

When Lancaster arrived in New York City in August 1818, American enthusiasm for his system was at its peak. Well-meaning philanthropists in cities such as New York, Philadelphia, and Boston had long tried to establish more charity schools. For decades, their efforts had felt inadequate. By 1818 Lancaster's promises gave reformers new life. During the 1810s and 1820s, they opened a spate of new tuition-free schools. They charted enrollment and attendance with bated breath, hoping at long last to win their desperate numbers game, to build enough charity schools to contain all the low-income children in their growing cities. At first, they thought they had succeeded.

Reformers charted their success with numbers: numbers of students educated, numbers of dollars spent, numbers of criminal careers averted. From Philadelphia, for example, a report by the Controllers of the Public Schools capitalized their conclusions to demonstrate their enthusiasm: their Lancasterian schools had educated "SEVEN THOUSAND EIGHT HUNDRED AND NINE CHILDREN" in their first three years alone.[59] A Pennsylvania State Senate committee carefully tallied attendance in Philadelphia's new Lancasterian public school system. When the system opened in 1818, it served 1,507 white boys and 1,338 white girls. The next year, the schools welcomed 1,677 boys and 1,591 girls. In 1820, the schools grew to 2,594 boys and 2,775 girls. But the trends of 1820 did not last. Attendance would plummet and never regain its peak, but in the early 1820s that future was not yet apparent. Pennsylvania's Lancasterians trumpeted their successes in squeezing thousands of students into free public schools. Most important, in their eyes, was that they had been able to slash the cost per student. Since implementing Lancasterian methods, Philadelphia's public school price tag had dropped to less than four dollars per year per student. Before then, it had hovered at above eleven dollars per child.[60]

In New York, by 1818 the system seemed to have worked. In 1806, the city's Free School Society—an organization inspired directly by Lancaster's promises—opened its first free school for white children on Lancasterian lines.[61] In 1810, the society opened its second school.[62] By 1819, it had opened two more, one in Greenwich and one on Rivington Street.[63] By 1821, the four schools enrolled a total of 2,589 white students. The society's School Number One was all boys. Number Two was mixed, and in Numbers Three and Four boys and girls were separated into different rooms with different teachers.[64] A few years later, in 1825, the system had grown to six free schools, enrolling 4,059 students.[65]

For a few years, their numbers looked good. As the trustees bragged to the state legislature in 1822, they had taught more than fourteen thousand students. Of those children, as the trustees told the tale, all of them from "the lowest classes in Society," there had not been one criminal. As the trustees put it, "not one of them is known to have been convicted of an offence against the Laws." Yet there was still more to do. As the trustees told the legislators, there were still "more than six thousand" unschooled poor children prowling the streets of their fair city. Without more support from the state, the New Yorkers worried they might yet lose their numbers game.[66]

For New York's Black population, the Manumission Society operated a smaller network of segregated "African Free Schools." Its first schools opened in 1795, teaching with traditional methods.[67] By 1817, leaders of the society worked closely with leaders of the Free School Society to operate two schools along Lancasterian lines. By 1834, the society had expanded to seven schools, which merged into the system of all-white public schools.

Cracks began to appear right away. As with all charity schools, enrollment and attendance were often seen as the measure of the Lancasterian miracle, yet enrollments at the two African Free Schools were frustratingly hard to track for society leaders. School visitors told the trustees that attendance was far below official enrollment figures. For instance, on July 25, 1818, one visitor noted with alarm from African Free School Number One, "Boys, 101; Girls 85 = 186 which is less than yesterday by 50."[68] The theme of low attendance was distressingly, dismally constant. Every visitor to every school, year after year, found similar problems. For example, on February 22, 1822, visitors to School Number Two found 229 students actually present, compared to the official enrollment figure of 414.[69] Drooping enrollment and attendance was one of the first signs of the collapse of inflated Lancasterian promises. Leaders struggled to explain it, but they generally did not yet realize the scope of the problem. In February 1822, the visitors explained away the low attendance by citing poor weather and the lack of warm clothing among the students.[70]

By then, Lancasterian schools had opened in many cities, with varying degrees of success. Boston added Lancasterian elementary schools to its existing network of public schools in 1818.[71] Baltimore tried for years to establish Lancasterian schools, finally succeeding in 1825.[72] The movement was strongest in the Northeast, but Lancasterians made inroads elsewhere as well. For instance, Savannah, Georgia, had operated a Lancasterian school since at least 1817, though, unlike the funding mix in most northern cities, the school was always exclusively funded and operated by a private philanthropic organization.[73] As historian Carl F. Kaestle has traced, there was at least talk and planning for Lancasterian schools throughout the nation. In North Carolina, a committee report recommended Lancasterian schools to the state legislature in 1817, though there was apparently no follow-through. Virginia claimed Lancasterian schools in eight cities, and Kentucky claimed them in two. In the West, Detroit and Cincinnati opened Lancasterian schools as well. By 1825, reformers shared stories of Lancasterian schools across New York in Albany, Poughkeepsie, Hudson, Troy, Schenectady, and Utica. In Connecticut, New Haven, Hartford, and Guilford boasted Lancasterian schools. In Pennsylvania, outside of Philadelphia, there were Lancasterian schools in Harrisburg, Pittsburgh, Erie, New Castle, and, of course, the town of Lancaster itself.[74]

In many ways, the story of Lancasterian schooling in Philadelphia offers the clearest example of the trajectory of reform. Of course, every city was different. Every city had different funding patterns from state and city governments, different constellations of existing charity organizations, and different individuals pushing a wide variety of plans and proposals. It would be far too simple, then, to see a city like Philadelphia as a simple stand-in for the Lancasterian reform overall. However, thanks to the anxious tracking of attendance by Philadelphia's numbers-obsessed school leaders, the Philadelphia experience can illuminate the Lancasterian crash.[75]

Recall that Philadelphia's reformers—white and Black alike—had a long tradition of charity schooling. Since the 1790s, leaders such as Richard Allen and various abolition societies had run free schools for African American students.[76] By 1800, church schools, especially schools run by Quakers, ed-

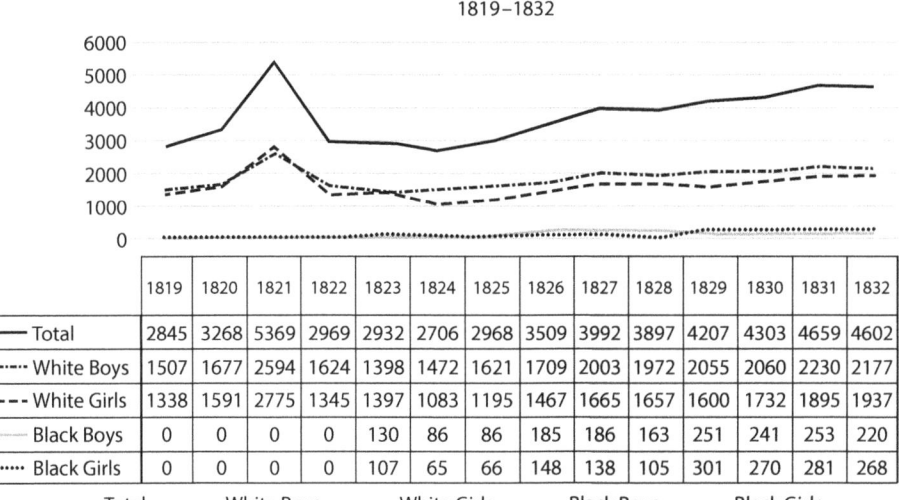

Philadelphia Lancasterian Public School Enrollments, 1819–1832

	1819	1820	1821	1822	1823	1824	1825	1826	1827	1828	1829	1830	1831	1832
Total	2845	3268	5369	2969	2932	2706	2968	3509	3992	3897	4207	4303	4659	4602
White Boys	1507	1677	2594	1624	1398	1472	1621	1709	2003	1972	2055	2060	2230	2177
White Girls	1338	1591	2775	1345	1397	1083	1195	1467	1665	1657	1600	1732	1895	1937
Black Boys	0	0	0	0	130	86	86	185	186	163	251	241	253	220
Black Girls	0	0	0	0	107	65	66	148	138	105	301	270	281	268

For enrollment-obsessed reformers in 1820, Lancaster's promises seemed to be coming true, only to face a disappointingly mediocre future. Data from *Annual Reports of the Board of Controllers of Philadelphia's Public Schools*, Historical Society of Pennsylvania; *Report on the Subject of Education, Read in the Senate of Pennsylvania, March 1, 1822* (Harrisburg, PA: C. Mowry, 1822), American Antiquarian Society.

ucated dozens of low-income white students as well.[77] In 1801, the Philadelphia Society for the Establishment and Support of Charity Schools laid the foundation for Lancasterian schooling. By 1817, the society operated two free schools, one for white girls and one for white boys. The girls' school had used Lancasterian methods since at least 1813, and by 1817 the boys' school did so too.[78]

The peak of Lancasterian excitement in Philadelphia came in 1818. In that year, just as Lancaster himself was arriving in the United States, the state of Pennsylvania passed yet another law mandating tuition-free public schooling for Philadelphia. The law established Philadelphia and the surrounding county as the state's first public school district. Directors of the district would be elected, and they would appoint a new board of controllers. The schools in the new district were specifically mandated to follow "Lancaster's system of education, in its most improved state."[79]

The Board of Controllers, led by the energetic Roberts Vaux, established

THE MODEL SCHOOL
East Side of Chester Street, North of Race Street

Photo by F. D. E., 3-21-1913

Philadelphia's Model School, constructed in 1818, as it still looked in 1913. From Franklin Davenport Edmunds, *The Public School Buildings of the City of Philadelphia from 1745 to 1845* (Philadelphia: self-pub., 1913), 52.

six schools immediately. They built a new Lancasterian Model School to introduce Philadelphians to the promise of Lancasterian education and to train new generations of Lancasterian teachers for Philadelphia's new schools. It wasn't cheap. The Model School cost a total of $15,131.01, including the furniture and the building lot.[80] It is always difficult to compare dollar values over time, but even with a very conservative comparison, this outlay equaled nearly $2 million in twenty-first-century terms.[81] Vaux and his allies thought that it would be well worth it. They could not anticipate how difficult it would be to work with Joseph Lancaster. They did not know how difficult Lancasterian reform would prove to be. In 1818 they saw endless possibility.

Starting with six school buildings, Philadelphia's public schools added another in 1820, then one for Black students in 1822. Enrollment leaped up at first, from a total of 2,845 students in 1818 to 5,369 in 1821. By 1825, the district ran a total of nine schools, with two segregated schools for Black students, one for boys and one for girls. But the enrollment numbers had crashed, never to regain their peak from 1821. From a total of 5,369 students in 1821, enrollment dropped to 2,969 the next year. By 1824, it fell to only 2,706. It inched back upward after that, but the city's Lancasterian schools failed in their most important expectation: they did not serve thousands upon thousands of students at a low price. In the end, they failed where it mattered most: they lost the numbers game.[82]

There was no simple explanation for the failure. Students, teachers, parents, and taxpayers complained about various aspects of the overhyped Lancasterian dream. Philadelphia's Board of Controllers found themselves by the late 1820s in a very different situation than the one they had imagined. At the start of the Lancasterian revolution, they thought they would soon welcome Lancaster himself to their city. They thought that their main problem would be finding enough buildings to accommodate the explosive growth of their world-changing school system. Instead, they discovered that Lancaster himself was unmanageable and that his system never lived up to its promise.

Students stopped coming. Parents complained. Teachers left.

Losing the Game

When Philadelphia's Lancasterians found themselves holding only the residue of Lancaster's inflated expectations, they scrambled. The long-term contribution of the Lancasterian movement, in Philadelphia and every other city, was not in its ballyhooed scientific precision. Rather, Lancaster's scientific-sounding promises and his expensive newfangled gadgets were merely a lure. They never worked as promised, though they did have some successes here and there. Nevertheless, the system's promises had lured reformers into a sense of new possibilities. They lured leaders such as Roberts Vaux in Philadelphia and De Witt Clinton in New York to pour money and energy into the project. They lured students and parents into expanding their visions of the possibilities of public education. They incited state and city governments to establish elected boards of public school administrators.

In the end, Lancaster's system could never make good on all its promises. Like Lancaster himself, the system made endless promises but could never follow through.

In Philadelphia as elsewhere, the importance of Lancasterian methods was primarily accidental. Lancaster's unwarranted confidence convinced American cities to buy into the promise of tuition-free schooling for all. Reformers in cities around the United States had leaped to implement Lancaster's ideas based on sketchy evidence. They did not look too closely at Lancaster's promises, largely because they assumed that their modern world could produce a system like Lancaster's. Reformers had long hoped to provide tuition-free school for all the children in their cities, and they latched on to Lancaster's system as the modern solution to their intractable problem. Based on his promises, city leaders promised free schooling for all. Once that genie was out of the bottle, leaders such as Roberts Vaux could only manage it, not squeeze it back in.

5

A Growing Disorder

To casual observers in 1809, especially to those looking from a long distance, the new Lancasterian schools looked impressive. From his vantage point an ocean away, for example, New York's De Witt Clinton thought that the London system was working exactly as promised. He was delighted by the "celerity in instruction" he heard about in Lancaster's English schools. He celebrated the "rapid improvement" and "purity of morals" among the pupils.[1]

For anyone more intimately acquainted with Lancasterian schools, however, some fundamental problems became immediately apparent. As one girl complained in 1808, it was absolutely impossible for her to carry out her assigned monitorial duties at the Lancasterian school in Maiden Bradley, about a hundred miles west of London. The primary characteristic of the school was the "unmethodical untrade-like way in which orders are still attended to."[2] Similarly, in 1811 a visitor to another early Lancasterian school in Maidstone, forty miles to the east of London, noticed with alarm a "growing disorder" at the school. If things were not fixed—and fixed fast—this observer worried it might cause a fatal "hurt to the sistem [sic]."[3]

Insiders in the United States were just as dismayed by the flaws in Lancaster's plans. Those flaws became painfully apparent as soon as the system moved from the printed page to real world schools. In New York, for instance, by 1817 the leaders of the Free School Society noticed a disastrous structural problem—namely, they could not get their monitors to monitor. As soon as any youth climbed to the top of the monitorial system, he or she usually left. New York's Lancasterians could never find a solution, though they considered some far-fetched proposals. At the time, the leaders of New

York's Lancasterian schools kept their worries to themselves. They still hoped they could quietly fix the system.

By the middle of the 1820s, however, even casual observers had noticed that the system was not working as promised. Most outside observers did not know how difficult it was for administrators to retain monitors, but they noticed other significant problems. By that time, the malfunctions in Lancasterian schools were so egregious that they had become obvious to all. They could no longer be wished away or blamed on temporary glitches. For instance, one visitor to a Lancasterian school in Boston found that the school was atrocious. Unlike the always-working students depicted in Lancaster's pamphlets, at this real-life Lancasterian school students languished every day in "a long interval of idleness." "This school on the whole," the observer concluded, was "in very bad condition."[4]

By the mid-1820s, the sad fact had become apparent to anyone: the system as a whole was in a perilous state. The dream of perfectly synchronized educational progress could not survive the complicated, messy nature of real schools. It was more than Lancaster's failure to predict that advanced monitors would drop out. It wasn't only that Lancaster had not imagined the damage that could be done by lazy, uninterested teachers like the one in Boston. It was bigger than the steady losses leaders racked up in their desperate numbers games.

The problems with the system were far more basic, more deeply rooted in Lancaster's utter misunderstanding of actual schools. In New York, for example, a new Lancasterian high school found out the hard way in 1825 that students did not fit into their neat Lancasterian categories. As the leaders of the school explained, real students showed up with "great diversities in acquirement." It proved impossible for the school's leaders to wedge these students into "proper classifications." Students could not move up the Lancasterian ranks, because there were in real life no clear ranks, only a messy mix of various abilities and backgrounds.[5]

One visitor to Baltimore's new Lancasterian school found a similar problem. "The doubt was irresistibly awakened," the visitor explained, "whether the diversity of human talent and mental acquirement were not too various to be thrown together, in such concert."[6] This visitor had traveled from Louisville and toured Lancasterian schools in New York, Boston, Philadelphia, and Baltimore. When he started his tour, he had been thrilled by the Lancasterian promise. By the time he finished, he was not so sure. In addition to all the problems he did not know about—monitors leaving, teachers lazing, costs rising, enrollments drooping—the schools he witnessed obviously differed enormously from the schools he had read about. In real life, he wrote, Lancasterian schools "seemed to carry the principle of classification to a degree of injurious amalgamation."[7] The system, in other words, relied on students fitting into a theoretically perfect network of round holes, but most real-world students were square pegs of one size or another.

As Lancaster was making an embarrassment of himself between 1818 and 1823, the problems in the Lancasterian system also became glaringly obvious. Yet the solutions were nowhere to be found. The biggest problem might have been the one that was first apparent: the imagined savings of the system were only imaginary. In practice, Lancaster's cheap solution was not so cheap after all. The traditional funding mix for tuition-free charity schools— philanthropy plus tuition dollars topped off with government largesse— proved inadequate. For one thing, teachers needed to be paid, and without tuition fees those salaries were very difficult to meet. And even if reformers could somehow find money to pay them, teachers needed to learn the system. But how? Lancaster, to no one's surprise, tried to monopolize teacher training. Yet there was no way he could supervise enough teachers to meet the needs of a multicity reform plan. Without teachers who knew the system, Lancasterian dreams had no chance. But that was not the worst of the system's failings. Monitors refused to work for free. The very heart of the Lancasterian promise proved to be a simple-minded delusion.

Not So Cheap

At first, Lancasterian reformers in the United States hoped that their problems would only be temporary. When costs ran far higher than predicted, some leaders assumed that the system would soon right itself. In Philadelphia, for instance, the leaders of the Lancasterian Adelphi School fretted in 1810 that they could not survive long financially. Enchanted with Lancaster's promises, they had budgeted for only four dollars per year per student, but they were actually paying out much more. If only they could run their school at full capacity, they figured, they would drive down costs per student. They were currently losing their endless numbers game, serving two hundred students and paying far too much to educate each one. If they could only attract a hundred more, they thought, the system would realize its financial promise. If not, they might not be able to keep the promises they made to their donors to educate three hundred students at a revolutionarily cheap rate.[8]

A decade later, the leaders of Philadelphia's public schools were still stuck in the same wistful trap of "if only." They reported that their costs had surged far above their budget in 1820, but that was only because they faced the exorbitant start-up costs associated with the Lancasterian system. In order to realize the system in its most perfect form, they had had to purchase real estate and construct made-to-order Lancasterian school buildings. They were stretched far beyond their means, but it would all be worth it if only the system worked. If only they could attract enough students, they reported, they would soon recoup the savings Lancaster promised. If only.[9]

Their first move was to build a new Model School to Lancasterian specifications. They had hoped to finish it by the time Lancaster himself arrived in town, but there were endless construction delays. They hired Ed Baker as their first teacher, paying him a generous annual salary of $1,200. Baker had been one of Lancaster's apprentices at the Borough Road School and followed him across the ocean to ply his teaching trade. They also tried to hire Lancaster, for a well-paid position as their superintendent, to help train new teachers and oversee the school's general operations. The Philadelphians asked him to run the new school they were planning for girls. They tried everything to include Lancaster in their plans.[10]

Lancaster did not make it easy. When the school board initially offered him the unheard-of salary of $120 per month to help get their schools up and running, Lancaster accepted the money, but he refused to do the work. He seemed offended that they would think of him as someone who would simply run a school. And the proposed salary, he told board leader Roberts Vaux, was "very little above the value of the salary of a common teacher and much less than those in New York and some other places."[11] At the time Lancaster said so, he knew very well that he was telling an outright lie. As we'll see, teacher pay was one of the main reasons why the Lancasterian system never worked very well. In 1817, New York paid its top Lancasterian teacher an annual salary of $1,000.[12] By 1819, reeling from a nationwide financial panic, the trustees of the New York Free School Society realized they needed to drop that number to $800 at the most.[13] When possible, they tried to hire women teachers for the much lower salary of $300 annually.[14] Lancaster knew that. Roberts Vaux knew that. Worst of all, Lancaster knew that Vaux knew it. Yet he did not scruple to lie right to Vaux's face.

When the Philadelphians offered Lancaster the chance to direct their new girls' school in 1819, Lancaster again balked. The salary they offered, he sniffed, was only eight dollars above his monthly costs.[15] "I am grieved," Lancaster wrote, "that there should be any controversy or discussion on subjects of finances."[16] In the end, he briefly agreed to teach at the girls' school, but he attempted to delay the full opening. Until the school board finally dismissed him in March 1819, he ran the school on a temporary basis, not allowing any additional teachers in to learn the system.

Why would Lancaster make things so difficult? Throughout his career Lancaster tended to see enemies everywhere. He always did his self-destructive best to turn his friends against him. In the case of Philadelphia's school board, Lancaster seemed miffed that they did not treat him with more deference. Yes, he wanted more money, always more money. But perhaps just as importantly, he expected the city's elites to come to him on bended knee, to defer to his superior genius. As he wrote to Vaux, he was startled to find he was not being "kindly attended to" in the negotiations. It had been "both unpleasant and painful to my feelings," he explained, that the other members of the board had not shown him "that general kindness of attention of which I hope I have done nothing to render myself unworthy."[17] Lancaster seemed to feel personally slighted by his treatment at the hands of the school board. In November 1818, for instance, several members of the committee visited the school while he was there. They toured the building—it was still under construction at the time even though Lancaster had promised it could be up and running the previous month—yet none of them stopped to pay special respects to Lancaster himself.[18] It is impossible to tell for sure from the archival record; Lancaster only told Vaux that "several of the committee were at the School." He complained that "none of them called on me."[19] But it is easy to imagine Lancaster huddled in his corner of the building, waiting for the visitors to visit him, planning to appear busy at work, too busy for an interruption—and then hearing the door slam behind the visitors as they left.

What's more, Lancaster thought he had better options. While the Philadelphia board was preparing its first model school and offering Lancaster a plush salary of $120 per month to supervise, Lancaster was dreaming of greener fields. In Boston, he told his daughter Betsy, a new Lancasterian school promised to rake in tuition payments of $6,000 in its first year. The leaders of that city, he bragged, would not nitpick the way the Philadelphians did. Rather, "the Institution will be altogether my own." The city leaders in Boston, he wrote, did not refuse Lancaster's salary demands, even though "the price I have named is <u>double</u> the price of Philadelphia Public Schools."[20]

Of course, that was not true either. For its new Lancasterian schools, Boston had no more need of Lancaster himself than did Philadelphia. Perhaps a gentler, kinder person might have found a comfortable home in Philadelphia, working to make the new schools succeed in spite of the obstacles and glitches in the system. That was not Lancaster's approach. Instead, as he had done in London, Lancaster alienated even his closest friends with his vicious and wholly unnecessary antagonism. He attacked everyone around him. Immediately upon his arrival in Philadelphia, for instance, he denounced his former apprentice Ed Baker—the teacher the city first hired—as "the most stupid ignoramus" they could have found.[21] For their crime of not recognizing his superior genius—and for not being willing to pay him for it—Lancaster blasted the Philadelphia school board as no "gentlemen" but rather "a parcel of milksops." It was only because of his personal loyalty to Roberts Vaux, Lancaster averred, that he had not taken steps to destroy them publicly. As Lancaster put it, if not for Vaux, he would have attacked them in the newspapers, and Lancaster bragged that his criticism would have instantly discredited his opponents politically.[22]

Lancaster's bitter denunciations soon escalated beyond the private meetings of the school board. Tired of Lancaster's endless delays, one member of the school board—Ebenezer Ferguson—visited the girls' school in late February 1819. Ferguson asked Lancaster to allow some women to observe the school in action, so that they could learn the Lancasterian system. Lancaster refused. As Lancaster told the tale, Ferguson "attempted to intrude them on me . . . a measure premature and ill-advised." According to Lancaster, Ferguson then "<u>threatened</u> me in the presence of the children." Ferguson soon followed with "profane swearing."[23]

Lancaster demanded Ferguson's removal from the board. As he huffed to Roberts Vaux, he was not willing to put up with such indignities. With his usual blend of delusion, anger, and intoxicating self-importance, he told Roberts Vaux, "Either he or I must quit the school."[24] By that point Lancaster's threat to leave was accepted with alacrity. The school board agreed finally to pay him an additional bonus of $490 if he would quit their schools entirely.[25]

With Lancaster making himself a problem elsewhere, the trustees of New

York's Free School Society were free to tackle other distressing issues. In private meetings, the trustees spoke frankly about their desperate financial situation. As early as 1817, the trustees confronted the fact that their actual costs far exceeded their Lancasterian expectations. In August of 1817, they cut their budget to the bone. They eliminated rewards for monitors, eliminated the post of assistant teacher, and added a new job for their own committee: a full-time budget hawk, dedicated to making sure that all expenditures were as frugal as possible.[26]

It didn't work. No matter how much they scrimped and saved, they were never able to make ends meet. At the outset of 1819, the trustees still blamed themselves. As one committee reported, it was time for the trustees to recognize "the imperious necessity of a more rigid adherence to the economy of the Lancasterian System of Education."[27] They still believed they could make the system work the way Lancaster described; they still dreamed the Lancasterian dream of a "School for the Cheap Education of Youth."[28]

By the summer of 1820, the trustees confronted the harsh reality: they could not in fact close the gap between Lancasterian dreams and harsh financial realities. Even with the strictest financial discipline, there was simply no way to run Lancasterian schools on a Lancasterian budget. Sure, the monitors worked for free, but the resulting savings were never as decisive as Lancaster had imagined. Even without actual salaries, maintaining monitors proved expensive. In 1819, the board discovered that it cost almost $300 annually just to support one advanced monitor—to pay for clothes, food, and lodging.[29] They imposed the strictest cuts they could imagine, but they could not get that number below $200 per monitor per year.[30] Despite the use of unpaid child labor, the board found that its numbers just would not add up. In that summer of 1820, the trustees made the first moves toward abandoning the basic premises of the system, though they still tried to keep the Lancasterian plan alive. From 1820 on, the advanced monitors would no longer be given room and board. Students would no longer be rewarded with tickets and prizes. Teachers had been teaching extra classes for advanced students, but those classes ended. At the time, New York's trustees did not admit that they were abandoning the system as a whole—they merely thought they were tweaking it to match dire financial realities.[31]

Those realities were harsher than Lancasterian reformers had imagined. It was not just that they underestimated the costs of buildings and monitors. More importantly, at the beginning of the Lancasterian crusade, reformers in New York and Philadelphia were still organized into traditional philanthropic organizations, which simply could not handle the financial exigencies of modern urban life. As the historian Michael B. Katz described, before the Lancasterian movement, traditional urban charity schools had been operated by a system of "paternalistic voluntarism." Leaders such as Roberts Vaux in Philadelphia and De Witt Clinton in New York engaged in school administration as part of their expected roles as benevolent elites. These voluntarists considered their ad hoc organization not a weakness but a sign of the purity of their intent; in Katz's words, they "scorned the need for elaborate organization, state control, or professional staff."[32] But as the financial and organizational flaws in Lancaster's system became apparent, so too did the weaknesses inherent in this model of philanthropic schooling.

For one thing, philanthropists such as Roberts Vaux were simply spread too thin. Vaux was involved in so many organizations that a handwritten list of the "public offices and Societies in which Roberts Vaux has served" ran to a full four pages of tight script. He was involved in everything from the Academy of Natural Sciences to the management of the Pennsylvania Hospital.[33] Obviously, neither Vaux nor anybody else considered his commitment to any single philanthropic group as full-time professional administration. Rather, prominent citizens like Vaux were celebrated for their willingness to lend their names and their prestige to a huge variety of worthwhile causes. They were never expected to bring relevant expertise to the role. Rather, they were only expected to lend their imprimatur to the various enterprises, to signal to other wealthy elites that these organizations deserved their support.

When American reformers first imagined a network of Lancasterian schools in their cities, they assumed that it would be run by traditional elites like Vaux. When the Philadelphia Society for the Free Instruction of Indigent Boys opened its first charity school in 1799, for instance, it was funded entirely by the personal donations of its nine members. As the society grew and opened more schools, it maintained its old funding system. By 1801, members paid a dollar each per month to cover costs for the society's tuition-free schools.[34]

Similar philanthropic financial models were the norm for all benevolent organizations, though the details sometimes differed. For example, one organization funded a school for Black children by charging its elite white members three dollars each for an annual membership.[35] A women's group fined its members twenty-five cents for every missed meeting.[36] Most common was the solicitation of subscriptions. Every philanthropic group published long lists of subscribers, in which elites announced to the general public how much money they had donated to a variety of causes.[37] In Philadelphia, for example, the founders of the Adelphi School published in 1810 a five-page list of subscribers, starting with those who had donated fifty dollars and dwindling to those who had given a quarter.[38]

The details differed in different cities, but the principle was the same. Before the Lancasterian system was widely adopted, tuition-free schools were generally seen as the responsibility of churches and public-minded elites. For a while, the old philanthropic model managed to cobble together enough funds to set up Lancasterian schools. When wealthy patrons died, they sometimes supplied a windfall, as when Christopher Ludwick in 1801 left the huge gift of $8,000 to the Philadelphia Society for the Free Instruction of Indigent Boys.[39] Philanthropic groups also counted on personal connections and celebrity appeal to meet their financial obligations on a school-by-school basis. For instance, when the Philadelphia society wanted to build a new school in 1803, Vaux and other well-known elites enlisted the help of famed physician Benjamin Rush to lead a fundraising campaign. In a short time, Rush was able to solicit a subscription of $2,800.[40]

Donations, Legacies, and Munificence

In their first flush of Lancasterian enthusiasm, elites believed that the savings promised by the system would allow them to expand their network of tuition-free schools without fundamentally changing their fundraising traditions. They assumed they could attract enough bequests and donations to pay for a greatly enlarged school system because they believed Lancaster's promises of dramatic per-pupil savings. When those financial savings proved illusory, however, Lancasterians were confronted with a dilemma. They needed to find ways to pay for their new schools, which were not actually as cheap as they had been led to believe. Before they finally hit on the winning formula we'll see in chapter 7, Lancasterians struggled to scrape together enough money to keep their schools financially solvent. As the case of the New York Free School Society demonstrates, reformers continued to rely hopefully, in the words of one 1820 report, on "the donations and Legacies of charitable Individuals, the bounty of the Corporation [city government] and the munificence of the Legislature."[41]

Even before Lancaster himself arrived in New York in 1818 and the movement kicked into high gear, New York's Free School Society leaders found it difficult to pay for their growing network of Lancasterian tuition-free schools. As they planned to expand from two schools to three in 1817, for instance, the trustees assumed they would rely on "subscriptions" to foot the bill.[42] At the time, they still managed to cover costs—barely—by regular philanthropic subscriptions, annual city payments, and the occasional bequest bonanza, as when John van Blarcom died in 1817 and left $500 to the society.[43]

Trustees of the Free School Society saw their role, at first, as fundraisers. They spread out into the city, subscription books in hand, willing to make themselves pests among their wealthy friends and connections. They asked for funding for specific enterprises, such as the opening of a third Lancasterian school. And they promised to publicize the names and amounts of subscriptions, as when Henry Rutgers donated a full hundred dollars to the goal in 1818.[44]

As they soon discovered, however, those aging networks of philanthropic largesse could not meet the financial needs of their expanding urban school systems. By 1819, the New York reformers realized they were in dire financial straits. At the beginning of the calendar year, they were running a dizzying deficit of $11,465. They had only $2,235 in their treasury.[45] They regularly received money from the city government, but in 1819 it only amounted to $3,619.20. Even worse, as they stared their deficit in the face in January, they knew they would not receive their city funds until September.[46] Desperate, they made what they thought would be a one-time application to the state legislature in Albany. They asked for $10,165. The trustees were careful to frame their request in the old language of charity and benevolence. The New York school leaders pleaded with the state legislature for the money as an act of state philanthropy, a single expenditure that would allow New York to "prevent the vices and crimes of European Cities from visiting our own." In 1819, older notions of the proper relationship between government and education still prevailed, at least among the white-haired trustees of New York's Free School Society. They did not yet see themselves as providing a service that ought to be fully funded by taxes, but rather as a benevolent organization pleading with other elites to extend "the hand of Charity."[47]

Alas, state legislators met the request with "much opposition."[48] The trustees were not new to the ways of state politics, however. They sent an influential member to the state capital in Albany to lobby for their request, "to pay the necessary attention to promote its passage."[49] Even so, it was an uphill battle. Though eventually the legislature approved a $5,000 donation,[50] in the meantime the trustees took out a bank loan of $2,000 to cover immediate costs.[51]

The lessons were clear for the trustees as well as the legislators. Tuition-free schools—whether they were called "charity" schools or "public" schools—could no longer count on old philanthropic networks to pay for their expanding costs. State legislators responded with half measures. They sent half the requested funds, for instance, and they also established a special lottery to help fund charity schools.[52] But those half measures were never enough. In 1819, the Free School Society gladly accepted $1,000 from the new lottery fund, but its costs and debts soared much higher.[53] For those who had hoped that Lancaster's system would allow them to educate thousands for the same amount they formerly needed to educate hundreds, there was no mistaking it: the system had failed.

Liberal Salary &c.

One of the most disappointing failures, financially, was the continuing high cost of teacher salaries. In theory, Lancaster's system dramatically slashed costs by dramatically reducing the number of teachers needed. In practice, the cost of teacher salaries was always too high, even when teachers themselves felt woefully underpaid. The dilemma of teachers' salaries put reformers in a tricky situation: if they paid too much, they could not meet their budgets; if they paid too little, they could not keep their teachers.

One of the first budget-cutting moves the New York trustees made was to cut teachers' salaries. In 1819, for example, they cut the teacher's salary at School Number One from $1,000 to $800 annually.[54] Not surprisingly, teachers left. It became commonplace for experienced teachers to hunt around for the best offers. Ed Baker—Lancaster's former student-apprentice at Borough Road in London—jumped around quite a bit. He led a Lancasterian school in Albany until at least 1816, served a brief stint in New York, and then left for a better offer in Philadelphia in 1817.[55] William Smith taught for at least three years at the Free School Society's first school, but he also quit in 1817.[56]

What were administrators to do? One of the answers came relatively easily. Administrators could hire women, they thought, for much cheaper rates. In 1819 the New York trustees were able to hire Susan Pickton, the wife of teacher Charles Pickton, for only $300 annually.[57] In Boston, too, Lancasterian schools found much cheaper female teachers. One typical female salary in Boston was only thirty-nine dollars for a three-month teaching stint.[58]

But for reformers at the time, the solution of grossly underpaid female teachers was only partial. Just like men, women often left. As a result, students could find themselves with several new teachers every year, as female teachers came and went.[59] In addition, sometimes women teachers would be forced out even if they were willing to work for low wages. For example, as soon as a teacher got pregnant, as happened to Susan Pickton in New York in 1820, she was expected to leave her job.[60]

Even when administrators could hold on to teachers, the relationship between teachers and trustees was often rocky. For their part, administrators often assumed that one of the reasons for their schools' lackluster performance must be lackluster teaching. In New York in 1822, the board of trustees pinned the blame on teacher John Missing. To explain the low enrollment numbers at School Number Two, the Free School Society's trustees accused Missing of being "delinquent," of slacking off and scaring students away. The Free School Society tried to hold his feet to the fire. They placed Missing on a new salary scale, one that paid Missing a per-student rate instead of a flat salary.[61]

Unfortunately, the records do not include any evidence of Missing's feelings about this new pay system. We do not know for sure how he felt about the accusations made against him. We do not know if he resented the charges or accused the trustees of blaming him unfairly, when the blame should have been on the system itself. In a few other cases, however, we do have direct evidence of teachers' feelings. In Boston, for example, for at least one case we have angry proof. In 1829, teacher George Fowle quit. George was the brother of the more prominent Boston teacher William B. Fowle, whose career we'll examine in more detail in chapter 7. George didn't last as long in the job as William. Before he left, he penned an open letter to the administrators of his Lancasterian school. He had done his best, Fowle wrote, for the past two years to make their Lancasterian school a success. Thanks to his unappreciated labor, he had increased the attendance at the school to its maximum. He blamed the school board for their "lukewarmness," a lack of zeal and energy that had driven away students. He blamed them for underpaying him and for failing to recognize his years of hard labor. He refused, Fowle wrote, to throw "away my youthful days for such an inadequate return."[62]

Unfortunately for historians, most teachers never left any records about their experiences. The negotiations carried on between teachers and administrators were usually far more subtle. When a visitor from the school board toured New York's African Free School in 1828, for instance, the teacher just happened to show him a couple of job offers the teacher had received from another Lancasterian school. The teacher assured his boss that he was devoted to "our poor little company," but he made sure the visitor was aware of his many opportunities, including the fact that other schools offered a "Liberal Salary &c."[63]

Normal School

Teachers like the one at the African Free School knew they had their bosses in a bind. Once a teacher could credibly claim to have mastered the Lancasterian system, he or she became a rare and valuable human resource. From the beginning, Joseph Lancaster had promised that his system would train its own teachers in abundance, but in practice, there were never enough. Reformers disagreed strenuously about the kind of training needed. Hungry administrators insisted that teachers could learn the system in a few short weeks. Other reformers insisted that it would take years. Not surprisingly, Joseph Lancaster himself tried to monopolize the training of teachers, demanding that only his personally trained apprentices deserved to be considered proper Lancasterian teachers.

In his earliest publications, Lancaster envisioned a self-perpetuating network of teacher training. As students became monitors and monitors became adepts, each Lancasterian school would generate the next generation of Lancasterian teachers, at least in theory.[64] However, in real Lancasterian schools the process of teacher training was far slower. As early as 1812, the growing network of American Lancasterian schools struggled to find enough teachers. In his Georgetown school, Lancaster's former apprentice Robert Ould worked at "qualifying" as many new teachers as he could, as fast as he could, but he could not keep up with demand. As he told Lancaster in 1812, "the demand for schoolmasters is great."[65]

Part of the problem, as usual, was Lancaster himself. Wherever he went, he insisted on the sole authority to train new teachers in the system. Before he left for the United States, Lancaster received letters from all over the United Kingdom, begging for trained teachers.[66] Lancaster sent his handpicked former apprentices out to various schools across England and Ireland, but he never moved fast enough to satisfy the demand.

Across the United States, meanwhile, the lack of trained Lancasterian teachers became an unexpected bottleneck for reformers. A group of philanthropists in Savannah, Georgia, for example, had done everything necessary to open a new Lancasterian school. At least, they thought they had. They raised money, bought manuals, rented a schoolroom, and furnished it according to Lancasterian specifications. Before they could open, however, they realized they could not find a properly trained teacher. They wrote anxiously to their reform allies in New York. Could they send a trainee to one of the New York Lancasterian schools to learn the system?[67]

The Savannans assumed that their teacher-in-training would need two or three months to learn the system.[68] But this was wishful thinking. One ardent Lancasterian from Delaware argued that no one could be considered a true Lancasterian teacher unless she or he had trained for at least five years. "It cannot reasonably be expected," he sniffed, "that a few weeks or months should communicate the whole manner and spirit of any proper system of education."[69]

The desperate administrators of New York's Free School Society saw things differently. For obvious reasons, they tried to create a fast track to Lancasterian certification for anyone willing to try. In 1818, they opened their schools as free training centers for potential teachers. At no cost, willing candidates could come to New York for a six-week experience.[70] At the end of six weeks, if the candidate had "passed through the several monitorial grades," he or she could apply for a formal "certificate . . . signed by the President and Secretary." The brief, free training, the trustees insisted, was enough to create new teachers "thoroughly versed in the Lancasterian system."[71]

Purists scoffed, especially those who had a strong self-interested reason to insist on long, expensive training for any potential competitors. Before his break with his former mentor Joseph Lancaster, teacher Ed Baker claimed that teacher training must be rigorous and extensive. "No person," Baker wrote in 1816, "is qualified to teach by [the Lancasterian system] who has not been instructed in some school which emanated from [Lancaster's school]." He himself had spent years laboring under Lancaster's abusive tutelage and apparently did not want newcomers to enjoy any shortcuts. Baker had painstakingly compiled a dossier of his own credentials, a packet of what Baker called "convincing documents that [Baker] taught a large School in London to the satisfaction of hundreds of Parents."[72]

Extensive training would slow down reformers' ability to spread Lancaster's system. It would be expensive. But it might generate rich new revenue for the trainers. As usual, when a conflict emerged between spreading his ideas and cashing in on them, Lancaster fought hard for the latter. After his move to the United States, he had received requests from potential teachers around the country. As one wrote from Chillicothe, Ohio, the local school board would not see him as a "genuine" Lancasterian unless he studied directly under Lancaster. How much, this teacher asked, would Lancaster charge for genuine training?[73] Lancaster was quick to recognize the potential. If teacher training could become a lucrative part of his system, Lancaster would fight to control the process. It would not be enough for teachers to merely observe for a short while, he argued. And it would never be acceptable for teachers to learn the system from anyone else. As he put it to Roberts Vaux in 1818, the "training of teachers is a most important part of the great object." Only those he trained directly could count as reliably certified Lancasterian teachers.[74] He promised the Philadelphians he would train teachers in abundance, but in practice he refused to let potential teachers observe him in action.[75]

Bound to Fail

As Lancaster made himself difficult in Philadelphia, however, Lancasterian reformers all over the United States realized they had a bigger problem. Not only were trained teachers hard to find. Not only did the market for those teachers drive up salary costs, shattering the dream of low-cost education for thousands of low-income students. Beyond those enormous real-world obstacles to achieving Lancasterian perfection, there loomed a more fundamental challenge—namely, the central premise of the system fell apart.

As we've seen, it fell apart almost immediately, but it took a while for administrators to recognize how intractable their problem was. From the very beginning, advanced monitors left their schools. Quite reasonably, as soon as they stopped learning, they considered their time at school complete. Once monitors thought that the school had nothing left to teach them, their parents pulled them out. After they left, sometimes the departing children taught in non-Lancasterian schools for pay, instead of teaching at Lancasterian schools for free. Sometimes they found other jobs, using their new skills to earn good money as professional secretaries, actuaries, or business managers.[76] It seems like an obvious result in retrospect, but it was something neither Lancaster nor his adoring fans had considered.

That was not how the system was supposed to work. It was supposed to thrive on the cheerful free labor of monitors of all ages. Without that labor, the system was not a modern marvel but simply a traditional failure. By the end of 1817, the trustees of New York's Free School Society acknowledged the severity of the issue. It wasn't just one or two monitors here or there who decided to leave. It was a general trend.[77]

Trustees' first instinct was to buckle down. In order to stem the loss of precious child labor, they considered a traditional remedy: binding their monitors as apprentices. After all, the practice had been the norm at Lancasterian schools in England. At least until his hostile break with the British and Foreign School Society in 1814, Joseph Lancaster bound his apprentices to him for specified periods of time. As one supporter described it, using the old terminology, "Mr. Lancaster claimed power over these lads as Master." At that date—1813—Lancaster's apprentices still had formal "indenture" forms signed by their parents, giving Lancaster full legal power over their work, usually until boys turned twenty-one or girls turned eighteen.[78]

Lancaster made the most of it. As more Lancasterian schools popped up across England, Lancaster dispatched his apprentices as he wished. He was able to exert full authority over the young teachers: their training, their work, and their earnings. Anyone who did not satisfy Lancaster could be removed from their teaching post, giving up the promise of future earnings. All power was in Lancaster's hands. The children were not consulted; their work was not their own until their indentures had expired.[79]

Naturally, some of them complained. After all, the ancient system of apprenticeship had broken down significantly by the early 1800s. For all laborers—white and Black, free and enslaved, young and old—it became increasingly repugnant to serve as unfree workers. Specifically for white children, employers had an increasingly difficult time justifying bound apprenticeship contracts.[80] Plus, white children had more attractive options. Published manuals and cash wages took away much of the secrecy and personalism of old crafts. Instead of devoting years to intense training at the hands of an acknowledged master, young people increasingly expected to earn pay for their labor and learn trades from a variety of manuals and instruction books.[81] Nevertheless, many white parents still clung fast to the old ways. As one parent wrote to Lancaster in 1813, there was no reason for Lancaster to consult with the parent. For this father, at least, the old system was in full effect. "Your master may dispose of you in any way he pleases," the father told his son, "he has my hearty concurrence." And to Lancaster, the father made himself clear: "Sir do with my Child as you see fit my liberty and blessing you have <u>For ever</u>."[82]

The cash-strapped trustees of the New York Free School Society remembered such attitudes with undisguised yearning. What if they could solve all their problems with the simple expedient of legally binding apprenticeship contracts? The board of trustees first considered the idea in the summer of 1818. All their monitors, they imagined, could simply be "apprenticed to the Boards."[83] The apprentices would no longer be free to leave anytime they wished. Their parents would no longer have legal authority to pull the children out of Lancasterian schools.

By fall, a subcommittee had hashed together the details of a plan. They created a sample indenture form, by which a child (and his parents) would agree to "put himself apprentice to the Free School Society of New York." The child would "learn the art or business of a teacher." In return, the apprentice would promise to stay for a specified number of years, or until they reached the age of twenty-one for boys or eighteen for girls. The subcommittee spelled out the rules: no fornication, no marriage, no freedom to "traffic or haunt ale houses, taverns, or play-houses or other places of diversion." Most importantly, apprentices would not be able to leave, no matter what job offers they might receive.[84]

It was a fairly standard apprenticeship agreement, but New York was not London and 1818 was not 1813. The proposal proved embarrassing to the trustees, and "several members" made strenuous but unrecorded "objections" to the idea.[85] They did not discuss it any further and quietly dropped the plan in March 1819.[86]

But abandoning the unworkable solution of legally bound apprenticeship did not leave them with any workable solutions. The board had tried everything. They had tried to improve conditions for their monitors, if they could do it without spending more money. They tried to replace expensive food and lodging with cheaper cash prizes for monitors. At the same time, they increased the amount of time monitors would spend as students, so that parents would think that Lancasterian schools still had plenty to teach them.[87] The trustees tried pressuring parents—they considered a plan to ask parents to simply sign an "agreement," not an indenture, that the students would remain in school.[88] They tried lecturing parents—they sent home a long tract warning parents about the dangers of ignorance and reminding parents that they "cannot but feel a weight of obligation to the friends and patrons of so valuable an institution."[89] Parents, however, rarely felt the weight of that obligation as much as the trustees hoped they would. Trustees knew there was only so much benefit to be gained by harsh lectures and one-sided agreements.

And the trustees were forced to cut costs again and again. In 1820, they decided they needed to squeeze monitors even harder. They could no longer continue offering free room and board to monitors; they could no longer afford to offer cash prizes for academic achievements. In short, they could no longer afford to run a Lancasterian school.[90] Over the next few months, the trustees wrestled with the implications of their impossible financial situation. By the beginning of 1821, they had sketched out a new plan. They would simply pay monitors a salary.[91]

It wouldn't be much of a salary. In 1821, the three current monitors-general would each receive a hundred dollars for the year. Future monitors would earn fifty cents per week.[92] Even these skimpy promises were too much for the Free School Society to actually fulfill. By the end of 1821, the head monitor of School Number Three finally quit. He had been promised nine dollars per quarter, but he had not received any wages all year. So after six years of unpaid labor in his Lancasterian school, the fourteen-year-old teacher walked out to try his chances on New York's job market instead.[93]

Even when salaries were not paid as promised, the switch to wages for monitors spelled the death of the Lancasterian promise. The system was built on the idea of revolutionary savings due to revolutionary efficiency. In theory, a Lancasterian school could educate a thousand children with only one teacher salary. In theory, children would provide free enthusiastic labor, knowing that their teaching was an intrinsic part of their learning. In practice, however, children and their parents were not theoretical cogs in Lancaster's vast imaginary educational machine, but reasonable people with hard-earned skepticism about the promises of elites. When theory met practice, theory died almost immediately, but it took a while for news of that death to spread.

Nobody said it out loud—yet. But the system had collapsed from the weight of its own impracticality. The difficulties faced by the trustees of New York's Free School Society were broadly and grimly shared elsewhere. In order to maintain Lancasterian schools, leaders in New York, Philadelphia, and every Lancasterian city had had to abandon the central premises of Lancaster's theories. Children would not work gleefully for free. Teachers would not be easy to find. Savings would not match Lancaster's sleight-of-hand promises.

Even when elite leaders failed to admit the failures, students and parents proclaimed them loudly and repeatedly. From the very beginning students shrugged off the impractical constraints of Lancaster's imaginary system. Sometimes students simply voted with their feet and stayed away from Lancasterian schools. In other ways, students and their parents made their concerns known, forcing the changes that created modern urban public school systems.

6

The Truant Plan

It took a while for school administrators to admit it publicly. For years, they tried to cope and manage, to fix the fundamental failures of Lancaster's system before people noticed. But students and parents often figured it out right away. From the beginning, they registered their complaints in the most effective manner available: they stayed away from Lancasterian schools. Elite reformers had a difficult time understanding why. Their first instinct was to blame the parents instead of blaming the system itself.

Sometimes, parents and students must have felt exasperated at the cruel indifference they heard from Lancasterian reformers. In 1810, for example, Joseph Lancaster blasted critics for their "silly phrensy" about his methods of punishment.[1] Parents, especially Black parents, had been dismayed by the thought of their children being forced into the humiliating discipline we saw in chapter 3, including shackling long chains of students in leg irons and forcing them to parade around the classroom. In retrospect, their reasons seem obvious. At the time, the cruelest image of the American slave regime was the sight of long coffles of enslaved Black people sold down the river, chained and shackled together, torn away from their lives and family and lashed toward a future of certain suffering. Among white families, too, the leg iron represented the hostility and injustice of institutions such as poorhouses and almshouses. In the Lancasterian era those physical punishments were rarely used on white inmates, yet the image of them remained a potent symbol of the humiliations that could be forced on the poor in the name of benevolence. It reeked of cruelty and imposition, not self-improvement and economic advancement.[2]

When parents refused to allow their children to be punished with Lancaster's "logs, shackles, caravans, &c," we might think that Lancaster and his followers would understand. We might suppose that school leaders would apologize and recognize that shackling together children by the ankles and forcing them to march around the school was a terrible, traumatic experience. Instead, Lancaster mocked outraged parents as mere *"conspirators* against the education of youth"; he ridiculed them for misunderstanding his use of such devices on the "HAPPY children" in his schools.[3]

It would not have taken much for Lancaster or any of his followers to notice that their students were often not happy at all. After all, students had made clear their distaste for Lancasterian methods. As one student at New York's African Free School described in verse, the punishments were unpleasant even if they did not impose the contrivances of slavery and almshouse on young children. As one student declaimed in 1819,

> If any do the truant plan,
> They suffer the ensuing day;
> Their coats are turn'd, and they are made;
> All round the school room to parade.[4]

The "truant plan" was a common one among students. They stayed away in droves. And their absenteeism ended up being the most effective method they used to communicate their dislike for Lancasterian schools. During the 1820s, elite reformers tended not to listen to students and parents when they complained about the methods and attitudes of Lancasterian schools. Reformers tended to assume that the problem was with the parents, not the schools themselves. It proved difficult or impossible for parents and students to get school leaders to heed their words. But when students stayed away— when they engaged in the truant plan—reformers were forced to take notice. There was no way to educate hordes of urchins if those urchins refused to enter their schools.

Most lower-income families valued schools and formal education in general, but they had plenty of reasons for avoiding Lancasterian schools in particular. The humiliating and offensive punishments were one. In addition, parents often thought that the academic offerings at Lancasterian schools were too basic. Yes, they wanted their children to learn to read and write, but they also wanted them to have the opportunity to learn more advanced subjects. Moreover, parents resented the stigma that tuition-free schooling suggested. They did not want to be labeled "paupers" who sent their children to "charity" schools. They wanted the kinds of schools that had become common outside of cities by that time—village schools that responded to the demands of parents and devoted more resources to education. And perhaps most importantly, even schools that did not charge tuition were not free. Children in school were not available to work for wages to boost family income, nor were they home to help with childcare or other nonpaid jobs. For many low-income families, school had to be very attractive to overcome the need to have children at work elsewhere.

For Black families, all these reasons were compounded by the profound racism of white reformers. Like Lancaster, many white elites could not understand that their "shackles, caravans, &c." would be offensive to Black parents. For years, organizations such as New York's Manumission Society—the white-dominated elite group that operated the city's Lancasterian African Free Schools—had blithely insulted the city's free Black population, warning in 1808 of their tendency to "looseness of manners and depravity of conduct."[5] Adding more insult, some white school leaders expressed frank surprise at the academic talent of their Black students. They hired white teachers who openly scorned their nonwhite students and stopped their ears against the requests of parents for change. And they did not imagine that Black parents might resent their attitude. Moreover, the skepticism of lower-income Black families was heightened by long-standing tensions within urban Black communities. Some families embraced Lancasterian schools, even as they tried to fix the many faults in the Lancasterian system, while others stayed away.

The changes and improvements parents demanded from Lancasterian schools were not particularly original, nor particularly surprising. As we'll see in this chapter, ideas about the proper goal and role of public education had been shifting for decades, in ways that were difficult to trace but easy to notice. Especially outside of cities, public schools had been growing and evolving since even before the Revolution, yet the Lancasterians had their eyes focused solely on London, never thinking to look in their own backyards instead.

Non-elites made their voices heard in a variety of ways. Historians have long argued about the political power, or lack thereof, of urban free African Americans and working-class whites.[6] As Monique Bourque has argued, in the first decades of the 1800s the poor themselves "assumed an active role in shaping the welfare system to their own needs."[7] To whatever extent lower-income groups made their political voices heard, they had one unmistakable method at their disposal to make their voices heard about Lancasterian schools, one method that elites could never ignore: the "truant plan." By the end of the 1820s, parents, students, white working-class pundits, and Black community leaders forced a reckoning. It took years for parents and students to puncture the self-assured complacency of white elite reformers, and even of some Black reformers. By the end of the decade, however, even the most dedicated Lancasterians had to acknowledge that their Lancasterian dream had never been feasible. They had to recognize that their beloved system was not the modern miracle they had been looking for. In the end, it was not the confident assumptions of elites that mattered most in shaping emerging urban public schools; instead, it was the enduring activism of students and parents that forced public schools to take their modern shape.

Ding-Dong of Change

In the first decades of the 1800s, the Lancasterian dream was only one expression of a commonly shared idea—namely, lots of Americans, not just elite urban reformers, felt that public schools needed to change, somehow. Why wouldn't they? Everything else was changing—there were new ideas afoot about citizenship, about families, about the economy, about everything. When the Lancasterian promise proved illusory, the dream of a new kind of public school didn't fade. The families and activists who pushed for changes in Lancasterian schools did not need to invent their demands out of thin air. They could tap into a growing sense that public schools needed to be something more than the meager Lancasterian vision could provide.

To put it most simply, in the first decades of the 1800s, more people expected more out of public schools. For one thing, they wanted more out of government as a provider of public schools, though people generally assumed they would pay part of the cost if they could afford it. They expected urban public schools to be as responsive as the community village schools they remembered (or read about) in smaller towns and rural areas. They expected more out of public schools in general—more advanced subjects, longer school terms, and better options for students. And more and more often, Americans tended to agree that being a full-fledged American meant attending a certain kind of public school, one that brought together children from richer and poorer families into a healthy republican institution, open to all—at least to all white boys. Most of all, they insisted that public schools should listen to them; they would only accept a public school that reflected the needs of the public itself. As we'll see in the next chapter, that desire—the desire for a school that listened—was so powerful that Lancasterian schools thrived for decades if their leaders managed to listen to community demands. In this chapter, we will listen to the city dwellers who rejected the Lancasterian model, people with expanding dreams for public education that could not be contained by Lancasterian blueprints.

A growing appetite for a certain kind of public education was one of the hallmarks of the era. As one historian put it, the "expansion of education" went "hand in hand" with other distinctive trends of the early 1800s, such as "religious awakening . . . interest in science, and technological progress."[8] Events such as the War of 1812 and the Panic of 1819 caused important shifts in the ways Americans tended to think about schools. In the words of historian Mark Boonshoft, the Panic "made public schools appear both more pressing and less radical, when compared with redistributive economic reforms."[9] The changes were broad and hard to pin down, but in the memorable words of a writer in 1830, the very air at the time was filled with a "never ceasing ding-dong about reform and change in our public schools."[10]

As we've seen, elite reformers such as Roberts Vaux and De Witt Clinton assumed that the source of successful reform ideas would have to be other cities, bigger cities. Even more specific, they were transfixed by the London roots of the Lancasterian system, the great city synonymous with both the dangers and the promise of modern urban life. Their utterly unexamined assumptions about the leading role of cities in reform lingered long after the Lancasterian movement crashed and burned. Even a century later, prominent historians such as Arthur Meier Schlesinger shared the assumption that cities were the "dynamic" part of culture, dragging the "static" countryside into the future.[11]

Later historians noticed the obvious: that American cities and their "hinterlands" were often joined together as economies and governments evolved.[12] It wasn't that cities were modern and villages weren't, and it wasn't that cities had solutions and villages had only problems; rather, both were linked together in an uneven stumble toward the future. In the case of Lancasterian reform at least, the connections between city and village were vital. Elite reformers might have been tightly linked to their peers in London and other world cities, but the families that used city public schools were more closely connected to their friends and relatives in the nearby countryside. As historian Thomas Dublin noted, children who moved from rural areas and smaller towns to mill towns remained a vital part of their extended families, "always in touch with one another and sharing the latest developments in their lives."[13] Families with children who attended Lancasterian schools were never cut off by city walls from developments in smaller towns and rural areas. They knew that their country cousins had different sorts of public schools, and they knew that Lancasterian ideas were not the only possible solutions to modern school problems.

In the case of urban public school systems, the solutions to Lancasterian failure were not imports from London but local products from the American countryside. Unlike the empty urban Lancasterian schoolhouses, children in smaller towns had long been attending common schools in ever-greater numbers. In the state of New York, for example, as historians such as Carl F. Kaestle, Maris Vinovskis, and Nancy Beadie have related, public school attendance had been shooting up since even before the turn of the nineteenth century, but mainly outside of the cities. Taking available evidence from sixteen of twenty-three counties in New York, for instance, not including New York City, the percentage of people under twenty years of age who attended school for at least part of the year increased from 37.1 percent in 1798 to 47.5 percent by 1815, and then to 57.4 percent by 1820.[14] In central New York, one town's school was packed in 1825 when *all* of the town's children showed up, including even some toddlers and older teens.[15]

Things were different in larger towns and cities, which had a mix of public schools and entrepreneurial pay schools, but even when taking attendance at nonpublic schools into account, children in cities attended less school than their village cousins. In New York City, for instance, in 1796 only 24.7 percent of children attended school, with nearly 90 percent of that attendance at nonpublic schools. By 1829, overall attendance had grown, but only to 32 percent, while the percentage of students in pay schools dropped to 62.2 percent.[16] The same pattern held for Massachusetts. In 1826, towns with fewer than 1,250 inhabitants had a 75.9 percent enrollment rate for their public schools. In larger towns and cities, that number was much lower. In Salem (population 12,875) only 20.9 percent of children went to the public schools. Boston, with a population of 54,154, had an attendance rate of only 30 percent.[17] As Kaestle and Vinovskis concluded, the surge in school attendance between 1800 and 1830 "was substantial, even when private schooling is accounted for, and it took place not in the cities but in the towns and villages of the hinterland."[18] Just as Lancasterian educational factories stood empty, modest one-room village schoolhouses were bursting. Why?

It's too simplistic to single out any one reason as the cause, but some features seem clear. It was not that village schools would have likely satisfied the desires of urban families for more advanced subjects and better-trained teachers. Village schools, after all, were notorious for their limited offerings and underqualified itinerant teachers.[19] And as historians such as Carl F. Kaestle noted long ago, those small-town and rural schools never managed to offer a modern "system" of schooling the way Lancasterian schools did.[20] Yet even with all their shortcomings, village schools tended to have two features Lancasterian schools did not: they listened to family feedback, and they enjoyed increasing financial resources from tax funding, not scraps from outdated philanthropic networks. When people felt more control over their schools, they supported them more strongly. As economists Sun Go and Peter Lindert found, in areas in which political power was relatively broadly shared—as in many communities in the rural North—there tended to be greater support for public schools.[21] In rural and small-town New York State, for example, as Benjamin Justice demonstrated, public schools became overwhelmingly popular in the years immediately following 1814 because a new funding plan "created a means of community control of education and a sense of permanency to the endeavor."[22] And, as Johann Neem has argued, between 1803 and 1853, in Ohio at least, a range of factors led people to invest more in public education, which led them to expect more from public schools, which in turn tended to lead to an even larger increase in funding.[23] It was not in London or any other modern urban metropole that the solution to Lancasterian failure was found, but rather in the tight connections between school and community in smaller towns and villages. People wanted more out of public schools, but not if it meant more schools that did not listen to their needs or provide for their expanded educational ambitions. As the Lancasterian dream fell apart, urban families could look to villages and towns for a model of public education in which community expectations were listened to. As more and more of their relatives outside of cities spent more and more time in schools that looked very different from Lancasterian ones, urban families recognized that Lancasterian answers were not the only possible ones for their educational problems.

Empty Seats

Though these trends and sweeping social changes seem relatively clear in historical perspective, there was absolutely nothing obvious about them to reformers at the time. It took decades for ardent Lancasterian reformers to admit that they could not simply patch and tweak their plans to meet families' demands. At first, reformers thought that the truancy issue had a quick fix. Students weren't coming to school. Perhaps, as the trustees of New York's Free School Society considered in 1818, parents could simply sign an agreement to guarantee their children's attendance.[24]

As it turned out, the solution would never be so simple. In the early 1820s, as the challenges of building new schools turned into the challenge of day-to-day operations, Lancasterian reformers recognized that their attendance problems did not go away. By 1821, New York's Lancasterian leaders were still struggling to understand why so few children showed up. Reformers blamed the parents; they told themselves that "parents among the poor . . . appear . . . to be insensitive of the importance of education."[25]

It was not only in New York. At his Lancasterian school in Washington, DC, Lancaster's former apprentice Robert Ould wondered why so few parents enrolled their children. Perhaps they were simply "bigots," Ould told Lancaster, with their prejudiced eyes closed to the glories of Lancaster's system. Perhaps, Ould mused, they simply had not had enough exposure to Lancaster's ideas, so they did not yet fully value their revolutionary potential.[26] Bigots or no, parents kept their children away from Lancasterian schools. In Philadelphia, the Controllers of the Public Schools announced in 1821 that the "only cause of regret" with their aggressive implementation of Lancasterian reform was that students did not show "regular attendance."[27]

The case was the same at schools for white and Black students. In New York's segregated African Free School Number One, white leaders noted low attendance numbers right away. In 1818, visitors could not help but see that official enrollments were much higher than actual attendance.[28] They could never figure out why. On March 9, 1821, for example, white visitor Robert Cornell dropped in and, in his words, "investigated the cause of the disparity between the number of scholars on the Register and of those attending the school." The teacher offered a few possible reasons, such as widespread illness among students, parents keeping students home to help with household tasks, or students dropping in and out throughout any given school day.[29] Time after time, visitors registered their dismay that the school was only "thinly attended,"[30] or "not well attended."[31] When the second African Free School opened in 1820, white visitors found that the attendance there was also too "small."[32]

Though Lancasterian reformers tried to keep their questions to themselves, the wider public soon caught wind of the problem. As one anonymous "Lancasterian" asked in a Philadelphia newspaper in 1822, why weren't the Controllers admitting their low numbers? This anonymous critic said he supported "this plan of public education," but on his visits to Lancasterian schools the students were noticeably absent. From what "Lancasterian" could tell, on any given day there were only about half as many students present as the Controllers claimed on their enrollment books.[33]

By 1823, Philadelphia's Lancasterian leaders admitted it. Too many children of "the poor" skipped school. "Instead of being placed in the public schools," Philadelphia's Controllers of the Public Schools complained, these children "are wandering about the streets and wharves, becoming adepts in the arts of begging, skillful in petty thefts, and familiar with obscene and profane language."[34] Year after year the Controllers noticed the same trend, yet they never managed to find a good explanation for it. In 1824, they wondered why so many children "have voluntarily denied themselves" their opportunity for tuition-free schooling.[35] In 1825, they lamented again that "a great number of the youth of both sexes, are withheld from the benefits of instruction, by the obliquity of their parents."[36] In 1826 they noted again that too many children "have been withdrawn by their parents."[37] In 1829, they publicly wondered why so many children, "notwithstanding the ample opportunities" for free schooling, were instead "wholly neglected, [and] wander as they list."[38]

It must have been intensely frustrating for the reformers, in Philadelphia and elsewhere. They had founded their schools precisely because they worried about the large numbers of uneducated poor children prowling their streets and wharves. They had listened with some skepticism to the rapturous promises of Joseph Lancaster, finally daring to believe in his supposedly scientific system. For years, they had cajoled their wealthy white friends and connections to subscribe to the wholesome project of tuition-free public schools. Yet by the 1820s, when those schools had finally been opened after so much toil and expense, the students stopped coming. In the end, after years of Lancasterian effort, they had not arrived in the Lancasterian promised land. Instead, their modern new schools sat half as full and twice as expensive as they had hoped.

Privately among themselves, Philadelphia's Lancasterian reformers shared some possible explanations and solutions for their low attendance numbers. One friend and ally of Roberts Vaux, James Ronaldson, wondered why parents were so "listless" about their children's regular attendance. Perhaps if the schools required some tuition payments from parents, even merely symbolic ones, the schools could get greater parental buy-in. After all, Ronaldson fretted, with free tuition, low-income parents did not think they were "throwing money away for nothing when the children are absent from the schools."[39] Or maybe Vaux could stage an old-fashioned "exhibition of the schools," Ronaldson thought. A public showing might increase parents' appreciation for the hard work of reformers like Vaux, Ronaldson argued.[40]

Improper Punishments

Remarkably, even as Lancasterian leaders in Philadelphia, Washington, New York, and other cities conducted discreet private inquiries into the reasons for their disappointing enrollments, they ignored the obvious answers. As we've seen, one of the most common complaints concerned the cruel practices of Lancasterian classroom discipline. There was nothing secret or new about those complaints. In England, pundits and critics had harped on the predictable consequences of switching from corporal punishment to a system based on public humiliation. As the poet Samuel Taylor Coleridge argued in a public lecture in 1811, what student or parent wouldn't be dismayed at Lancaster's punishments? Far better to have a quick and simple physical punishment, Coleridge believed, than a lingering public humiliation. As Coleridge put it, "What would a parent think if he saw his child punished" with Lancasterian methods? How would they feel when the "feelings of the child" were assaulted and the humiliation forced the child to be "associated with the sentence of the most abandoned criminal"?[41]

Looking back, the blithe equanimity with which Lancasterian schools punished children seems truly shocking. It does not seem to require any explanation that students and parents would not relish the idea of their children being shackled or, even worse, suspended in a basket or cage above the schoolroom, subjected to the taunts of their peers. Yet Lancasterian reformers had a remarkable ability to ignore such criticisms. In New York, for instance, the Free School Society's trustees received numerous complaints from students about "improper punishments." By 1821, the complaints had piled up to such an extent that they could no longer be ignored. The trustees appointed a committee to inquire into the veracity of student complaints, but in October 1821 the committee reported that the students' complaints had no merit.[42] Instead of examining the practices in their Lancasterian schools, the trustees concluded that students simply didn't like being educated.

In schools for Black children, punishments were harsher and white reformers seemed even more dedicated to ignoring families' complaints. By 1817 the published manuals of the Lancasterian system no longer recommended the most egregious punishments. Gone was the "basket." Also gone was the "fool's coat," which Lancaster had recommended in his 1810 manual.[43] Though Lancaster had dismissed objections about "logs, shackles, caravans &c.," his followers and former friends had quietly eliminated them from Lancasterian instruction manuals after 1812. For white children, at least, Lancasterians implicitly agreed that those punishments were too cruel, even if they worked. Instead, after 1812 Lancaster's manuals recommended an ever more complex system of merits and demerits, possibly including, at worst, "confinement after school-hours." Gone were the public parades and caravans. Gone were the attempts to mark young offenders out for ridicule by their peers. Instead, by 1817 Lancasterian reformers moved toward a gentler system of reward tickets. For white children after 1817, the recommended punishment for truancy was the forfeiture of four merit tickets.[44]

For Black students, the old regime remained in place much longer. Recall the complaints of the student in 1819 at African Free School Number One. He and other truants not only forfeited four merit tickets, as white students might have, but also were made to reverse their coats and submit to a humiliating Lancasterian parade around the schoolroom. If a student were to repeat their truancy, though the student did not give details, they would be subjected to "a punishment yet more severe." Any student caught lying would be "disgrac'd beyond the rest." They would have a placard attached to their shirt, "descriptive of a lying tounge [sic]."[45]

Informally, too, the regime of punishment and heavy-handed supervision was more onerous at New York's African Free School than at New York's Lancasterian schools for white children. At the all-Black schools, for instance, white visitors frequently conducted surprise inspections, meting out punishments to students who did not appear to behave properly. Even as late as 1827, one visitor popped in and felt he "was compelled to make an example of" some students who were "unruly."⁴⁶ As they never did at the all-white schools, white visitors frequently "admonished" Black students.⁴⁷

Even when they did not dish out admonishments and penalties, white visitors tended to speak about Black students and their parents in demeaning terms. In 1821, for example, two white visitors openly expressed their surprise that a Black student could excel in academic work. As these visitors reported, they were "astonished" to find that a former student had great "talent in poetry a specimen of which she gave us."⁴⁸ The white teacher of African Free School Number Two was just as bad at times. At a public exhibition in 1822, for instance, the teacher, C. C. Andrews, had two students perform an intensely awkward dialogue that the teacher had written. In front of an audience that included the assembled white elites, the top members of New York's Black elite, and the rest of the lower-income Black parents, the students described the unworthiness of Black families for the gift of tuition-free schooling. In the dialogue, one student was hurrying off to school. Another was lollygagging and delaying. When the first student upbraided the second for his attitude, the second explained that he did not need to go to school because his parents "seem to take but little concern."⁴⁹ His parents, the truant went on, simply "don't know the value of it [formal education]." In case anyone in the audience had missed the point, Andrews had the truant student declaim at the end, "Parents may be frequently the real cause of [students'] bad conduct, though insensible of it at the time."⁵⁰

Even if Black parents at the time could have swallowed these public insults, they had a much more serious cause for concern. In the busiest years of Lancasterian schooling in New York, roughly between 1817 and 1822, Black students were expelled at far higher rates than white students. The records are not exhaustive, but it is clear that Black students at the African Free Schools were kicked out more often, both in absolute terms (nine Black students expelled between 1817 and 1822 compared to six white ones) and relative to enrollments (an average of about four hundred Black students per year compared to about twelve hundred white students). Moreover, all of the expulsions of white students during that period were done in a single month, October 1817. After that, no white students were expelled, although in 1818 the trustees initiated a new policy, warning that white truants might be "immediately and publicly" expelled.⁵¹ However, no white students ever suffered that kind of punishment. Instead, teachers sent home a letter to white parents warning them: "The Rules of the school require that you should be informed that _____ will be expelled, unless in future he attends school regularly."[52] No such letters were sent home to Black families. Black students were simply kicked out, sometimes on the spot by implacable white visitors.[53]

Throughout the 1820s Black parents and pundits registered their complaints, with varying degrees of success. Among all the repeated insults, discriminations, and inequalities they endured, perhaps the most bitter might have been this: even as elite white reformers dismissed complaints and dished out harsher punishments to Black students, they noticed that Black students sometimes behaved better than white ones. In early 1818, at least, the trustees of the Free School Society wondered why white students at School Number One repeatedly made a "Nuisance" of themselves when they were dismissed from school. The neighbors had complained about their "noisy deportment." It seemed impossible to the white trustees that the white kids could not be brought under control, because, as they noted, "the Children of the African School can be dismissed without giving umbrage to the Neighborhood."[54]

If they could acknowledge the fact that Black students, as a group, behaved better than white ones, it might seem reasonable to think that the elite white reformers in cities such as New York and Philadelphia could recognize other facts as well. It might seem likely that they would connect their absentee problem with their continuing use of humiliating punishments. It might seem fair to assume that they would acknowledge the bitter inequities in their white and Black schools, or that they would wonder whether the explanation for their empty schools was somehow to be found in those schools themselves. That is not what reformers did. In the middle of the 1820s, before community complaints forced them to notice the true causes of their unpopularity, elite reformers did not find fault with Lancaster's system, but rather with the poor themselves.

This Class of Persons

They sounded harsh and vindictive, but the Lancasterians who heaped insults on the families of their students likely thought they were simply stating the facts. For years in the early 1820s, reformers—including both white and Black elites—blamed low-income parents for the withering Lancasterian schools. For instance, in 1823 Philadelphia's Controllers lauded the promise of their "School for the Instruction of Coloured Children." With proper education, the all-white school board explained, even "this class of persons" could be improved; they could be saved "from their ignorance and consequent depravity."[55] Yet to the eternal surprise of the white reformers, Black parents seemed not to appreciate the value of this free gift. The parents of eligible low-income Black children seemed indifferent or even hostile to the new Lancasterian schools, and elites assumed that the fault lay with parents' "ignorance" and "depravity." In the eyes of reformers, at least, the problems lay with "this class of persons," not with their schools.

Time and time again, reformers thought they could fix their attendance problems by cracking down on parents, by hectoring them, insulting them, and eventually forcing them to send their children to school. In 1819, for example, the trustees of the New York African Free School called a general meeting of students and their families. The white trustees read a list of problem students, especially those who had skipped school. Then, the trustees turned to the parents themselves and dished out "suitable advice" about how to be better parents.[56] We don't know exactly what that advice was, but it is hard to imagine that many parents were inspired to change by the endless accusations.

We do know that the tactics of "suitable advice" did not work. Attendance at the African Free Schools continued to dwindle in the early 1820s. Perhaps, reformers thought, they needed a better spokesperson. In 1823, the white visitors invited a group of forty-three of the most prominent Black elites in the United States to visit their students, including Bishop Richard Allen of Philadelphia's African Methodist Episcopal Church. Bishop Allen lectured the students about the "importance of the opportunity now afforded them" by the free school.[57]

It didn't help. Attendance remained low; students and parents still avoided the Lancasterian schools. By the end of 1827, reformers—both Black and white—came up with a more intrusive plan to force lower-income Black families to send their children to the free schools, especially to School Number Two. In consultation with white leaders of the African Free Schools, a group of twelve Black elites decided to hire a "special agent." This agent would visit Black families, "urging and beseeching them to send their children to school."[58]

Within a few weeks, the ad hoc committee of Black elites—the city's "respectable men of Colour"—had found their man: Samuel Cornish. Cornish was a prominent Black intellectual, a former editor of the weekly newspaper *Freedom's Journal*, a former minister, and seemingly well suited to spreading the gospel of free Lancasterian education.[59] He would visit all of the city's Black families in turn, accompanied by two local Black citizens of each neighborhood. Cornish would explain to his fellow Black New Yorkers the value of school; he planned to demonstrate the ways basic literacy and math education could improve the lives of everyone in the community.[60]

Some white trustees thought that the plan had worked. Throughout 1828, visitors reported that attendance was up. As one visitor wrote in March 1828, the school was almost full, and he gave credit to "the influence of the agent employed by the trustees to persuade the parents of Children to send them to school."[61] The truth was not so simple. The short-lived spike in attendance soon dwindled back down to alarming levels.

It took nearly as long for elite white reformers to learn the same lessons about lower-income white families. From the beginning of the Lancasterian crusade in the United States, wealthy elites assumed that low-income parents were defective and deficient. As early as 1810, for example, the Philadelphia philanthropists who ran the Adelphi School warned one another that the children of the poor tended to be difficult to manage, "and for this habit," elites explained to each other, "the parents are often to blame."[62]

Elite reformers thought, at first, they could fix the problem by lecturing white parents about the value of formal education. If parents did not make their children attend free schools, reformers assumed, it must be because the parents were too ignorant to appreciate the schools' value. For instance, in 1818 the trustees of New York's Free School Society sent a letter home to all parents of truant students. "Parents ought soberly to reflect," the letter told those parents, "on the great advantage it must be for their children to have school learning." A charity school, "free of expense," afforded their families with a great "opportunity." But if parents did not enforce attendance, they were ignorantly squandering this valuable gift.[63]

Frustrated by the lack of improvement in student attendance, the next year the trustees sent home a much longer and much more aggressive letter. In order for the free school to operate, the letter explained to parents, "much depends on your cooperation." It was not merely recommended but absolutely obligatory for parents to do a better job of getting their children to school every day. As the letter put it, "you are bound by every moral obligation, to avail yourselves of the advantages which your children may derive from a steady attendance at school." There was only so much the school could do on its own, the letter explained. If parents abused "Spiritous Liquors," then children would follow suit. It was vital for parents to set a good example. "Otherwise," the trustees hectored, "in vain may we labour to promote the welfare of your children." Moreover, too many mothers—specifically mothers—did not know that children should be kept clean. Due to their lack of "temperance and economy," the letter wrote, those mothers would be judged harshly. As the trustees explained, "the appearance of children exhibits . . . the character of the mother." The trustees were certain that too many parents simply did not give their children the necessary attention. The trustees, after all, had spent a great deal of time, money, and effort to establish these free schools. They presumed that the parents "cannot but feel a weight of obligation to the friends and patrons of so valuable an institution." The trustees ended this long list of accusations with a threat: parents must make sure that their children showed up on time, and that they showed up every day. "Otherwise," the letter ended, "they are liable to be punished for your neglect."[64]

In Philadelphia as well as New York, elite reformers assumed at first that they could lecture parents into better appreciation of their Lancasterian schools. In 1820, the Controllers of the Public Schools in Philadelphia recommended a more thorough "admonition to parents on the utility of sending their children to school."[65] The next year Philadelphia's leaders again noted their problem of low attendance. Once again, they suggested that the solution could likely be found by explaining to ignorant, low-income parents that schools were important. The goal of reformers, the board suggested in 1821, should be "to impress the minds of Parents and Guardians with a sense of the obligation they are under."[66]

It is not difficult to imagine the feelings of low-income parents who became the target of this barrage of insults and admonitions. It took several years, however, for elite reformers to question their own assumptions. Instead, those elites assumed in the early 1820s that their earlier letters home had been too gentle, too polite. As the trustees of the New York Free Society concluded in 1821, instead of only pleading with parents, there might be some way to compel "ignorant" parents to obey. Reformers might be obliged "to *enforce* on the minds of the poor, the propriety of sending their children to the Free-Schools." If parents were receiving "relief" payments, those payments could be cut off if parents did not heed "this advice."[67] It wasn't a brand new idea. In 1818, one Bostonian suggested a similar plan. If low-income families would not send their children to school, they could be cut off from financial assistance.[68]

As Philadelphia's Controllers worried in 1822, it would be extremely "difficult to determine" how to legally withhold financial assistance from the families of truants.[69] By 1826, however, in Philadelphia elite reformers had come up with a new plan. If low-income parents were too ignorant to recognize the value of education, and lecturing them did not help, perhaps there was another possibility. Reformers such as Roberts Vaux considered a more heavy-handed approach. Perhaps the "vicious children" of such "indolent and worthless parents" could be forced by "Legislative enactments" to be incarcerated in an educational "House of Refuge" until they learned their lessons.[70]

Family Business

Roberts Vaux was not only worried about parents who allowed their children to roam the streets; he and his elite reform colleagues were also worried that parents would be lured by the "inducement of wages" to allow their children to work in factories.[71] They noted with alarm that paid employment in burgeoning factories was drawing students out of schools.[72] After all, in the early 1820s, a white child in Philadelphia could earn anywhere from fifty cents to $1.25 per week in those factories, and the factory owners were always on the prowl for more workers.[73] Vaux and his colleagues on the Board of Control of Philadelphia's public schools lamented the fact that so many parents were willing to put their short-term financial interests—what Vaux called their "private gains"—above the long-term social benefits of formal education.[74]

And though Lancasterians did notice that many city children were being lured by the inducement of wages into factories, they tended not to notice that they actually faced a much larger problem. Even when children were not getting formal factory jobs, for example, families often had a financial incentive to keep them out of schools. In the case of Black children, elite reformers misunderstood most of the calculations that kept them out of school. In most cases, Black children were barred from the higher-paying formal factory jobs.[75] But that hardly meant they were not out in the streets working for cash. Some of the hardest, dirtiest, most dangerous jobs were reserved for Black children. Most famously, chimney sweeps often employed squads of Black boys, small enough to worm through the vertical brick tunnels of Philadelphia and New York.[76] As one 1808 travel booklet warned tourists in New York, the poor little chimney sweeps were "unpleasant to the sight, clothed in rags, and covered with soot." As even tourists could lament, this "necessary and suffering class of human beings" would be better "employed in getting learning," but the financial exigencies of modern urban life forced them into this terrible line of work instead.[77]

In the first decades of the 1800s, the streets of US cities were full of children hustling to make money. Kids hawked all manner of goods on the streets: fruit, matches, rusks for tea, and more.[78] Tourist guides made clear that these street trades were open to kids both Black and white. In New York, for example, tourists might come across Black girls selling baked pears.[79] This "honourable and honest" work was held up as a model for all children "white or black," who might be tempted instead into lives of crime and thievery.[80]

Even when children weren't bringing home cash, they were often vital to their family's economy in other ways. Though it is hard to trace in the archival record, elite reformers got occasional glimpses of the many financial reasons children could not attend school. One visitor to the African Free School, for example, noted that low attendance one day was likely due to the fact that "many are kept at home by their parents to collect fuel."[81] Similarly, visitors often noted that children were kept home to help with other tasks. In the 1800s, for instance, May 1 was "Moving Day" in New York City.[82] Leases ran out for most renters on the same day. As a consequence, as one visitor noted, school attendance could be "small owing to it being moving time and the children being detained at home to assist their parents."[83] Even more common, presumably, was the long list of less dramatic jobs that might require children's help at home, such as watching younger siblings, cousins, and neighbors, or helping with cleaning, shopping, and cooking. The list could be nearly endless and seems glaringly obvious.

Yet the elite reformers who established Lancasterian schools never fully acknowledged the financial calculus faced by low-income families. Though they noted with chagrin that parents kept children home to work, for wages or not, reformers like Vaux never truly accepted the plain economic facts of life for urban families—namely, that even "free" schools were not really free for families. Families faced a stark choice: either forgo the economic help of children, or give their children a formal education. Instead of coming up with real solutions, reformers like Vaux tried instead to coerce families into sending children to Lancasterian schools.

As early as 1822, Vaux proposed legislation in Pennsylvania to prohibit child labor in factories.[84] As Vaux saw it, the problem was clearly one that needed a forceful solution. Selfish parents might prefer the quick cash from child labor, Vaux reasoned, but in his view "the moral culture of a healthy race, is more important to the State than any revenue arising from juvenile labour."[85] Vaux was willing to consider some alternatives. For instance, he supported the idea that factories—the ones that "employ large numbers of young persons"—could simply be required to provide all child employees with sound basic educations.[86] As a general rule, however, Vaux preferred simply to find ways to force parents to send their children to school, utterly heedless of the desperate financial dilemma imposed on low-income families.

Much Depends on the Teacher

Though Roberts Vaux did introduce a bill along those lines into the Pennsylvania legislature in 1828, by that time the tone of the public debate about Lancasterian schools had shifted.[87] By the end of the 1820s, parents and pundits from lower-income groups forced elites to reconsider their assumptions about Lancasterian schools. In African American newspapers and white working-class ones, writers explained the many reasons why parents and students did not flock to Lancasterian schools. It was not due to ignorance about the value of education, these writers insisted; it was due to the failings of the Lancasterian system itself.

At the very least, Black pundits hoped to refute the charge that their community did not value education. Black newspapers such as New York's *Freedom's Journal* made a constant refrain of the need for improved education for all African American children.[88] Along with "economy" and "union," the editors claimed, "education" was one of the "three wants" of the free Black community.[89] Other community members agreed. The notion of "moral suasion" had a strong appeal for middle-class and wealthier Black urbanites. If only enough Black citizens could prove their ability to live sober, industrious lives, the thinking went, surely white prejudice would wither with time.[90]

As "Philanthropos" wrote in *Freedom's Journal*, formal education was the primary need for "our too long neglected race." Even if educated Black children could only get manual labor jobs, Philanthropos argued, it was worthwhile for families to devote themselves to the cause. Eventually, with perseverance and sacrifice, Philanthropos thought that education would destroy "prejudice."[91] The glorification of education for its own sake was a common refrain in the pages of *Freedom's Journal*. As "Amicus" wrote in 1827, "The cause of education is the great cause of man."[92] Some writers argued that it was also the great cause of woman. As "Matilda" put it, African American women did not have the same advantages as white women, "but we can improve what little we have." If they did not have access to education, she pleaded, "how can we be expected to form the minds of our youth"?[93]

In cities throughout the United States, Black communities came together to push for increased access to higher-quality education for their children. And the law was often on their side. In Boston, for example, public schools had been legally open to African American students even before the city's 1789 school law.[94] In New York, the 1795 school act specifically required free schools to be open to children of "White parents or [those] descended from Africans or Indians."[95] Pennsylvania's school laws of 1802, 1809, 1812, and 1818 all specified that the tuition-free public schools should be open to all, if segregated by race and gender.[96]

Yet time and time again, Black activists found their efforts to enforce the laws unsuccessful. In Philadelphia, for instance, a tuition-free public school for African American students did not open until 1822.[97] Instead of waiting for their legal rights to be enforced, African Americans opened their own schools. At times, those efforts were met with more than foot-dragging. Historian Kabria Baumgartner has documented at least ten physical attacks on Black schools in the Northeast between 1830 and 1845.[98] In the Lancasterian era, too, builders of Black schools had to deal with white violence. In Providence, Rhode Island, Black activists raised money and built a schoolhouse, even in the face of what they called "certain discouraging circumstances."[99] In 1820 they managed to open their school, in spite of "violent opposition from some."[100]

As in Providence, Black communities in cities such as Chillicothe, Ohio, chipped in to build their own segregated schools. Contributions came from the entire community, not only the more affluent members.[101] In bigger cities like New York, community members came together in organizations such as the African Mutual Instruction Society and the African Infant Schools committee to establish schools for all ages.[102] Across the river in Brooklyn, community members held their own educational exhibitions to bolster the underfunded offerings at the segregated public school.¹⁰³ Even schools that charged tuition, including Stephen Gloucester's school in Philadelphia, usually also relied on "liberal patronage . . . from a generous public."¹⁰⁴ Even without great wealth and even in the face, at times, of "violent opposition," African Americans of all income levels and all educational levels sacrificed to provide schools for their community.

In the early decades of the 1800s, then, anyone even slightly familiar with the culture of Black communities in northern cities in the United States would have known of their commitment to the causes of schooling and formal education. Charges from white Lancasterian reformers that Black parents and community leaders did not value education must have stung, both for their viciousness and for their ignorance. Even beyond those issues, however, Black leaders had cause to complain about the meager offerings at Lancasterian schools. In the girls' school in New York, for example, Black students asked to learn more advanced skills in sewing. But they were met with open discouragement from elite white visitors who warned the girls away from their interest in "ornamental" work. The white visitors lectured the students that such skills, while vital to the education of white girls, were not "essentially necessary" for Black ones. In the eyes of the white women, Black girls ought instead only to learn "knitting and plain sewing."¹⁰⁵

For boys, too, Black activists in New York complained that segregated Lancasterian schools only offered "a little smattering" of education. The Lancasterian free schools did not include any "higher schools" that might elevate the intellect.¹⁰⁶ Community leaders looked jealously to Philadelphia, where Stephen Gloucester's school offered a variety of programs, from basic literacy all the way through natural philosophy, Latin, and Greek.¹⁰⁷ At the African Free Schools in their city, in contrast, the editors of New York's *Freedom's Journal* lamented that there was "no public opportunity for obtaining the higher branches." Instead, Black New Yorkers were supposed to be satisfied with only basic literacy education. For the editors, that was not enough, no matter what the income level of families. The editors wanted all Black children to be pushed "up the steep hill of science."¹⁰⁸

It was not only the editors of *Freedom's Journal* who complained about the meager academic offerings at New York's Lancasterian African Free Schools. As far back as 1808, one alumnus of the free school had publicly complained that his education was "not great." For decades, graduates of the school pointed out the limited academic offerings and berated the schools' leaders.[109]

The problem was not limited to New York. As they surveyed the academic offerings at free schools around the nation, the editors of *Freedom's Journal* found them sorely wanting. They accused Lancasterians nationwide of thrusting "dull and stupid instructers [sic]" upon Black communities. The editors pointed out that the failures of Lancasterian schools were not due to the "dulness [sic] and stupidity" of the students, as some had alleged. Rather, they explained, "much depends on the teacher, as well as the pupil." They protested against the typical policy of hiring laggards as teachers. If such teachers, they accused, were "placed in any other than a coloured school, [they] would hardly be considered as earning *their salt*." Unfortunately, it seemed that white leaders believed that "*any one* who possesses a few qualifications . . . is . . . fit to keep a school for us." Subpar Lancasterian teaching, they protested, created "unequal advantages for education" for Black children.[110]

Yet members of African American communities did not all agree. Unlike the white population that was split between higher-income elites who sent their children to pay schools and lower-income families that had no option but Lancasterian free schools, among African Americans there were far fewer choices. Certainly, some pay schools for Black children existed, but they were few and far between. As a result, Lancasterian schools such as New York's African Free Schools run by the Manumission Society tended to combine children from the small Black professional class with students from lower-income families. And that combination led to some predictable tensions.

The affluent white leaders of the Manumission Society tended to exacerbate those tensions by both word and deed. For instance, white leaders constantly differentiated between middle-class Black families, what they called the "most serious and influential" members of the city's Black community, and lower-income ones. White leaders repeatedly warned that Black elites needed to do more to control "the disorderly and riotous conduct of some of their colour."[111] Moreover, the white leaders of the Manumission Society had alienated the entire Black community in 1809 by firing the long-serving Black principal teacher of the African Free School, John Teasman, as a result of his growing public advocacy for immediate abolition.[112] The white leaders of the Manumission Society had instead promoted a gradual end to slavery.

The attitudes of elite white school leaders put Black intellectuals in a difficult position. Certainly, Black pundits may have disagreed with their white allies about firing John Teasman. They may have winced to hear white school leaders voice their astonishment at Black students' academic talent. And as we've seen, Black pundits such as Samuel Cornish never shied away from demanding better free schools with broader academic offerings. Further, as historian Patrick Rael has argued, Black leaders like Samuel Cornish developed their own ideas about "uplift and elevation," but at times they sounded very similar to white elites.[113] For example, Cornish was just as convinced as his white allies in New York's Manumission Society that the first goal of reform must be "social elevation."[114] That is, Cornish shared the conviction that lower-income African Americans must improve themselves individually. He placed the burden on lower-income people to work and sacrifice to make a better world for themselves and their children. He had little patience for free Black Americans who lagged behind. Like his white allies, Cornish voiced a confident distinction between "the civilized and enlightened man"— the one who made sure his children attended school—and "the savage," who did not seem to care.[115] At other times, Cornish agreed that better-off African Americans had a duty to assist their lower-income brethren, but that duty was strictly limited. If and when Black families behaved badly, "our hearts feel but half that pity . . . and our hands give but half what they otherwise would."[116] Too often, lower-income African Americans brought their trouble on themselves, Cornish argued, by ignoring simple rules of decorum. Lower-income African Americans hurt themselves and all free Black Americans by drinking, carousing, and allowing their children to engage in the truant plan.

Samuel Cornish was not the only prominent member of the Black middle class to hector and insult lower-income members of the broader Black community. In 1827, "Philanthropos" again took to the pages of *Freedom's Journal* to voice his disgust at the ignorance and apathy of lower-income Black parents. Their continued indifference to their children's education, Philanthropos argued, brought nothing but "mortification" to "our reflecting brethren." When a few bad apples gave in to "loose and depraved habits," he wrote, it brought shame to "our whole community." Why were so many Black children skipping school? Why were they avoiding the tuition-free opportunity that had been provided for them? Just as did white elites, Philanthropos put the blame squarely on parents. The children were running wild, he wrote, due to "their present parental government which indeed is no government at all."[117]

It was a common accusation by the city's Black elite.[118] In 1828, for example, the Reverend Peter Williams, an Episcopal priest and graduate of the African Free School, pleaded with his fellow Black New Yorkers to send their children to school. Parents who allowed their children to do the truant plan were guilty of a "criminal remissness," Williams charged. If any community member should see a Black child skipping school—missing out on the opportunity for social elevation offered by the tuition-free schools—he exhorted them, "do use your influence with their parents, to have them sent to these fountains of wisdom."[119]

Just like white reformers, Black ones played a desperate numbers game. As Williams fretted, there were twenty-five hundred Black children of school age in New York, yet only about six hundred attended the free schools.[120] At the time, those figures were in fact optimistic, because on any given day far fewer than six hundred students actually showed up to the African Free Schools. Yet the idea of six hundred students out of twenty-five hundred children haunted African American elites. At the end of 1828, for example, Samuel Cornish worried that those numbers were "discreditable to our community at large." Such rampant truancy would, Cornish warned, "discourage the most zealous of our friends."[121]

Yet for all their intense interest in statistics, Black elites ignored some realities just as thoroughly as white elites had. Pundits like Samuel Cornish insisted that Black families needed to live up to respectable norms, with mothers staying home to care for children while fathers paid the bills.[122] At the time, hard realities made those exhortations meaningless. Establishing single-family households, for instance, was an impossibility for many families, due to the simple fact that the bleak job market pushed many Black adults into low-paying jobs as domestic servants. Many servants were required to live in white households: in Philadelphia in 1800, up to half of Black adults were in that situation; in New York City between 1800 and 1820, the number hovered around a third.[123] How could families establish two-parent households when at least one parent had to live in another residence? Moreover, in cities like New York, the legacy of slavery meant that women made up about 55 percent of the Black population.[124] With women outnumbering men and restricted from well-paid jobs that could support a full household, living in small nuclear families—much less families in which female adults could refrain from outside employment—was simply impossible. As historian Jane A. Dabel has charted, nearly half of Black households in New York City in the 1800s set up some variety of "augmented" status, with multiple adult women, boarders, and a shifting arrangement of family relationships combining to meet the financial needs of the household.[125]

The Black intellectuals who wrote for *Freedom's Journal* might insist that the proper role of Black women was to set up respectable homes, on the "absolute necessity of making and keeping that house really a home," but such instructions were simply irrelevant to the conditions in which urban Black families lived.[126] Lower-income Black families were able to ignore the pleas and insults of Black elites just as easily as they had ignored those of white leaders. The best evidence of their attitude toward Lancasterian schools is their continued use of the truant plan. When schools did not meet their needs, or when schools humiliated their children or taught only scanty basic curriculum, lower-income parents did not force their children to attend. School had to be worth its cost, even when there was no tuition to pay. It is very difficult to trace those family-level decisions in the archival record, but lower-income parents periodically voiced their disapproval of Lancasterian schools.

In 1827, for example, one Black New Yorker sent a plea to the editors of *Freedom's Journal*. Certainly, education was a good thing. Expanding schools was a worthy goal, this man wrote. But he added a warning to Black elites like Samuel Cornish. "Every Man," he wrote, should be allowed to "Mind His Own Business." If a family chose to keep its children home, that was their business. If they chose to wear less expensive and less respectable attire, that was their business.[127] The writer's frustration came through clearly. He had had enough of lectures from Cornish and his Black peers. It was time for higher-income Black New Yorkers to stop looking down on their neighbors.

Even more intriguingly, members of New York's Black elite hinted at the divisions among the city's African American community. In 1828, an anonymous female reformer took to the pages of *Freedom's Journal* to warn against "suspicion" and "persecution" of white school leaders by unnamed members of the Black community. Those lower-income Black citizens, she admonished, must "keep still, if they do not wish their names and deeds held up to the contempt of all the wise and good."[128] Apparently, in the eyes of this anonymous member of the small Black middle class, there had been too much murmuring among lower-income African Americans. She had heard enough complaints from her lower-income neighbors to worry that white allies would become offended.

While it certainly made sense for lower-income Black parents to resent the constant insults from members of the "wise and good," whether Black or white, it is important not to overemphasize the divisions among the African American community in the time period. In the 1820s, after all, hurt feelings and differences of opinion within the reform community took place in the brutal context of far harsher attacks from less sympathetic white groups.[129] Yet without a doubt, though their public statements in publications such as *Freedom's Journal* were rare, lower-income Black families made their attitudes known in a variety of ways. They complained loudly enough to cause middle-class Black reformers to worry. And most importantly, when Lancasterian schools did not meet their needs, they simply stayed away. The voices of lower-income community members are hard to hear in the historical record, but their children's attendance is relatively easy to track, and it provides the best proof that lower-income families were not pleased with Lancasterian schools.

Attendance rose and fell with the changing attitudes of parents and students. Elite reformers—white and Black alike—tried a variety of schemes to get lower-income children into their schools. As we've seen, in 1827 white and Black elites began a program of aggressive visits to every Black family in the city. Samuel Cornish certainly thought that his visits produced the intended effect, and some members of the board of the Manumission Society agreed. However, the numbers don't quite add up. In the opinion of at least one white visitor of the African Free Schools, the increased attendance of the late 1820s "is entirely without the aid of Saml E. Cornish or any other agent."[130] Unfortunately, this visitor was angry but not loquacious. He did not provide his own theory of the true causes for increased attendance in the last years of the decade. Certain other factors make it seem likely he was right about Cornish's lack of effect. If the visits of Cornish and other elite agents were truly the cause of increased attendance, we would expect them to continue as long as the visits continued, but that was not the case. Instead, in 1830, attendance plunged again.[131]

Why? It is not easy to know for sure why parents sent their children more often during 1828 and 1829, only to have attendance numbers drop off again in 1830. One factor was probably the visits of Cornish and his cohort, yet the angry white visitor who disputed Cornish's influence was likely partly correct. After all, other causes probably played a significant role. In 1825, for example, as we'll see in more detail in chapter 7, New York's white Lancasterian schools underwent a dramatic transformation, opening to all white families, no matter what their income. Perhaps Black families hoped that similar changes were afoot for their own Lancasterian schools. It is even more likely that New York's final abolition of slavery in 1827 played a role. The state had passed a gradual emancipation law in 1799, but only in 1827 did the last legally enslaved New Yorker gain their freedom. Certainly, as the city's Black community celebrated, it might have led to a burst of optimism in the possibilities of post-slavery New York society.[132] Perhaps more families felt compelled to send their children to school to take advantage of what they hoped the future might bring.

One of those hopes was always fuller citizenship. As Hilary Moss has argued, in the eighteenth century white Americans broadly agreed that public schools were a necessary part of training for republican citizenship, but that widespread agreement tended to freeze Black families out of the equation. If citizenship were only for white men, the thinking went, it did not seem important to many white leaders to offer schooling to Black children.[133] Indeed, the connection between citizenship rights and literacy skills was so strong that an emerging possibility of Black citizenship in northern states by the 1820s led nervous white leaders to reduce the availability of schooling for Black children. By that same logic, however, the connections between citizenship and literacy for urban Black children led many Black activists and their allies to double down on the importance of schooling for their children.[134]

Whatever their reasons for sending their children to the African Free Schools in greater numbers during 1828 and 1829, the policies and attitudes of white teacher C. C. Andrews soon discouraged parents once again, and attendance dipped sharply in 1830.[135] Andrews tended to exacerbate divisions among the Black community. Among better-off members of the Black professional class, Andrews was often seen as a crucial ally in their long-term strategies of moral suasion and social elevation. Writing decades later about his experience in Andrews's classroom, for instance, prominent physician James McCune Smith testified that Andrews's stern tutelage inspired generations of low-income Black children. It led them to believe that they, too, could become learned members of society.[136] McCune Smith believed that Andrews was truly "in sympathy with his scholars." Some students, Mc-

Cune Smith remembered later, believed that the white schoolteacher "even regarded his black boys as a little smarter than Whites."[137]

To fans like McCune Smith, Andrews's effectiveness as a teacher was proven by the outstanding academic and professional success of his students. By 1830, a handful had graduated from colleges such as Amherst, Columbia, and Bowdoin.[138] Others, like Philip Augustus White, went on from Andrews's African Free School to careers in medicine and public service.[139] As one historian put it, the Free School nurtured and encouraged Black accomplishment; it educated "a roll call of prominent northern black leaders."[140]

But Andrews was not universally popular among Black families. He openly and proudly discriminated against lower-income members of the community. For instance, he liked to praise the children of middle-class families, reveling in their "neatness of dress and person, [their] propriety of manner, and [their] ease of carriage."[141] Children from lower-income families who could not afford such neatness and propriety, on the other hand, met Andrews's deep scorn. He was disgusted by their appearance, calling it little better than that of "those who drag out a miserable existence as pests in our streets." He called lower-income students "uncultivated, unpolished, [and] heathenish." Lower-income children, Andrews explained, had a telltale "idle, vacant, stupid look."[142]

Andrews seemed utterly unwilling to recognize the challenges of urban life for his students and their families. Throughout the 1820s, finding adequate, affordable housing was impossible for many Black New Yorkers. In 1820, up to a fifth of Black families had to crowd into dank cellar apartments.[143] As one cellar dweller remembered, low-income families packed into small "dank and noisome hole[s]."[144] As this resident told a journalist, their cellar had a floor made only of "loose boards, and the black mud and slime used to ooze up through the cracks all about." There was no light, no air, and the smoky darkness was always damp, always noxious. "The damp," the resident explained, "used to come out on the walls, and stand there year after year, in big, gummy drops."[145]

Living in such conditions, undoubtedly health problems must have kept children at home. In 1820, for example, an unspecified "fever" swept through New York City. Of 562 Black New Yorkers living in one neighborhood, 112 were living in squalid, damp cellars, and due to such conditions, over 50 died.[146] Even if this specific fever outbreak did not impact large numbers of students, it was only one of the many health problems that racked cities like

New York at the time. City children—especially children crowded into damp airless cellars—experienced illnesses such as cholera, typhus, and smallpox. Given such conditions, it often took a great deal of struggle and sacrifice for lower-income Black New Yorkers to get their children to school, and those children were often struggling through sickness, cold, and want, all while trying to concentrate on learning basic literacy and math skills.

It is not difficult to imagine parents' and students' dismay when Andrews mocked and belittled students' cheap and smudged clothes or their difficulties in staying focused. Though children from better-off families might have felt nurtured and challenged by Andrews, it seems likely that lower-income parents would have resented Andrews's cruelty and prejudice against their "uncultivated" offspring. And those parents were not alone. White reformers had long looked askance at Andrews's performance as a teacher. For years, white visitors had noted Andrews's shoddy record. On many visits, he was simply not present, having left the second African Free School in the hands of child-monitors. Andrews made a variety of excuses. Sometimes, he said he was sick. Other times, he claimed to be out visiting families.[147]

Yet for many years Andrews held on to his position, presumably making enough parents and children happy to convince the trustees of his value. By 1832, however, Andrews crossed a line and lost the last of his support among Black elites. Stories and traditions differ about Andrews's final ouster. According to some, in 1832 Andrews voiced support for colonization for freed African Americans. Among the city's Black elite, by the 1830s this idea had become anathema, and protests forced Andrews out.[148] According to another tradition, the final straw came when Andrews whipped a student. It was not the whipping that galled Black parents; rather, it was the cause. The student had described a visitor to Andrews as a "gentleman." When Andrews saw that the visitor was Black, he exploded with rage—Andrews considered it a severe breach to describe a Black man as a "gentleman." When the story got out, Black parents protested once again, and the absentee teacher found himself out of a job at the African Free Schools.[149]

Whatever the cause, Andrews's removal helps prove how unpopular he was among lower-income Black New Yorkers. When the Manumission Society replaced Andrews in 1832 with Black teacher James Adams, enrollment and attendance shot up once again.[150] Though the voices of lower-income Black New Yorkers are often hard to trace, their approval and disapproval of Lancasterian schools are easy to see in their continuing use of the truant plan. When Lancasterian schools and teachers insulted their children, humiliated them, or wasted their time with go-nowhere basic education, families stayed away. When, on the other hand, the free schools offered them real chances at professional advancement, as well as a feeling that they could indeed be "smarter than Whites," families were enthusiastic.

Although this gets ahead of our story somewhat and we'll find out more details in the next chapter, the pattern of attendance booms and dips continued throughout the 1830s. In 1834, the Manumission Society merged its African Free Schools into the broader network of white public schools run by the Public School Society. The white leaders of the Public School Society reduced the academic offerings at all but one of the segregated Black schools and fired many of the Black teachers. The result was predictable: attendance and enrollment crashed once again, though it went up correspondingly at a new private school run by one of the fired Black teachers.[151]

Pretended Philanthropists

The tension between families and elite Lancasterian reformers played out differently for white students, but many of the issues were similar. In cities such as New York and Philadelphia, communities of working-class whites called out the many failings of the Lancasterian schools. Just as they had with African American complaints, elite white Lancasterian reformers tended not to hear the strident accusations from the class of people called at the time "mechanics," "working-men," or simply "operatives." The emerging political power of working-class whites manifested itself in a variety of ways, and battles over the nature of public education became one of them.[152]

The failure of elite reformers to heed the complaints of white working-class families was not due to working-class reticence. Working-class pundits had voiced their opinions in no uncertain terms. For example, one speaker at a working-class convention blasted Philadelphia's elite Lancasterian reformers for their "illiberal and injudicious management" of the city's public schools. Left in in the hands of these "pretended philanthropists," this critic warned, those schools had not served their intended, benevolent purpose, but rather had caused great "injury to the children of the Operatives." The public schools, paid for by taxes—"funds wrested from us"—ought instead to be run by the public themselves. Elite reformers such as Roberts Vaux, this speaker argued, were "the last men on earth to whose guardianship the children of any generation ought to be entrusted."[153]

Unfortunately, in the long run, reformers such as Vaux were also the last people in Philadelphia to hear the message. It was not that Vaux's lower-income neighbors did not value education for their children. Indeed, in many cases working-class pundits shared the exaggerated utopian faith of wealthier reformers. What Vaux and other reformers failed to understand was that working-class complaints were targeted specifically at Lancasterian schooling. Like African American pundits, working-class white critics accused Lancasterian schools of cruel and unusual punishments. They criticized Lancasterian schools as too rudimentary, not offering anything other than basic literacy. Unlike Black writers, white working-class ones often also derided Lancasterian schools as un-American for isolating the children of the working class in separate schools. Black leaders generally grudgingly—or strategically—accepted the idea of segregated schools, if those schools could be improved. White working-class writers, in contrast, attacked the principle of separate schools for lower-income children. By the end of the 1820s, white working-class voices were calling for a new vision of public education: funded by all, attended by all—at least all the white children.

At times, working-class writers sounded just as optimistic about the potential of universal education as did elites. As one Philadelphia worker wrote to the working-class newspaper *Mechanic's Free Press* at the end of 1828, he believed that modern schools could soon eliminate "the whole dark and undigested mass of ignorance, superstition, intolerance and vice." Thanks to modern improvements in "physical and moral science," he argued, a bold new day was "near at hand," though much work still needed to be done to spread the gospel of modern learning.[154]

Like their more affluent neighbors, working-class writers viewed universal education as key to the functioning of republican society. As "Yorick" wrote in 1829, "every freeman should have an education which would enable him to judge for himself as regards the qualifications of all candidates for office." In the pages of working-class newspapers, this was a common plea. As another writer put it, "the character of your rulers depends on the character of those who are ruled." Only by educating the workers could America hope to raise up a generation of good leaders.[155] It was a "moral obligation" for every voter to learn, one worker wrote from Washington, just as it was an obligation for society to provide a good education for those voters.[156]

If universal education was done correctly, working-class pundits argued in the 1820s, it would provide a way for the children of mechanics and operatives to improve their lot. Indeed, one worker, "R.D.O.," called education the most vital "cause of the people." With good public schools, R.D.O. enthused, even the poorest parent could rest secure, knowing that their children faced an improved future. With good public schools, after all, the children would be "participating in the same advantages . . . as the wealthiest children in the land!"[157]

In practice, however, those advantages were not distributed evenly. By the end of the 1820s, white working-class writers condemned Lancasterian schools forcefully. Yes, education was to be valued, but Lancasterian schools were not providing the kind of education desired by parents and pundits. The most commonly voiced complaint was that Lancasterian schools in the 1810s and 1820s isolated the children of the poor. Instead, working-class writers insisted that public schools must mix all white children together, "the poor equally with the rich."[158] Unlike early Lancasterian schools, which were open only to the poor, working-class writers argued that public schools— truly public ones—could only function if they were attended "by both *rich* and *poor*; otherwise we lay the foundation of *inequality*."[159] After all, one speaker told an 1830 convention of Working Men of the City and County of Philadelphia, it was true that "the main pillar of our system is general education." But that pillar could only support its weight if it included both "the children of the poor and the rich."[160] In New York, too, speakers to "Mechanics and Working Men" repeated the claim. "PUBLIC EDUCATION," one man pronounced at an Independence Day speech, could only do its proper job if it lay "within the reach of children of the poor man as well as the rich."[161]

To be fair, there had always been among Lancasterian reformers a minor theme of republican equality. As early as 1812, for instance, Lancaster's former apprentice Robert Ould boasted that his Lancasterian school in Georgetown was a boon "to all classes of society, equally beneficial to the wealthy, and accessible to the most indigent."[162] In Philadelphia, reformers in 1817 dreamed of a Lancasterian revolution—one that would make good the promises of the American republic. In Lancasterian schools, they promised, "all the children of a village or a neighbourhood may meet together on the same footing." These wonderful schools would provide an "equality that no other system can afford." The miracles promised by Lancaster, the Philadelphians dreamed, could create "Public Schools for the education of ALL CHILDREN, the offspring of the rich and the poor."[163] Similarly, the Lancasterians of Portsmouth, New Hampshire, imagined their Lancasterian schools as a new kind of public education, one that would bring together the classes instead of isolating poorer children in charity schools. In 1818, they hoped that the efficiencies of Lancaster's system would allow their public schools to "level the artificial distinctions of society."[164] In their new schools, they dreamed, children of all classes "would mingle" and would eventually "unite." They dreamed of a new type of school, one in which "all meet on equality; on the broad and delightful ground of the pursuit of knowledge."[165]

However, critics were not wrong when they accused Lancasterian schools of being merely corrals for children who could afford nothing better. And as ideas about schooling changed, the notion of a divided system of schools rankled. As the 1800s advanced, it seemed clear to increasing numbers of Americans that public schools should be for everyone, at least everyone white. As historian Mark Boonshoft has noted, as the nineteenth century matured, more Americans wanted a new kind of public school for their new republic, rather than elite schools for a few and Lancasterian literacy factories for the many.[166]

Only by mixing white children together, working-class thinkers agreed, could public education escape the deadly stigma of separate "charity" or "pauper" schools. One speaker at a working-class convention in Philadelphia in 1829, for example, blasted Lancasterian schools as "a puny, a degrading, and a humiliating system, on the principle of charity or public bounty, for the poor only." Truly public schools, he claimed, were not a gift to the poor, but rather a fundamental "right . . . withheld hitherto by venal and aristocratic legislators."[167] Another speaker asked pointedly whether American "Working Men" deserved true education, or only lower-quality schools "tinctured with the name of charity."[168] By 1830, if elite reformers still did not understand why so many lower-income parents kept their children out of Lancasterian schools, one working-class speaker tried to make it clear. Anyone attending Lancasterian schools was thought of as a mere "pauper," and it was the duty of all Americans to "reject a proffered bounty that connects with its reception a seeming disgrace." No, this speaker told elite Lancasterians, the problem in Lancasterian schools was not with the parents. The problem was with the schools themselves.[169]

Like African American intellectuals, white working-class critics also took issue with specific elements of Lancasterian schooling. The punishments were far too harsh, even if they avoided physical beatings. As one speaker at a working-class convention explained in 1828, at Lancasterian schools "the children are treated as the convicts of a work-house."[170] Another writer blasted Lancasterian "systems of punishment" as unfit for a republic, with cruel discipline "which would disgrace a despotism."[171]

Also like Black critics, working-class white writers attacked Lancasterian offerings as far too basic. "Working Men," one writer argued, wanted schools "not merely to learn reading, writing, and arithmetic." Rather, truly American schools must equip even the poorest child for any career, any profession.[172] Another writer warned that "the Lancasterian plan" taught merely mechanical repetition, "without ideas." To this writer, the system seemed far too basic to be accidental. Rather, he suspected a grand scheme, a plan "calculated to blind the working classes by a specious show of Education, to keep them in the bondage of ignorance, and mental imbecility."[173] There was nothing too advanced for the children of the working class, wrote one pundit from New York. Whether it was "mathematics, astronomy, history, the modern languages, chemistry, physiology, comparative anatomy, drawing, [or] music," he wrote, if they were good for the children of the rich, they were good for the children of the poor.[174]

By the end of the 1820s, white working-class writers called for all this and more. They demanded truly public schools, which from their perspective meant schools that combined all the children of the white public. Moreover, they demanded schools that removed the "charity" label but maintained the public funding. As one writer wrote in late 1829, truly "republican education" required public funding; it must "relieve parents from the expense of educating their children."[175] There was plenty of public money available, according to working-class pundits. In 1829, one suggested using the sale of public lands or, if that wasn't sufficient, simple "taxation" to fund Philadelphia's public schools. In addition, those schools must be governed publicly—not by philanthropic elites but by "persons chosen by the people of each district."[176]

In effect, what working-class pundits demanded by 1830 was nothing less than modern public education systems. But these pundits did not dream up their proposals out of thin air. Rather, changing ideas about the proper nature of public schooling had been gaining popularity for decades. By the end of the 1820s the gross structural failures of Lancasterian schools made these fixes seem not only worthy but necessary, and even the most fervent Lancasterian reformers were forced to acknowledge the justice of critics' claims.

The Classes for All Classes

Though elite Lancasterian reformers had never truly recognized the real, obvious reasons for their low attendance figures, by the end of the 1820s the answers seemed clear. The voices of parents and pundits, as well as the truancy of so many students, had forced most elites to acknowledge the obvious truth—namely, that the reason for low attendance was not due to parental "ignorance," nor was it due to "depravity" or "savagery." No, the reasons for low attendance were far simpler yet far more difficult to fix.

Families wanted schooling for their children, but they did not want Lancasterian schools. They did not want schools that separated their children from others and labeled them as "paupers" or cases for mere "charity." They did not want schools that offered only basic skills in reading, writing, and math. They did not appreciate the excruciating and humiliating punishments that Lancaster recommended. And they did not want their children to spend their time as unpaid teachers. If they were going to make the necessary financial sacrifices to send their children to school, they wanted the children to be students, not monitors. In short, they wanted modern public schools, not the outdated fantasy of Lancasterianism.

Over time, parental complaints and the truant plan forced city leaders to make changes. It wasn't a simple or clean process. Rather, by an agonizing series of trials and errors, leaders in every city scrambled to find solutions that would fix problems that many leaders had never acknowledged in the first place. It was out of this complicated muddle of parent complaints, student absenteeism, and public school experimentation that modern urban public school systems were finally born. The Lancasterian movement provided the impetus to start, based on Lancaster's incorrect prescription. When those solutions proved woefully faulty, it was out of the pieces of Lancasterian schools—including the school buildings, the child-teachers, and especially the goal of universal attendance—that modern public schools emerged.

7
Public School Society

From the beginning, Lancasterian reformers knew that it was not going well. In every big city, after the initial enthusiasm wore off, Lancasterian schools sat half empty or worse. Students had rejected Lancaster's system by refusing to act like the theoretical automatons Lancaster had described, or simply by staying away. Parents and pundits had rejected it in essays, letters, petitions, and complaints. The reformers who had fallen in love with Lancaster's illusory promises had no idea how to respond. The fact of failure was clear, but not the solution. Ardent Lancasterians tended to assume that their problems could be fixed with patches and half measures. They hoped they could address the protests of low-income families by adjusting some details here and there. By making those changes—adding more advanced classes, paying and training monitors, securing funding through taxes, and opening their free schools to middle-class families—Lancasterian reformers created the first modern public school systems. It took a while for them to acknowledge it publicly, but the emergency solutions patched together in the 1820s ended up becoming systems that lasted for centuries.

Some reformers, including—not surprisingly—Joseph Lancaster himself, preferred not to fix the problems in the system or even to acknowledge their importance. The problem, they told themselves, was not with Lancaster's vision, but rather with the concerted plotting of vague powers of darkness, a vast conspiracy to foil the system, to thwart its revolutionary potential. To cite just one example, as soon as Lancaster got off the boat from London in August 1818, he received the following warning from an anonymous "Friend of Lancaster": Beware, the tipster told him. Though "your system is highly approved of, if properly taught," there were scammers and schemers in the United States. There were "<u>certain</u> teachers," he or she told Lancaster, who pretended to know Lancaster's system but in fact were "without talent, qualification and common honesty." Due to the epidemic of false Lancasterianism, the "Friend" explained, the "system <u>has been</u> abused, and a large and respectable School dwindled down to nothing."[1]

It wasn't clear precisely which "large and respectable School" the writer was talking about, but it didn't really matter. Most Lancasterian schools had dwindled down to nothing. It must have been tempting to accept this kind of conspiratorial explanation for the low attendance at Lancasterian schools, because it shifted the blame away from the flawed system itself and onto malicious teachers. Most Lancasterian reformers, however, recognized that they had bigger fundamental problems. The beautiful, perfect system they had seen in their Lancasterian dreams never survived the harsh light of day. An imagined system that relied on free teaching from child-monitors actually had to shell out money to pay its teachers. Real children never acted like the cheerful drones Lancaster had described; when Lancasterian schools didn't meet their needs, children simply stayed away. And that was not all. Joseph Lancaster hadn't learned any lessons from his London experiences. His humiliations had never humbled him, never taught him any lessons in generosity. Instead, he continued chasing after his selfish dream, chasing a financial bonanza that never came. Moreover, even without the unpleasantness of Lancaster himself, free schools had only the most tenuous grasp on political support. New York's Free School Society long had to beg and scrimp to meet its budget, as it acknowledged in 1825. As they put it, "the parents who are taxed to support the Free Schools, complain and justly complain that they are denied the benefit of an institution, to which they are compelled by law to contribute."[2]

What to do? Lancaster himself offered no help at all. His career in the United States had become a dismal charade, as he veered ever farther away from reality and left his family and former apprentices to clean up after him. Lancasterian reformers were left on their own, and they tried everything they could think of. In New York, for example, the trustees of the Lancasterian Free School Society changed their name to the "Public School Society." Instead of limiting their schools only to the children of low-income white families, they opened their doors to all white children, including the children of the middle-class parents who justly complained. The leaders of the Public

School Society hoped that this move would be enough to overcome the "truant plan"; they hoped that it would convince white parents of all income levels to send their children to the Lancasterian schools.

The New York experiment was one of a long line of awkward developments that plagued Lancasterian reformers throughout the 1820s. In every city, school leaders were hampered by their own inability to listen and by the slow pace at which they responded to parental and community complaints. They assumed that the system could still be perfect if they could just get it right. The problems that they encountered, reformers assumed, would disappear with tweaks and adjustments. But those tweaks were not tweaks at all, but rather major alterations to the basic structure of public school systems. School leaders fundamentally abandoned the premises of Lancasterian promises and built instead the kinds of modern school systems that lasted. Yet during the awkward 1820s, Lancasterians never took credit for their revolutionary changes. Instead, they pretended they were not changing much at all, only patching and fixing, not scrapping and rebuilding. They were not able to acknowledge that their school plan—the sparkling receding horizon of the Lancasterian promise—was a mirage.

One of the reasons for reformers' confusion is relatively easy to understand, even two hundred years later. Instead of looking at structural issues like funding, teacher training, and teacher pay, they tended to focus on adjusting the details of Lancasterian classroom methods. Reformers at the time assumed that the most important aspects of Lancasterian schools were the issues Lancaster had raised in his instruction manuals, such as classroom organization, schoolhouse architecture, classroom technology, and extravagantly detailed disciplinary procedures. Like Lancaster himself, reformers assumed that their schools would work perfectly if only they could deliver the system perfectly.

Yet the teaching methods were never the main problem. At times Lancasterian methods worked wonderfully. In New Haven, Connecticut, for instance, Lancaster's former apprentice John Lovell ran a thriving Lancasterian school for years. In Boston, too, though many Lancasterian public schools suffered familiar setbacks, William B. Fowle ran a school very successfully using a Lancasterian approach.

The successes of Fowle and Lovell, though far from typical, are key to understanding the troubled story of Lancasterian reform. Success did not result from an ever more perfect articulation of the system. Instead, success came from providing the kinds of schools communities wanted and devoting adequate resources to families' expanding appetite for education. As we've seen, when parents did not approve of Lancasterian schools, they effectively exercised veto power over them. By keeping their kids home, all parents—lower- and higher-income, white and Black—had the ability to stymie the plans of elite reformers. Without students, there could be no schools. By focusing on fixing the details of Lancasterian classrooms, urban reformers missed the obvious. They did not understand that merely changing classroom organization was not enough.

In their own ways, elite reformers tried a variety of experiments to solve the problems in their schools. They tried, for instance, to make sure that their Lancasterian schools offered more than just basic literacy and math education. They tried to find better ways to pay for their schools. In addition, they hoped to attract and keep monitors without abandoning the monitorial system. Most importantly, they tried to answer the questions that had never been answered—namely, they tried to figure out whether their tuition-free schools were meant for all children, or only the children of the poorest citizens. Were they trying to provide universal education by opening charity schools for only the poorest students, or were they trying to provide universal education by creating public schools for all?

Knowing, as we do, the end of the story, it can be painful to watch well-meaning reformers struggle to recognize the obvious. We know, in the end, that the only solution that lasted was to acknowledge and address the real concerns of families. Public schools only succeeded when they created schools largely as we know them today: schools with trained, adult teachers; schools broken up into classrooms each led by one teacher; schools funded reliably—if not yet exclusively—by tax money; and schools, most importantly, open to all and paid for by all. It can be tempting to skip ahead, to ignore the years in which reformers pretended that their non-Lancasterian public schools were simply fulfillments of Lancasterian promises. Yet only by watching the struggle of reformers to discover those solutions (as obvious as they seem in hindsight) and recognizing the reluctance with which reformers abandoned their Lancasterian dreams can we adequately acknowledge the real relationship between dreams of school reform and the much messier realities.

Public school systems were not born at the stroke of Lancaster's pen, yet the story of their birth would have been vitally different if it weren't for misplaced Lancasterian zeal. Only by examining the hesitant zigzag path of school reformers in the 1820s can we hope to unearth the complex roots of urban public schools: they were not built as deliberate systems at all, but rather as a series of compromises between gritty reality and glittering Lancasterian promises. They did not spring from the genius of Joseph Lancaster, but rather only came about when Lancasterian arrogance was humbled and overhauled to meet the demands of real families.

Pecuniary Advantage

Meanwhile, Joseph Lancaster himself only plunged to new depths of delusion and narcissism. He never seemed interested in solving the problems of his system, but only in feathering his own nest. His goal was always the same: to parlay his fame and reputation into riches and a life of comfort. It might seem surprising to twenty-first-century readers that any teacher might hope to get rich, but it was not unusual in Lancaster's time. As historian Kim Tolley has demonstrated, in the early 1800s schoolteachers commonly expected to be able to secure high salaries, especially if they had desirable skills such as training in music education.[3] Indeed, in the early years of the 1800s, as one admirer noted sadly to Lancaster, too many teachers had reputations as people who merely sought their own "pecuniary advantage."[4]

Before the Lancasterian movement transformed urban public schooling, popular teachers could earn as much as the market allowed. If they could attract enough tuition-paying students, an entrepreneurial teacher could expect at the very least to earn a good living. With a little luck and a few credentials, teachers—especially male "masters"—had a chance to acquire property and lodge comfortably in the upper echelons of urban professionals.[5]

Lancaster always assumed that he deserved even more. One might think that he began his career selflessly and only became greedy as he aged. That was not the case. Even in his earliest London notebooks, he reminded himself to "Obtain a scale of Master's and mistresses Salaries."[6] Lancaster's eye had always been on the bottom line. He never quite mastered the finances involved in operating a school, but he always assumed he could use his system to pad his bank account.

In the earliest days, at least, success seemed possible. While Lancaster feuded in London with the Royal Lancasterian Society, his friends in the United States enticed him with tales of American bonanzas. In 1812, for instance, his former apprentices Robert and Henry Ould wrote to Lancaster from Washington, DC. The Lancasterian system was so popular in that city, the two brothers told Lancaster, that in just a few short weeks reformers had raised a whopping $30,000 to fund new Lancasterian schools.[7]

When Lancaster arrived in the United States in 1818, he was disappointed to find that those figures were not really typical. Yet he still assumed he would be able to amass personal riches from his system. As we have seen, Lancaster was shown the door in Philadelphia, but he assumed that another city would soon fulfill his extravagant financial demands. As he wrote his daughter from Boston in 1819, enthusiasm for his methods was so robust that he planned for a quick and dramatic payoff. Other private schools in the city, Lancaster told Betsy, charged as much per quarter as he planned to charge for a full year. He assumed that he would immediately have "Scholars enough to produce 2 to 3000$ down on the nail."[8]

He dreamed big. Certainly, he told Betsy, she might have to take on adult responsibilities at the age of fourteen. She might need to delay payments to the grocer and the landlord. She might be required to dodge creditors and flee from city to city to avoid punishment for debt. But fear not, Lancaster told her in the first years of their American sojourn; their time was always coming soon. In the summer of 1819, as Betsy struggled to keep the household together in Philadelphia, Lancaster announced he had made an important contact in New York. His new rich friend, Lancaster assured Betsy, would soon turn around the family fortune. "The time is not far distant," he told her, "when I may tell my Jewell, that she has a choice home of her own."[9]

Later that summer, Lancaster promised he would soon be "rich and independent." He told Betsy that his first move would be to secure a "small estate for thee."[10] He did not forget about his own comfort. Once he received his fair reward, he planned to purchase "a Chaise of my own."[11]

As always, Lancaster spent more energy on dreams than on details. Throughout his feverish summer of 1819, he told Betsy he planned to earn the outlandish sum of $50,000 that year, all without working too hard.[12] To put that sum in contemporary financial context, the school board of Philadelphia had initially offered Lancaster a "munificent" salary that same year of $1,440, more than double what it paid another Lancasterian teacher in its system and far more than the $1,000 annual salary earned by the head teacher in the New York Free School system.[13] Lancaster ruined his chances at that kind of stable salary by feuding with the Philadelphia trustees. If Lancaster truly had been able to earn $50,000 in a single year, he would indeed have been able to fulfill his financial promises to Betsy. But he was soon forced to moderate his dreams of avarice. In 1821, for example, he confided to Philadelphia's Roberts Vaux that he would soon earn $2,000. Even that radically reduced figure, Lancaster calculated, would provide him with the "capital" to "place [him] in usefulness and domestic comfort the remainder of my days."[14] The actual numbers of Lancaster's presumed payout seemed to dance uncertainly in his head, but one element of his spectral finances remained constant. He repeatedly promised Betsy the arrival of a single enormous payday, a windfall that would allow him to "settle all at once" the family's ever-burgeoning debts.[15]

"You Are Now in Arrears"

Alas, for Lancaster's "Jewell" that day never came. Young Betsy was left to manage a difficult household without any financial help or guidance from her father. Her mother, also named Elizabeth, had long struggled with mental health issues. Elizabeth's physical health was also shattered by long years of struggle, and her time in the United States would be best measured in months, not years. Before her death in late 1820, she was never able to offer adult guidance. So Betsy made do.

First, the family hoped to live in New York City. As soon as they arrived in New York in August 1818, Joseph Lancaster happily absconded for a series of lectures. Betsy, meanwhile, found the family an apartment on Dey Street.[16] By the end of the year, however, Lancaster had instructed them to move to Philadelphia, where he assured Betsy he would have a more lucrative reception.[17] At the time, the family consisted of the absent father Joseph, mother Elizabeth, daughter Betsy, and two of Lancaster's former London apprentices, Richard Jones and John Lovell. In Philadelphia, Joseph's brother William lived with them as well, unhappily. William has a spotty presence in the archival files, but he was apparently another irascible and irritable Lancaster who made Betsy's home life continually awkward and tense. During the first few years of their American stay, Jones and Lovell often traveled with Joseph Lancaster, assisting him with his speeches.[18] Eventually, both of them moved on to schools of their own: Lovell opened a Lancasterian school in New Haven, Connecticut, in 1822, and, as we'll see in this chapter, his successes help explain the mysteries of Lancasterian reform. Jones remained longer with the family, throughout the tribulations in Philadelphia and Baltimore. In the end, Betsy and Jones built a new life for themselves in Mexico City, as we'll see in the next chapter.

During their early, desperate struggles in the United States, those futures were not at all predictable to young Betsy, Richard, and John. Instead, they found themselves living hand to mouth, supporting Mrs. Lancaster, flattering Mr. Lancaster, and struggling to evade angry debt collectors and the unpredictable Uncle William. For his part, Joseph behaved no better than he had in London. He spent his time on the road, giving speeches about universal education and wheedling bits of vague praise from strangers. He accumulated a backlog of ever-deeper debts and a sheaf of ever more threatening warnings from creditors. He owed money to the printer, to the haberdasher, to the landlord.[19] He owed money to the grocer,[20] as well as to the ship captain who brought John Lovell over from London.[21] He owed everyone.

When he finally ran out of excuses in Philadelphia in 1820, he instructed Betsy to move the family to Baltimore, where he expected a friendlier reception.[22] It never happened there either. By the beginning of 1822 the family's Baltimore landlord had had enough. "You are now in arrears," he warned Joseph Lancaster. The landlord was no longer willing to excuse $220 in back rent, plus $125 for the coming month.[23] The time for excuses had run out. The landlord had begun legal proceedings. He even sent appraisers to Lancaster's failing Baltimore school to estimate the value of the furniture. It would all be seized soon, Lancaster's lawyer warned him, unless some quick solution could be found.[24]

Lancaster's only solution was to flee once again. His strategy was to dodge and delay, to shift responsibility to his daughter and former apprentices, and to spin promises of a better financial future just over the horizon. For as long as he could, he gave creditors just enough to keep himself out of court.[25] He used all the tricks of the trade, including endless promises that he had already sent payments in the mail.[26] He shamelessly threw his few remaining friends under the financial bus. For instance, David Holt was a supporter from Manchester who had generously raised funds to pay for Lancaster's travel to the United States. In return, Lancaster told his Philadelphia creditors that they could bill Holt directly for Lancaster's continuing household expenses. Lancaster ran up tabs based on false promises that he had a letter from Holt authorizing the arrangement. As one frustrated Philadelphia merchant wrote to Lancaster, "This Letter [from Holt] I shall be glad to receive. . . . I have no Letter from him on the subject."[27]

Under such conditions, friends did not remain friends for long. Unfortunately for Betsy and the rest of Lancaster's youthful household, they had no escape. They became experts at managing Lancaster in order to survive. In her letters to her father during their first years of American travail—1818 to 1823—Betsy always wrapped her requests for help in thick layers of flattery. For instance, she addressed her letters not to "Father" or even simply to "Joseph Lancaster" but rather to "Joseph Lancaster, Founder of Education."[28] She always began by thanking him for the dribs and drabs of financial support that he did manage to send. It is difficult not to hear a sarcastic tone in some of her letters, as when she had begged him to send money to settle hundreds of dollars of debt and then thanked him for the eleven dollars he finally contributed.[29] She always asked for his approval for decisions, even though he never offered any substantial help or advice. For example, when they were plunged into debt in Philadelphia in the summer of 1819, a summer plagued by fever and countrywide financial panic, she pleaded with her father to allow her to move the family into a smaller, cheaper house. Lancaster forbade the sensible move, requiring Betsy to keep up appearances.[30]

It wasn't only Betsy who was left on her own. When Lancaster's former London apprentice John Lovell followed the Lancaster family to the United States in late 1819, he thought that Lancaster would pay for his passage. Indeed, Lancaster had promised he would pay; he told Lovell he would have money waiting for him in New York, but when Lovell arrived, there was no money.[31] Instead, Lovell had to deal with the increasingly angry demands of the ship's captain for his payment. All the while, Lovell was charged with caring for Mrs. Lancaster, whose behavior had grown erratic and even dangerous. Moreover, Lovell felt compelled to assure Lancaster that he was not angry about the money.[32] Instead of chastising him for leaving him high and dry, Lovell comforted Lancaster during Lancaster's negotiations with the Philadelphia school board. Perhaps the Philadelphians do not adequately recognize "your merit," Lovell told Lancaster, but "it appears they are Men," not angels. Lancaster should be indulgent with his inferiors, Lovell wrote, and be confident that he was "in a fair way to success."[33]

The longer Lovell lived with the family, however, the more dismayed he grew about their financial situation and Lancaster's inattention. After a year of life in Philadelphia, Lovell warned Lancaster more bluntly that "something must be done respecting the Rent." The landlord had come to warn of taking "violent measures" to collect the debt, Lovell warned. The tailor, too, kept coming to the house to demand back payment. As Lovell put it, he "seems quite importunate."[34]

The family's flight to Baltimore in early 1820 did not solve any of their problems. Within a few months, the bills piled up once again. By August, Lovell informed Lancaster that their Baltimore bank was demanding at least $117.06, or dire consequences would ensue.[35] Just as with Betsy's letters, it is difficult to read Lovell's pleas without hearing a tone of bitter sarcasm, but Lovell was apparently perfectly sincere when he wrote Lancaster, "I am very pleased that you are enjoying yourself." Back home, however, Lovell reminded Lancaster that the situation was desperate. "I shall be very glad to get a dollar or two by next post," Lovell wrote as the bank threatened eviction and Lancaster enjoyed his speaking tour. At the time, Lovell mentioned, he felt a terrifying uncertainty about the future, "having but 50 cents in the world."[36]

Wild Nonsense

For his part, Lancaster never lifted a finger to help at home. He offered vague and unrealistic suggestions. For instance, as Betsy and the boys begged to be allowed to move to a cheaper house, Lancaster suggested instead that they take in boarders to help defray costs. As Lovell gently reminded Lancaster, such a plan would require even more out of Betsy, now aged fifteen. Her mother was utterly incapable of self-control; she would never be able even to talk civilly with boarders, much less manage their meals and rooms.[37]

Similarly, Lancaster suggested that they allow his brother William to contribute more to the household finances. Betsy hated the idea. As she wrote to her father in the summer of 1819, she had finally been forced to borrow money from her uncle. She was concerned about asking any more from him, because she knew he would expect her to "keep house" for him. Though Betsy was willing to put up with great indignities to manage the household, the thought of being "under obligation to him" was more than she could stand. "I have lived with him long enough," she wrote, "to know how disagreeable he is."[38]

Among the many impossible aspects of Betsy's situation, she was left on her own to mediate between her uncle and her mother. Her mother was prone to loud vocal outbursts, unpredictable and uncontrolled. Her uncle did not have much tolerance for it. He had apparently reacted angrily to the elder Elizabeth's shouts, and Betsy told her father plaintively that she and her mother were living in fear. What did Joseph Lancaster do? Nothing, as usual, except to send from Boston some useless advice: that Betsy keep her mother quiet. If Elizabeth could simply be kept from making any "disturbance in the house," Lancaster advised lamely, William "will not interfere with her."[39]

By the time Betsy was forced to play referee between her mother and her uncle, Lancaster could not plead ignorance about the difficulties of his wife's mental health. It is unclear what forms of mental distress Elizabeth suffered, due to the way it was described and discussed in the early 1800s. Even by the standards of the day, however, Joseph Lancaster's response was cruel and callous.

To differentiate her from daughter Betsy, for example, Lancaster referred to his wife as "Eliza (the stupid one)."[40] Moreover, Lancaster manipulated Elizabeth's condition for sympathy and donations. In one public letter, for example, he bemoaned how "a relapse of her former mental illness" led to his financial "distress." To the public in general, he begged for financial support, lamenting that Elizabeth's mental illness had left him "destitute of the pecuniary means" to pay for Betsy's education.[41] Privately, however, he blamed Elizabeth for her own problems. As he told his daughter—as always, from afar—her mother had the power to "heal her mind," if she truly wished, by ending her habits of "idleness and foul suspicion."[42]

We can uncover only a very limited amount of information about Elizabeth's mental health problems. We know, for instance, that it began soon after the birth of Betsy in 1804. Elizabeth seemed depressed and hostile to the baby. She would not care for the child and apparently threatened her. As one diagnosis put it, "all joy—all happiness was then too much for her." A local doctor in 1807 declared her "incurably and constitutionally deranged."[43]

Until her death in Baltimore on December 6, 1820, Elizabeth Lancaster's life was punctuated by periods of lucidity and equanimity, always followed by a return of her erratic behavior. In 1807, Joseph Lancaster found a care home for her that he described as a "retired place." It failed to provide "proper care," so he brought her back home. As he traveled about the United Kingdom giving his first rounds of lectures about his marvelous system, he left her in the care of his Borough Road apprentices, who were children, unprepared for the task. They soon took her to the home of a local Quaker who had a reputation for treating people with mental illnesses.[44]

During Lancaster's glory years in London, when he was still well regarded by the city's elite, a member of the royal family suggested that Elizabeth might benefit from a "music cure," a treatment that had apparently assuaged the mental health symptoms of King George III. It seemed to work for a while—as Lancaster observed, "she appeared fully recovered"—but Elizabeth soon relapsed. Observers such as Joseph Lancaster's father and Elizabeth's brother agreed that she was not manageable; she was "such a trouble to them both" that they refused to continue caring for her.[45]

When Lancaster decided to move the family to the United States, he claimed that it raised Elizabeth's spirits temporarily. However, when they arrived in New York, he declared her "unfit for society." She apparently fumed angrily and even violently at everyone she met, including Betsy and the rest of the family. She seemed to hate the Queen of England, blaming her for Lancaster's repeated failures.[46] Why the Queen? No one knew. No one in the household could explain or control her behavior. According to John Lovell, throughout her time in Philadelphia Elizabeth Lancaster was utterly unable to control herself or act in a conventional manner.[47]

Lancaster never cared. He did not expend any energy on sympathy for Elizabeth, nor even for Betsy, John, and Richard as they tried to manage her care. He considered her continuing struggles to be self-induced. As he told Betsy in the summer of 1819, he was unwilling to tolerate Elizabeth's "wild nonsense which she can restrain." He did not offer any help or advice to Betsy, but he did insist that he would "never allow [Elizabeth] to be an annoyance, and interrupt our comfort or our business." He promised Betsy that if her mother became too difficult, "she must go."[48] Where she would go was unclear.

To Elizabeth herself, Lancaster offered only chastisement. He scolded her in early 1820 for her "spirit of infirmity." The true problem, Lancaster insisted, was not her health but her intellectual weakness. "I am afraid," he told her, "thou hast loved it." If she hadn't, "it would not have bowed thee down so long, and so much." Betsy had told him that Elizabeth had taken to hiding things around the house. He told her she must stop all her "nonsense" behavior immediately.[49]

Such scoldings did not help Elizabeth—they only deepened her depression. In a lucid period just before her death, she responded to Joseph with profuse apologies. Whatever she had done to anger him, she wrote, had happened "unguardedly, or accidentally." Her only goal was "to regain thy affection and kind regard for me."[50]

Sadly, she never could. He maintained his cold emotional—and physical—

distance until she died. Unless Lancaster were willing to come home and intervene, there was little he could do. The one thing he could have done he never did: he never sent the money he always promised. He apologized vaguely for his brother's temper, but he only sent excuses.[51] He pocketed letters, like one from Richard Jones after the family had moved to Baltimore. The family was desperate, Jones wrote. In order to stay afloat, they needed at least $400. "If you could get this sum in a lump," Jones pleaded, "it be of service to you."[52] Like Betsy and John Lovell, young Jones was trying his best to keep Lancaster's head above financial water and Mrs. Lancaster safe and well. He was trying to help Betsy find her lonely way through an impossible situation. Lancaster never responded. He had no money to send and no time to spare for the worries of his family back home.

More Rigid Adherence

While Lancaster dodged creditors and blame, his fans and followers tried to dodge the obvious fact that his system simply didn't work. For years, throughout the late 1810s and early 1820s, Lancasterian reformers tried to explain away their problems by blaming poorly trained teachers and by pointing to rare successes. As did the trustees of New York's Free School Society in 1819, for a while reformers exhorted themselves to a "more rigid adherence" to the details of Lancaster's system.[53] If they could only do so, they promised each other, they could solve all their difficulties at once.

Especially in the 1810s, Lancasterian enthusiasts often assumed that the drastic problems they saw in existing Lancasterian schools were merely due to a lack of training, whether intentional or accidental. Writing from London in 1815, for instance, one supporter of Lancasterian reform noted that even the best schools "will still depend on their due administration."[54] It was in the administration of the system that the problems could be found, this supporter argued, not in the system itself. Some of the British schools, she admitted, were not very good at all. However, these problems were "not ascribable . . . to any defect in the system, but to a defective administration of it."[55]

Too often, Lancasterians in the United States agreed, the reputation of the perfect system had been besmirched by its "defective administration." From Albany, New York, for instance, Lancaster's former apprentice Ed Baker warned that merely reading Lancaster's guidebooks was not enough. Too many readers, Baker explained, had tried to open schools, but they "were not practically acquainted with" the true system.⁵⁶ The dangers of such dilettantish attempts were severe, Baker believed. Indeed, the "ignorance of pretenders," Baker wrote, might lead the reputation of Lancasterian schools to be permanently "tarnished." If reformers were not careful to weed out such scammers, Baker warned, the great "cause of universal education" might suffer from these "abortive attempts of incompetent teachers."⁵⁷

In the early years of Lancasterian enthusiasm in the United States, some reformers groused about the schemes of fake Lancasterians. Writing from Louisiana, for instance, one Lancasterian teacher warned that he had been undercut by a rival teacher who was only out to make money. The problem, in the Lancasterian teacher's view, was that con men and swindlers had turned fake Lancasterian teaching credentials into an "object of traffick." It was far easier and cheaper to buy a fake Lancasterian credential than to go through the hard work of truly learning the system. As the Louisiana Lancasterian told Lancaster, his school adhered to the rigid requirements laid out in Lancaster's manuals, but his rivals' schools did not. With such a thriving, unchecked market in cheap forged credentials, this teacher warned, "mischief ought to be expected."⁵⁸

It should come as no surprise to anyone who knew Lancaster that he embraced this kind of explanation. He continually dodged blame for any failures with his system. Instead, he pointed the finger at "mischief" and schemes. As he warned President Monroe in 1820, the failures of his system were never due to the system itself, but rather to the machinations of "cold hearted, keen calculating men." There were indeed false Lancasterians stalking America's cities, Lancaster warned President Monroe, "professing to import the system from Europe" and flaunting their fake credentials.⁵⁹

Lancaster clung to these conspiratorial explanations far longer than anyone else. Even at the end of the 1820s, by which time city leaders had acknowledged the obvious flaws in the system, Lancaster was blaming "erroneous practices" for any problems. These practices, Lancaster claimed in 1829, were never a part of his true, perfected system but were the result of poorly trained, money-grubbing pretenders. Such backhanded infringement of the true system, Lancaster admitted, might "become productive of serious injury" to the reputation of the system, but it never represented the system itself.⁶⁰

By 1829, most Lancasterians had given up on such delusions. By that time, reformers in US cities had instead taken to fixing and adjusting the system in order to address its serious internal flaws. In early years, some reformers still found reasons to hope that the system could be fixed with only minor adjustments. In New York, for instance, one white visitor to the African Free School noted in 1818 that the school was woefully underattended. Among the students who showed up, though, there was a "pleasing aspect of diligent application, obedient compliance and contented deportment." Even better, since this visitor's last visit, students had shown "some advancement in learning."[61]

Similarly, up through 1819 members of the board of trustees at New York's white Free Schools continued to tell themselves that their plan was working. One visitor reported to the board that their second school was thriving. On one visit, the children were "assiduously engaged in their several employments" and the school hummed along with a very satisfactory sense of "order."[62]

In Philadelphia, too, in the late 1810s and early 1820s Lancasterian reformers held out hope that their dreams were salvageable. As the Board of Controllers told the general public in 1819, their students showed great "improvement in their learning, as well as encouraging evidence of advancement in their morals."[63] In 1820, the board admitted that their schools were far more expensive than they had predicted. But in spite of all their early challenges, the board still hoped and promised that the system would be worth it in the end. Once they had ironed out the wrinkles and assuaged their growing pains, the board predicted, "we may confidently look for that ameliorated state of society" that Lancaster had promised.[64]

In the early 1820s, however, their confidence was rattled. By 1823, Philadelphia's Board of Controllers took a notably defensive tone. Yes, they had serious problems. Yes, they had overshot their budget. Yes, their dreams of teaching all low-income students had been stymied by low attendance and enrollment. They recognized by 1823 the vast weaknesses of Lancaster's system, yet they insisted they "continue to believe it to be a duty to recommend the mode of instruction pursued." By 1823, unlike the heady 1810s, Philadelphia's leaders knew that the system was no panacea. Yet they did not abandon the system altogether. Rather, they continued to believe in it, though they did so in a defensive, apologetic way.[65]

A Genuine Lancaster School

Lancasterian reformers' first impulse in the 1810s and 1820s was usually to fix the system, to identify problems and solve them without abandoning the system altogether. At the time, after all, there were well-known examples of success.

Those successes, rare as they were, play a major role in explaining the seemingly paradoxical career of Lancasterian reform. These unusual Lancasterian success stories demonstrate that the definitive problem with Lancaster's ideas was not with the teaching methods themselves. Under the right conditions, the schools Lancaster imagined really could be created. Yet most reformers did not examine the conditions that led to the possibility of success. Instead, they believed Lancaster's false promise that his system could be successful anywhere, under any conditions. It took most Lancasterian reformers many years to recognize that they needed to change underlying structural problems like the lack of reliable funding and the unexpected costs of hiring trained teachers. It was never enough only to tweak the details. As the examples of John Lovell and William B. Fowle demonstrate, reformers who looked in Lancaster's guidebooks for solutions to their underlying structural problems were looking in the wrong place.

John Lovell escaped from the endless dysfunction of the Lancaster household in 1822, when he was invited to open a Lancasterian school in New Haven, Connecticut. The school was the dream of Yale College leaders, such as the famed theologian and former college president Timothy Dwight.[66] Except between 1828 and 1831, when Lovell moved to Amherst, Massachusetts, to teach at the short-lived Mount Pleasant Classical Institution, Lovell ran a very popular and successful Lancasterian school in New Haven until 1857.[67] We might think that Lovell would take a bitter satisfaction out of fulfilling the promise of Lancasterian education, a promise broken over and over by Joseph Lancaster himself. We might assume that Lovell would take revenge for his years of suffering under Lancaster's distracted tutelage, that Lovell would try to seize the Lancasterian mantle from Lancaster himself. But Lovell never did. Even when Lancaster died in 1838, by which time larger cities had abandoned the system, Lovell kept praising Lancaster's name, crediting Lancaster as the genius behind the successes of the system.[68]

Unlike Lancasterian schools in bigger cities, Lovell's never suffered from a lack of students. At the opening, he reported that he had admitted a full house and had to turn away at least sixty applicants.[69] Moreover, the school's leaders, chaired by President Dwight, agreed to raise Lovell's salary in 1823 to $1,000 annually, the equivalent of what New York's Free School teachers were earning.[70] The systems that were failing in cities such as New York and

Philadelphia were succeeding in New Haven. Students came in large numbers. There was plenty of money to increase Lovell's salary.

What was the key to Lovell's success? Most notably, the New Haven Lancasterian school was never intended to serve only the poorest children of the city. Rather, it was founded and run by community members for their own children and the children of their neighbors. The school enjoyed the solid financial base of traditional tuition payments, at least from those families that were deemed able to pay. In addition, unlike Lancaster, Lovell was very willing to work closely with his school committee to create the kind of school the leaders wanted. Whereas Lancaster fretted and fussed with the leaders of Philadelphia's public schools, demanding outrageous payments and picking fights with prominent leaders, Lovell was quick to agree to the New Haven committee's wishes.[71] He listened to their ideas and tailored his school plans to their vision. In the broader New Haven community, too, Lovell cultivated support. In 1824, for instance, while leaders in New York and Philadelphia were ignoring complaints from parents, Lovell instead organized an exhibition of his students' academic work. As Lovell told Lancaster, the exhibitions attracted "crowded audiences." Lovell hoped that these events would earn "some New Friends to the Institution."[72] Lovell's strategy showed how different his attitude was from Lancaster's. Instead of ramming his Lancasterian methods down the throats of hesitant parents and students, Lovell worked hard to earn their friendship, to deliver the kind of education families wanted. When parents asked for more mathematics curriculum, for instance, Lovell made it happen. By 1826, Lovell had published his own guidebook for teaching arithmetic.[73]

Even as larger urban school districts abandoned Lancasterian approaches in the later 1820s and 1830s, Lovell's New Haven school never did. Lovell proudly advertised his school as a "genuine Lancaster school."[74] He bragged that his curriculum was guided by "pure Lancasterian principles."[75] And in New Haven at least, those principles remained popular. The parents and school committee in New Haven loved their Lancasterian school.

The problems with Lancaster's ideas were not to be found in the details of his teaching methods. The problem was not with the use of monitors, or with the idea that children would teach one another. The problem was not with the use of one large communal schoolroom, with reading circles along the walls and writing taught on slates. When teachers like John Lovell used those methods in a way that was sensitive and responsive to community demands, their schools could succeed in ways the Lancasterian schools in other cities never did.

Like Lovell, William B. Fowle used Lancasterian methods long after they had fallen out of favor in larger school systems. Fowle started his teaching career in 1823 in Boston's public schools. After a year in the city's school system, Fowle left to run his own Lancasterian school, funded by private, individual tuition payments.[76] Just as at Lovell's New Haven school, the reliable tuition funding gave Fowle a sturdier financial base than the larger urban public school systems could claim at the time. But Fowle's success was not only due to the financial health of his school. Like Lovell, Fowle took pains to cultivate community support for his school and for Lancasterian methods.

For instance, when parents complained about "disorder" in Fowle's school, Fowle did not ignore them. Instead, he invited them to a gathering in which he addressed their concerns. The Lancasterian system, Fowle told parents, led to the opposite of disorder. Fowle promised that the system led to "so much love and harmony" that students naturally behaved in an orderly and polite manner.[77] Fowle understood that parents and community leaders had questions; he knew that they wondered whether his Lancasterian system was "really an improved mode of education or a speculation upon the credulity of parents."[78] He offered proof and demonstrations of the system; he never wanted parents to believe they were being gulled or disregarded.[79]

Perhaps most importantly, Fowle promised that his teaching methods would always be flexible; he promised he would listen to the desires of parents and community members. In 1828, when leaders of big-city public school systems were apologizing for their Lancasterian assumptions and ditching their Lancasterian schoolrooms, Fowle insisted that his school would remain true to the Lancasterian dream. In his school, however, the system would never be rigid. Rather, Fowle promised, it would be constantly "modified to suit the circumstances of the community."[80]

Fowle followed through on his promise. When parents worried that children in a Lancasterian classroom might not get enough attention from a trained, adult teacher, Fowle tried to soothe their concerns. Yes, the teaching was done by other children, Fowle admitted, but it was never left in their hands alone. Every child in his Lancasterian school, Fowle assured parents, would also receive plenty of attention from adult teachers. Children in his school would always be examined by "a careful instructor," Fowle claimed, so that the instructor's careful eye might "detect such faults as may have escaped the notice of their monitors."[81]

Similarly, when parents asked for more advanced subjects, Fowle obliged. For instance, in 1826 parents asked for Latin, so Fowle added it to the curriculum. When they wanted French, astronomy, and "Natural Philosophy," they got it. As Fowle claimed, far from limiting students to only basic academic skills, his Lancasterian approach exposed students to the very latest sciences. Students at his school, Fowle bragged, "performed experiments with their own hands." They benefited from studying a rare collection of "very valuable" minerals sent directly from Paris.[82]

There was nothing, in short, that students in Fowle's Lancasterian school would miss out on, academically speaking. And as Fowle continued to claim into the 1830s, when other Lancasterians had abandoned the system, students in his school received an extra benefit from Fowle's superior use of the Lancasterian approach. Bigger-city school systems, Fowle explained in 1834, had tried to tweak the system by introducing small salaries for monitors. In Fowle's opinion, the move to salaried child-teachers destroyed the very essence of the Lancasterian system. In his school, instead, Fowle offered what he called an "unmutilated" Lancasterian approach. His use of child-teachers, Fowle claimed, was never about saving money, the way it was in bigger-city systems. Rather, Fowle insisted he understood what other Lancasterians did not—namely, that when children taught other children, they were not only teaching but also learning themselves. They were learning more profoundly than they would have if they had only passively listened to adults; their monitorial duties were not an unfortunate departure from their own learning, Fowle argued, but rather the very best, most advanced way to learn.[83]

Fowle never acknowledged that he enjoyed a luxury the bigger-city school systems did not. He never publicly noticed that his success rested fundamentally on the fact that his school could rely on a steady stream of tuition payments. Perhaps because of his financial confidence, Fowle, like Lovell, was able to solve many of the problems that plagued other Lancasterians. He cajoled and wooed parental support for his plans. He listened to parental complaints and addressed them. He promised he would change his approach whenever necessary. In Fowle's hands, Lancasterian education avoided the pitfalls that bedeviled the schools of big-city systems.

And Fowle's success, like Lovell's, proves a crucial point. The failures of the Lancasterian model were not to be found in the details of classroom architecture or monitorial instruction. When those methods were used in well-funded, community-supported schools, they worked very well for decades. The failures of Lancasterian education were to be found elsewhere, in Lancaster's unfounded promises. Lancaster had promised a system that would run itself, without any need for teacher expertise. He had promised a system that would cost nearly nothing. He had promised a standardized, modern, scientific system that could be plunked down in any city and run immediately without any adjustment.

Those Lancasterian lies led to the mess that reformers had to clean up in the 1820s. Outside of the rare success stories in Fowle's school and in Lovell's, the ardent Lancasterians in cities such as New York and Philadelphia found themselves struggling to fix the major problems in their schools. Throughout the later 1820s, leaders experimented with a variety of patches and half measures. In the end, although no one at the time recognized it, those experiments accidentally created modern public school systems. By expanding academic offerings, shifting away from unpaid and untrained monitors, securing reliable tax funding, and opening up public schools to middle-class students, Lancasterians unintentionally turned the failed Lancasterian dream into a successful public school reality.

Advanced Learning

For one thing, school leaders expanded the curriculum of Lancasterian schools beyond the mere basics. Though it might seem surprising, due to the racism embedded in the system, Lancasterian free schools for African American students actually had a longer tradition of teaching advanced curriculum. Precisely because Black families had fewer schooling options, the children of more affluent and less affluent families often attended the same schools. As a result, at New York's second African Free School, for example, teacher Charles C. Andrews had long offered essentially two different tracks. In one, students learned only basic reading, writing, and mathematics. For other students, however, Andrews had always taught advanced subjects such as geography and astronomy. As one former student remembered, Andrews offered science and navigation courses as well, even hiring additional expert teachers to do so.[84]

Lancasterian free schools for white children expanded their curricula more slowly. At one Lancasterian school in New Hampshire, for example, leaders initially assumed they could not offer Latin or Greek using Lancasterian methods. Because those languages were key to attending universities at the time, the city planned to open a separate, non-Lancasterian free school to teach them. That way, city leaders assumed, "poorer children [will have] . . . facilities for admission to any university."[85] Among the New Hampshire Lancasterians, at any rate, the assumption in the 1810s was that Lancasterian methods could only be used to teach basic reading, writing, and arithmetic.

By the middle of the 1820s, Lancasterians tried bolder remedies to fix their ailing schools. Many reformers hoped to entice families into their schools by adding advanced curriculum into their existing Lancasterian school systems. At some level, they understood that middle-class families wanted "advanced learning" for their children, something that would equip them to deal with the changing economic realities of a new era.[86] In 1824, for instance, the leaders of a Lancasterian high school in New York insisted they would offer everything any advanced student could want, including Latin and Greek, as well as "the higher branches of useful science."[87] Lancasterian methods, they insisted, could be just as good in teaching astronomy, geology, and Latin as they were in teaching writing, reading, and basic arithmetic. Similarly, by the mid-1820s in Boston, Lancasterians were promising that their methods could work for any student, for any subject, at any level. As one Lancasterian gushed in 1826, the methods had triumphed at both basic and advanced levels. They would soon take over at colleges and become simply the standard way to teach any subject, no matter how advanced.[88]

For some reformers, offering advanced subjects seemed to have solved their problems. At New York's Lancasterian high school, for instance, leaders happily reported in 1825 that enrollment was much higher than anticipated.[89] And they insisted that their Lancasterian promises were being fulfilled. As one report crowed, "The monitorial method has triumphed."[90]

Yet it was a strange kind of triumph, one in which Lancasterian reformers quietly abandoned Lancasterian methods yet kept the label. At New York's Lancasterian high school, for example, students were lured in by the school's advanced curriculum, yet those advanced classes tended to use traditional methods instead of Lancasterian ones. For instance, even as the leaders of New York's Lancasterian high school were proclaiming the triumph of Lancasterian teaching, teachers were using lectures to teach subjects such as philosophy, science, French, and Latin. Instead of having monitors teach other children, supervised by a single adult teacher, the New York Lancasterians used multiple adult teachers—each of them specially trained and separately paid—to teach the different advanced classes.[91] Those classes were taught by what one observer tactfully called "senior instruction."[92] And in 1826, at the new high school for girls, reformers claimed to be teaching with Lancasterian methods, but in fact they moved the students into smaller groups, teaching small classes directly with adult teachers, instead of using child-monitors to teach other children.[93]

For a dream with such a dramatic origin, it died a remarkably undramatic death: lingering, ambiguous, and unacknowledged. Lancasterians shuffled along for years without recognizing the fact that they had abandoned the central premises of Lancasterian methods. By patching and fixing, making changes here and there to address the concerns of families, they had essentially created something different, something new, something Joseph Lancaster had never imagined. For a while, however, they claimed that each change was merely a triumph of the Lancasterian system, instead of its failure.

Any Boy Who Can Read

One of the first and biggest changes was the replacement of child-monitors straight from the benches with specially trained teachers. The monitor system had never worked very well in larger cities. Just as with the switch to offering more advanced subjects, the move away from the use of unpaid, untrained child-monitors was an unplanned, emergency solution that became a permanent part of urban public school systems.

In retrospect, it is clear that abandoning the use of monitors meant abandoning the Lancasterian system as a whole, but that fact was not clear to reformers in the 1820s. They thought they could tweak the monitor system but maintain Lancasterian schools, yet the use of unpaid, untrained child-monitors had been the core of Lancaster's original promise.[94] In real life, Lancasterian schools found themselves in an impossible situation. Real teaching required expert training, reformers discovered. And real teachers demanded a salary. In fits and starts, reformers addressed the problems in detail without acknowledging that they were actually discarding the heart and soul of Lancaster's system.

The shift toward using only trained teachers—whether those teachers were children or adults—happened over the course of the 1820s. As early as 1821, the New York Free School Society scrapped the original Lancasterian approach. It was simply not feasible to maintain unpaid monitors, so in that year the trustees of the Free School Society agreed on a standard salary for all monitors, as well as all adult teachers.[95] By the later 1820s, it became standard procedure in New York to pay salaries to monitors. Indeed, by 1827 the distinction between a "monitor" and an "assistant teacher" was difficult to discern. Monitors, as in the case of Sarah Tigall, could be paid a regular salary and could spend all their time teaching. In practice, for Tigall at least, the title of "monitor" had become merely an empty label, a different way of saying "teacher."[96]

Or, to be more precise, the label "monitor" came to mean *lower-paid* teacher, in most cases. By the 1830s, the old Lancasterian dream of unpaid child-monitors had faded to a fuzzy memory in the New York public schools. Consider, for example, the case of the pay scale at African School Number One in the school year 1835–36. The school employed a lead teacher at an annual salary of $600. An assistant teacher was paid $200. The head monitor's salary was one hundred dollars, and assistant monitors received fifty dollars each.[97] At the time, depending on the school, adult teachers might find their salaries closer to those of monitors than to those of lead teachers at larger schools. At Primary School 26, for example, the adult teacher in 1836 was paid $160, only sixty dollars more than the head "monitor" at African School Number One.[98]

The pay system was anything but systematic. Teacher pay reflected a range of factors, including the gender of both the teacher and the students, the ages of the students, and the race of the students and teacher. But one thing became clear: the most important distinction was no longer between "monitors" and "teachers," but between different types of employees, regardless of title. In 1836, for instance, the male lead teacher in a school for boys received a salary of $1,000. His lead male assistant got a salary of $500. Their head monitor, also a male, was paid a hundred dollars. At the same time, in the same building, the lead female teacher of female students was paid only $400, while the female lead teacher in the primary department received only $240.[99] By the end of 1840, a male teacher with the title of "senior monitor" at Public School No. 15 was paid $200, a salary that exceeded those of female teachers at other schools.[100]

Philadelphia's public schools experienced a similar unsystematic shift away from unpaid child-monitors. By 1828, leaders in Philadelphia promised that their monitors were no longer simply children pulled from their benches and turned into unpaid teachers. Instead, in Philadelphia the Lancasterian schools began using what the leaders euphemistically referred to as "permanent monitors." These teachers were still sometimes children, but they received training as teachers, not as students. They were expected to take on the roles of teachers, though they still bore the monitorial title.[101]

By the end of the 1830s, as we'll see in more detail in chapter 8, districts such as Philadelphia made it official. Like New York's, the public schools in Philadelphia had stumbled along for many years, using paid, trained teachers that it still called "monitors." Perhaps because of the death of long-time leader Roberts Vaux in 1836, the next year a new board president, Thomas Dunlap, announced the change that had actually happened years earlier, declaring in his inaugural annual report that the city's public schools would no longer use "juvenile monitors, taken from the classes."[102]

The announcement was a long time coming, but it only admitted what had been going on for years. Lancasterian reformers had shifted from using child-monitors to hiring paid, trained teachers. There was often a new hierarchy of teachers, and the lower-paid youngest teachers often kept the "monitor" label for a while, but that did not change the underlying reality. Almost as soon as Lancaster stepped ashore in New York in 1818, it was obvious that his promise was empty, that his system was full of holes. At least in the bigger-city school districts, there was no way to teach with untrained part-time children.

Pennies on the Dollar

Like the questions of teacher pay, the trickiest solutions to Lancasterian dilemmas came down to money. From the very beginning, several states provided tax funding for public schools, but the details were different and the money was always insufficient. By the 1830s and 1840s, in different ways, cities and states would iron out a new approach—namely, public schools would be paid for by taxes, not tuition. Throughout the 1820s, however, reformers scrambled to figure out how to pay for the schools Lancaster promised would not require any new taxes.

Tracing the evolution of tax-funded, tuition-free public schools is a difficult task. As historian Carl F. Kaestle has noted, in the first few decades of the 1800s states and cities pursued a wild variety of approaches.[103] And in cities as much as in rural areas, it can be difficult, as Nancy Beadie has argued, to "follow the money."[104] Nor have historians been the only ones who have struggled to find a unified set of policies or even a clear timeline of the shift to greater tax funding for public schools. As one contemporary observer complained in 1830, it was "impossible" to find "an accurate and comprehensive knowledge of the theory and operation . . . of the school systems of the older states." He had been sent from Kentucky to discover how New York, Connecticut, Pennsylvania, and Massachusetts organized and paid for public education. By 1830, however, he gave up, complaining about the "scanty materials" he had for research.[105]

Scanty for sure, but to make matters worse, even those few remaining materials in archives show that funding for public schools was never part of a single, coherent plan in any state at any time. In New York, for example, the state had passed a law in 1795 providing tax funding for public schools.[106] In New York City, the law left many things unclear. Could charity schools run by churches benefit? Could schools take both tax money and tuition funding?[107]

New York's Free School Society always battled for a bigger piece of the tax-funding pie, but despite its many political successes, the funding was never enough. In 1807, for instance, the society used a one-time grant from the state government of $4,000 and an annual fund of $1,000 to open its first Lancasterian free schools.[108] As we've seen, the Free School Society repeatedly asked for more money from the state legislature, with mixed results. By 1822, the society made a new proposal to the city and the state. In order to continue its ambitious plans to expand its network of Lancasterian free schools, the trustees proposed a new special tax. If every resident paid only a tiny proportion of their wealth, the society could quickly raise $5,000 and begin its building drive. The politically savvy trustees offered several different visions of how the taxes could work. One way to do it would be to scale taxes based on citizens' overall wealth. In this scheme, the poorest of New York's residents would only pay a tiny amount. Someone who currently paid only one dollar of tax annually would only pay an additional 1.6 cents. Someone who paid twenty dollars would add thirty-two cents to their tax bill. Or, the trustees suggested, all residents could simply pay a flat tax of four cents. If that was a nonstarter, perhaps real estate could be taxed instead. In short, Lancasterian reformers in New York City did not know exactly what to do to raise the money they needed, but they knew they needed money and they hoped they could get it through added taxation.[109] In 1822, at least, they couldn't. The mayor immediately squelched the proposal. No matter how they structured the tax, it was a political failure.[110]

Similar efforts elsewhere led to similarly mixed results. In Pennsylvania, for example, Lancasterians struggled to get more public money for their schools. From the very beginning, Pennsylvania's constitution had required tuition-free tax-funded schools for poor children, but in practice the money had been hard to secure. In 1828, state legislators considered a new fund, similar to the ones in New York and Connecticut. If they sold their western lands and invested in a statewide school fund, legislators believed, they could vastly improve their educational offerings for low-income children.[111] It was a popular plan—among state legislators at least—but into the 1830s the idea was still only a hopeful proposal in the state capital.[112]

Similar funding challenges beset reformers throughout the United States. In Baltimore, for example, city reformers raised funds for a Lancasterian school, but the state provided no financial support. Instead, Baltimore's urban Lancasterians sold subscriptions and appealed to public-minded philanthropists to support the school out of their own pockets.[113] In Louisville, similarly, in 1829 the citizens created a Lancasterian school for all children under the age of fourteen. Unlike Baltimore, this school was paid for by taxes, but only within the city's borders.[114] They appealed to the state for financial support, but at the time the state's "Literary Fund" was too small to provide much help.[115] The best they could hope for was that the state would shell out for supplementary materials for the Lancasterian schools, like special "apparatuses" to help teach advanced subjects. The Louisville school, for example, used state money to buy a large wall chart of the solar system.[116]

All Together Now

That kind of financial assistance was welcome, but during the 1820s it was never sufficient to maintain public schools, much less expand them to accommodate all children. Though the details differed in different cities, during the 1820s the idea of using tax money to pay for the education of all children seemed like a dream. It was only when reformers addressed the complaints of lower-income pundits that the politics of school funding changed for good.

As we've seen, white working-class writers had long insisted that public schools must mix together children from all classes. The reason they avoided Lancasterian schools, pundits explained, was that such "charity" schools were fundamentally un-American, anti-republican. To make their cases, pundits could draw on a long tradition of inclusive public schooling outside of cities; they could point to broadly changing ideas about what public schools should provide; they could, in short, argue that modern public schooling meant something different than the charity model embraced by Lancasterian reformers. In the early years of the Lancasterian crusade in the United States, however, most elite reformers were not yet convinced. They stubbornly clung to their old ideas about schooling for the poor, ideas that were already outdated by the time Lancasterian schools were opened in the United States. The New York Free School Society, for example, was from its very beginning in 1805 pledged to establish free schools specifically for "the children of persons in indigent circumstances."[117] Like many reform-minded elites at the time, Free School Society founding member De Witt Clinton simply assumed that only poor children were the "proper objects of a gratuitous education."[118] In Philadelphia, too, the original name of the group that became the Board of Controllers of the Public Schools in 1818 was "The Philadelphia Society for the Free Instruction of Indigent Boys."[119] The Lancasterian system, reformers in Philadelphia assumed, was meant only for children "of the humbler class of life."[120]

For many Lancasterian reformers, especially in the early years of the crusade in the 1810s, the assumption was so strong that it did not even need to be spelled out. These schools, reformers simply assumed, were only to be attended by children who could not afford any other options. In 1814, for instance, New York's Free School Society stressed that their schools were intended only for the "indigent population."[121] And the 1818 Pennsylvania law mandating Lancasterian schooling at public expense for Philadelphia spelled out the kinds of children who could attend. Only "indigent orphan children; [or] children of indigent parents" were eligible.[122]

By the 1820s, however, elite reformers acknowledged they needed to change their vision. They needed to build schools that families would attend. Maybe, they hoped, by mixing rich and poor together—though, as always, they only meant mixing all white children—their schools could overcome the "truant plan." In 1824, for example, a new, tuition-free Lancasterian high school in New York promised to bring "together all classes of society."

The school would be "open to all classes of society, to the children of want and misfortune, as well as to the heirs of competence and wealth."[123] By the middle of the 1820s, it was not only in their high school that New York reformers dreamed of common Lancasterian schools. Yes, the leaders of the Free School Society noted in 1825, their free schools had "conferred the blessings of education upon a large number of the children of the poor." What they really wanted, however, was a more fully "public school," one "where the rich and poor may meet together."[124]

The leaders of New York's Free School Society embarked on an awkward process of experimentation to achieve their new goal. They were far from alone. For years, Lancasterians in many cities had ranged far beyond the prescriptions of Lancaster's manuals in order to create a new kind of public school, a new vision of "universal" education that brought white students together in a new common education. They came up with new systems that they thought would amend the awkward blunders of Lancaster's instructions.

Several Lancasterian schools tried to bring rich and poor together by a variety of voucher programs. In Philadelphia, for instance, the Adelphi School used a system of vouchers in order to allow students to mingle on an equal basis. Instead of having students pay tuition fees directly as they arrived at school every day, as early as 1807 the Philadelphians issued tickets that students would use for admission. Some of those tickets were purchased by students' parents, but others had been bought by wealthy philanthropists and distributed among lower-income families. At least in theory, by using this system, students would not know who came from wealth and who did not. All the students would have the same tickets, whether their families paid any tuition fees or not.[125]

One Lancasterian tried a similar voucher plan in Virginia. Lancaster's former apprentice Elisha Wales founded a Lancasterian school in Petersburg, hoping that his scheme to mix students would overcome parental fears of the stigma of "poor or charity" schools. As Wales saw it, reluctant lower-income parents "might participate in a school upon the Lancasterian system with the more wealthy . . . without the least disadvantage to any." Just as at the Adelphi School, Wales proposed a blind system of vouchers. The school committee would issue vouchers for admission. Parents who could afford them would pay for them; parents with less means would get them for free. The tickets would be identical. No one would know who had paid and who hadn't except the committee. At least in Wales's imagination, this system would solve the problem of reluctant parents. As he told Lancaster, "the name of poor or Charity school would not be known; thus its popularity would be secured."[126]

Perhaps not surprisingly, Lancaster stole the idea and pretended he had invented it. Without crediting his former students or recognizing the earlier attempts to salvage Lancasterian education with blind voucher systems, Lancaster proposed a similar system to the Boston school committee. In order to bring students together in Lancasterian schools, Lancaster suggested, vouchers could be sold for ten dollars. Parents could buy them for their own children, or philanthropists could buy them. No one would know where an individual student got their ticket, and, in Lancaster's optimistic description, it would eliminate the problems associated with "a charity or free school."[127]

These ticket or voucher plans did not last for long, and there are no reports of long-term success. It seems safe to assume that they did not provide the blind equality that proponents had hoped for. Other Lancasterians suggested different ways to bring all students together. Many reformers thought that it would be best to charge everyone a nominal tuition fee. The goal, as some imagined it, was not really to raise money, but rather to eliminate the stigma of attending a charity school. If all parents paid something—no matter how little it was—then all parents would feel invested in the school and in their children's attendance. As one Lancasterian wrote from Uniontown, Pennsylvania, in 1822, the tuition would be a vital key to enrollment, "because pride has got such a hold of some people that they would rather have their children raised in ignorance, than to have them taught gratis."[128] Charging a tiny amount of tuition might not solve the financial problems of Lancasterian schools, but it promised to bring children of all backgrounds together and to avoid the perception that a Lancasterian school was only a holding pen for the poorest children.

In New York City, the Free School Society engaged in a decades-long set of unplanned experiments in order to achieve similar goals. Unlike elites in most cities, the trustees of New York's free schools were unable to charge tuition, even if they wanted to. The 1795 law that had established a state school fund had delivered the matching funds exclusively to the Free School Society, bypassing the more numerous pay schools. The rule was simple: only tuition-free schools could be funded with state money.[129] Under their original charter, the Free School Society could not resort to tuition or to voucher schemes. They had to come up with some other solution for their half-empty schools, some other way to entice students to attend.

Instead of acknowledging the complaints and petitions of students and parents, the trustees' first experiment was to try blaming the teachers for low attendance. In 1822, they came up with a new plan to increase student attendance by tying teacher pay directly to the number of students in seats.[130] If a teacher—a "delinquent teacher"—was so lazy that they regarded their job as a "sinecure," then they would presumably see no reason to drum up students. If students were not coming to the free schools, the trustees figured, perhaps lazy teachers could take a more entrepreneurial role. Teachers should "seek . . . amongst the families of the poor" to find students for their schools. Instead of rewarding lazy teachers with empty schools, the new plan would pay a salary tied to attendance. At the time, that meant that a teacher would receive two dollars per student per year up to two hundred students, then $1.50 per student between two hundred and six hundred students, then a dollar per student for every student over six hundred. Under the old system, the highest-paid teachers in the New York system received a salary of $1,000 per year. Under the new proposal, a teacher would have to fill his or her school to bursting in order to make that kind of money.[131]

This payment plan never worked, not least because it falsely assumed that teachers had the power to compel attendance. Yet it remained popular among elite reformers. In Philadelphia, for instance, one of Roberts Vaux's close friends and colleagues wondered aloud if this kind of pay-per-student plan might solve the problem of low attendance. When teachers received a flat salary, this friend mused, there was "no stimulating allurement to the teacher to push on." If teachers competed with one another for students, this market-friendly friend assured Vaux, every teacher would work their best to achieve a "high character and popularity." If more money were on the line, then "every teacher would exert himself" to create a popular school and to be promoted to even more popular schools.[132]

Like the blind-voucher plans, these teacher-pay schemes went nowhere. By the mid-1820s the New York trustees recognized that there was a far more obvious and effective solution to the problems of low enrollment. If parents kept their kids home because they hated the idea of a charity school, a school that isolated lower-income children and taught them only the basics, then maybe parents would send their children to schools that mixed richer and poorer students together. After all, in New York the trustees had long fought a two-sided losing battle. On one hand, they struggled to find enough students to fill their Lancasterian benches. Yet on the other, they had to sternly and awkwardly turn away children from higher-income families. As early as 1819, the trustees had reminded families with higher incomes that their children were not welcome in the free schools. As they put it, "The children of Parents who are able to pay for Schooling, cannot be admitted."[133] By 1824, the trustees recognized the obvious. They spent too much time "ascertaining . . . that [children] were the proper objects of gratuitous education."[134] Why not solve both problems at once? Why not beef up enrollment by simply admitting the children of wealthier parents who were already pleading for admission?[135]

In 1825, the trustees of the Free School Society made the switch. It was not easy. They had to appeal to the state legislature to change their charter. Their goal was twofold. First, by changing their schools from "Free or Charity" schools to "Public or General" ones, they would eliminate the stigma of pauper-only institutions.[136] Plus, they would boost enrollment by admitting the many students of families that had asked to enroll their children but were not deemed poor enough.[137] Not least of all, a school that mixed children of different classes could help create what one New York Lancasterian called "a perfect democracy."[138] A new kind of public school for New York City, trustees hoped, would solve all the glaring fundamental problems with the Lancasterian system, while keeping the Lancasterian teaching methods intact.

The plan seemed to work, at least for a moment. The trustees succeeded in getting their proposal approved.[139] They changed their name from the Free School Society to the Public School Society, and in 1826 their new vision of public schools got its start. Instead of schools only for the poor, the new public schools would welcome all white students and would encourage attendance by requiring a tuition fee from all students. However, enrollment and attendance soon crashed once again. From a high in 1825 of 4,059 students, attendance dropped to 3,759, even with the new all-tuition system.[140]

Not only did students fail to enroll, but those who did often chose not to pay. Though attendance bounced back up in 1827 to 4,565, only 2,874 students actually paid the mandatory tuition.[141] Once again, the plans of the reformers had left everyone unhappy. Lower-income students resented being marked out as not paying their way. And parents who paid tuition wondered why they were the only ones who paid. As the treasurer of the Public School

Society noted in 1827, the tuition-for-all system was a failure. It only brought in "a comparatively trifling sum" but it generated plenty of disaffection among parents.[142] In 1832, in response, the Public School Society finally hit on the plan that lasted: public schools open to all white students, none of whom would pay tuition. It was the only way to overcome parental resistance to the humiliations their children suffered from being isolated as paupers, unable to pay tuition.

In other cities, reformers took different paths but ended up in a similar place. By the end of the 1820s, the goal of common public schools for the children of all white families had become overwhelmingly popular. In Philadelphia, for example, by 1828 a state senate committee expressed the vision of common schools in unmistakable terms. Instead of setting up schools only for the poorest children, the senators wanted schools "open to all without distinction." In addition to teaching writing, reading, and more advanced subjects, these "common school houses" would provide a place for all children to meet "upon terms of the most perfect equality."[143]

By the beginning of the 1830s, the legislature of Pennsylvania had again endorsed the idea of mixed common schools for all white children. Anything else, one house committee declared, threatened to introduce "an insidious distinction between the wealthy and the poor."[144] Not only would common schools solve this moral conundrum, but they would also solve the fundamental flaws in the Lancasterian system. Mixed schools, the legislators believed, would encourage wealthier Pennsylvanians to support tax-funded schools. After all, it was a difficult political proposition to ask for more money for schools for other people's children. Moreover, common schools for rich and poor would solve the truancy problem, by assuring lower-income parents that they were not being looked down upon as paupers.[145]

Mistakes Were Made

In their debates, none of these lawmakers mentioned actual Lancasterian teaching methods. They did not debate whether or not children could make good teachers. They did not wonder whether large, open Lancasterian schoolhouses were the best way to structure learning space. They never discussed the pros and cons of corporal punishment, or student recitations, or any of the high-tech gizmos Lancaster himself was so fond of. The basic problems of Lancasterian schools were found elsewhere. Reformers assumed that tuition costs were the only thing that kept low-income students out of school. They assumed that monitors would relish the chance to work for free. They assumed that their philanthropic traditions could handle the responsibilities of a modern public school system. They had embraced Lancaster's flawed vision because it assured them that their assumptions were all right, but it did not take long for them all to be proven wrong.

In addressing those fundamental problems, reformers made fundamental changes. In practice, they created very non-Lancasterian modern public schools, even while they believed they were only tweaking and adjusting the Lancasterian system. For example, they paid and trained monitors. They dealt with unexpectedly high costs by negotiating new funding systems, systems that put more emphasis on taxes. They offered classes beyond the mere basics. Most importantly, they opened schools to all white students, richer and poorer. In short, they made all the changes—fundamental changes—that parents and families had demanded, but during the 1820s reformers did not yet acknowledge that fact. Nor did they recognize that their changes heralded the end of the Lancasterian system. For a while, they stumbled along with un-Lancasterian Lancasterian schools, schools that no longer relied on the free labor of children, schools that no longer promised to teach basic skills only to the children of the poor, schools that were no longer run as the philanthropic causes of urban elites but as a public service of tax-funded governments.

The tortuous trajectory of Lancaster's flawed vision has been difficult for historians to follow largely because reformers at the time abandoned the system while keeping the name. Historians have focused on the rise and fall of Lancaster's classroom methods, without noticing that those methods were, at most, a side issue.[146] As we've seen in this chapter, in at least two schools in New Haven and Boston, Lancaster's methods remained popular and successful for decades. The successes at John Lovell's and William B. Fowle's Lancasterian schools, however, were not due to a superior understanding or a perfected implementation of Lancaster's system. Instead, those successes happened because Fowle and Lovell built Lancasterian schools with plenty of financial support. They built schools that met community demands. At their schools, parent concerns were listened to and immediately addressed.

In the big cities, on the other hand, elite reformers refused to listen. They refused throughout the 1820s to admit the inadequacies of their Lancasterian dreams, no matter how forcefully they were pointed out by working-class pundits, no matter how painfully obvious it became that students were simply not coming. If we listened only to the words of the reformers in the bigger cities, we would think that their Lancasterian methods worked well throughout the 1810s and 1820s, until they suddenly fell out of favor and were replaced by trained adult teachers, smaller classrooms, and mixed common schooling with advanced curriculum. In fact, the solution to the mystery of Lancasterianism's failure can be found in its divorce from its own methods. In a few cases, the methods worked, because they were used in schools with plenty of resources, schools in which school leaders heeded community input. Yet without those resources, and without acknowledging that input, the methods never worked.

To make things even more profoundly confusing, even when the methods were abandoned in bits and pieces here and there, reformers kept the Lancasterian name alive, by calling their non-Lancasterian schools "Lancasterian." In practice, the system never really existed the way it had been imagined. In effect, the Lancasterian miracle never happened, at least in the larger urban districts. But that fact has been obscured by the messy realities of reform politics. Though their Lancasterian dreams never worked, reformers made them look as if they were a huge success, at first. They announced that they were enacting the system, but by the time reformers acknowledged the effective veto of lower-income families, they had in practice abandoned the central tenets of Lancaster's system long before. They had changed it so radically that only the name remained, along with the huge echoing Lancasterian schoolrooms. The end of the Lancasterian reform movement and the demise of Lancaster himself were both ugly affairs. Both lingered long after they had ceased to be relevant to the real practices and problems of urban public education.

8
The Next Big Thing

It was almost as if none of it had happened at all. By the time of Lancaster's ugly, violent death at the end of 1838, the world of urban schooling and school reform had moved on—so decisively, at times, that it was as if Lancaster and his empty promises had never existed. It had been over thirty years, after all, since the New York Free School Society had opened its first Lancasterian school in 1806. It had been two decades since Pennsylvania had passed its law requiring Lancasterian methods for Philadelphia's public schools. A new generation of reformers had taken over, and they sometimes thought that their challenges were brand new.

In Massachusetts, for example, a committee reported in 1835 that they had finally found a solution to all their educational problems. Heedless of any lessons from the Lancasterian debacle, the Boston-based reformers explained that they could find all the answers they needed in a modern European education reform, the "Prussian system." Thanks to this "well-devised plan" of schooling, the reformers explained, they could elevate the quality of "public instruction in this Commonwealth" without spending any additional money or requiring any additional taxes.[1]

In other ways, too, the school reform talk after Lancaster's death seemed to be a mere repeat of the language of the early 1800s and 1810s. During the 1840s and into the 1850s, ardent urban reformers warned that thousands of hapless children were learning dangerous lessons on the streets. Reformers looked in panic at the intractable problems of urban education; they had no idea how they could possibly afford to give basic schooling to so many street children.

In spite of these dispiriting echoes, everything about urban public education really had changed enormously by the late 1830s. Since the 1820s, in order to solve the unforeseen shortcomings of Lancaster's plan and to address the complaints of parents and pundits, reformers in cities such as Boston, Baltimore, Philadelphia, and New York had tinkered with Lancaster's impractical system. They had turned monitors into teachers, even if they didn't change their titles; they had added advanced classes and trained teachers in an effort to convince students to show up; they had cobbled together tax funding to pay for it all; and they had eliminated the stigma of charity schooling by creating public schools for rich and poor together. In doing so, they effectively abandoned the Lancasterian system long before they admitted they had. What happened at the end of the 1830s was not the failure of Lancasterian methods. Those methods had failed much earlier. No, what changed was the openness with which city leaders finally admitted their failure. By the end of the 1830s, larger US cities openly ditched their Lancasterian efforts.

In this chapter, we will take a quick glance at what the world of urban public education looked like after the last glow had faded from the Lancasterian promise. The changes were deep and profound—a casual observer in 1800 or 1818 would be amazed at the changes by 1838. But unlike the introduction of Lancaster's world-famous system in 1805, by 1838 there was no dramatic announcement of a single new approach. Changes were piecemeal and local. Reformers in 1838 did not have a grand new solution to their problems, though, as we've seen, many reformers had not learned to be more skeptical of grand new solutions. Because Lancaster's promises never came true, or even close, reformers found themselves asking similar questions about intractable problems of urban poverty and the possibilities of more equitable schools. The reformers of the 1830s seemed generally unaware of the scope of the vast changes that had taken place in the past thirty years. Yet even if the later generation of reformers did not know it, their paths had been smoothed by those who had gone before.

Dead in the Street

What about the man himself? Joseph Lancaster's end was as pathetic and as hard to understand as the end of the reform movement that bore his name. By October 24, 1838, he had alienated even his closest friends and thoroughly eliminated any chance that anyone might ever take his ideas seriously. On that day, he stood on the streets of New York City once again, hoping against hope to convince someone—anyone—to give him money for his school reform ideas.

He might have been pondering his latest humiliating rejection. He had come to New York City to pitch a new, secret, even better version of his reform plan to the leaders of the Public School Society. They wouldn't even meet with him.[2] As even his former friends admitted, by that point he had become a figure of sad pity, "a mass of obesity, unwieldy, and of feeble articulation, such as we occasionally see in individuals of objectionable habits, loaded with adipose deposits."[3]

He never had a chance to come up with another scheme: on that day in late 1838 he stepped out in front of a rushing horse carriage and was killed immediately. It was an inglorious end. For years, his misfortunes had never seemed to let up. After he had made himself impossible in Philadelphia in 1820, he moved to Baltimore to repeat the process. Then, in typically outlandish fashion, Lancaster soon began bragging that the newly independent government of Simon Bolivar in Gran Colombia—incorporating the later countries of Colombia, Ecuador, Panama, and Venezuela, as well as parts of Peru and Brazil—had offered him the princely sum of $20,000 to take over their Lancasterian school systems. They hadn't. He was eventually paid just over $1,300 to lead a school in Caracas.[4] Nevertheless, Lancaster moved to Caracas in 1824 to pursue his imagined payoff.[5]

It was a strange sojourn. Lancaster refused to teach at the Caracas Lancasterian school. Instead, he usually tacked up a sign on the door of the school saying he was "indisposed."[6] He spent his time endlessly writing ignored letters to Simon Bolivar pleading for the money Bolivar had never offered.[7]

It must have come as a shock to Lancaster during his squalid stay in Caracas that his daughter Betsy finally escaped. When he arrived in Caracas on May 24, 1824, he traveled with his daughter Betsy and former apprentice Richard Jones. Before they left the United States, however, Betsy and Richard changed the nature of their relationship. They had lived for years together in the Lancaster household. They had struggled together to manage Mrs. Lancaster's mental illness and Joseph Lancaster's delusions and depredations. They had abandoned rented houses in the middle of the night to avoid angry landlords, and they had put off the demands of creditors in every city and cleaned up the messes Lancaster made. Somewhere along the way, they became more than fellow sufferers, and before they left for Caracas they became husband and wife. Their marriage did not change much at first—they still bore the brunt of Lancaster's narcissism—but during their time in Caracas they finally found a way to escape the Lancaster household, though not the wider Lancaster influence.[8]

In the end, their opportunity for escape came from the unpredicted direction of Mexico. Like many governments around Latin America, the leaders of Mexico had long hoped to establish Lancasterian schools in their country.[9] Two Mexican officials had visited Caracas to talk with Lancaster about the requirements for free Lancasterian schools. Lancaster made his usual outrageous demands, which the officials ignored, but he did not manage to dissuade them from their goal.[10] When the country declared its independence from Spain in 1821, like Gran Colombia, it immediately established a national network of Lancasterian schools, and in 1824, the Lancasterian Company of Mexico City published its first Lancasterian manual.[11] Disgusted by Lancaster himself, the new government invited Richard Jones instead to guide their Lancasterian efforts.[12]

It was a unique opportunity for Jones, and he took it. Not only did he finally get away from Lancaster's domestic cruelties, but the job allowed him and Betsy to set up their own household for the first time.[13] It was not easy for them. Jones found the schools in Mexico City to be atrocious.[14] The young couple was without money or friends at first, without even a decent school in which they could teach. As usual, when they asked Joseph Lancaster for financial help, he offered none. However, the Joneses persevered and eventually opened a Lancasterian school in Guadalajara that thrived for decades.[15] As Joseph Lancaster veered and careened in his usual destructive way in Caracas, Betsy and Richard built a new life for themselves far away.

The Civilized World

To people familiar with the sad failures of Lancasterian reform and Joseph Lancaster's personal life, it might seem surprising that anyone would be recruiting Lancaster's followers. But urban reformers in the United States had not been the only ones to observe from afar Joseph Lancaster's early work at the Borough Road School in London. As early as 1808, Lancaster's manuals had been translated into German, and other languages soon followed.[16] During the 1810s, as Lancaster feuded with his former supporters in the British and Foreign School Society, Lancasterian methods were implemented around the world. Newly independent or soon-to-be-independent nations such as Haiti, Chile, and Uruguay established Lancasterian schools in the 1810s.[17] By the end of the 1810s, the British and Foreign School Society bragged that their Lancasterian schools already dominated in France. Schools had been established in Spain, Russia, Italy, and Belgium. They were huge in Canada. In India, Lancasterian schools had been established in Kolkata and Mumbai. In Africa, there was a Lancasterian school in Sierra Leone.[18]

By the 1820s, as they had in the United States, Lancasterian ideas had been implemented worldwide. The British and Foreign School Society reported that France and Spain had unfortunately withdrawn their initial enthusiasm, but the methods had been embraced elsewhere,[19] such as in Denmark, the Netherlands, Greece, Sweden, and Malta,[20] as well as in Liberia, around the Caribbean, and throughout the Ottoman Empire.[21] Around the world, there were both schools and rumors of schools. Often, the tales were exaggerated in the retelling. For instance, when one New York Lancasterian hoped to share the gospel of Lancasterian reform, he reported with more enthusiasm than accuracy that Paris had embraced the system and had opened several hundred schools in France, "which promised to rescue the lower classes from the deplorable ignorance in which they are too generally involved."[22] At the time, the better-informed and more modest leaders of the British and Foreign School Society had quietly admitted that, in fact, the news from Paris was "unfavourable" to the global Lancasterian movement.[23]

Not only did rumors often exaggerate global Lancasterian success, but also the purposes of Lancasterian schools were often different in different locales. As the leading scholars of the global Lancasterian movement have noted, there were vast disparities in the purpose and goals of Lancasterian schools.[24] Around the world, though, a few common themes emerged by the 1820s.

For instance, in ways that were never much part of debates in the United States, global Lancasterianism came to be seen as an anti-Catholic movement. In Canada, for example, the establishment of a Lancasterian teacher-training school in Montreal met with opposition from Catholic bishops, who objected to the idea that students would read the scriptures without suitable religious guidance.[25] Similarly, in Paris, the Bourbon government withdrew its support for Lancasterian schools in 1824 because it felt that the methods clashed with Catholic principles.[26]

Catholic concerns were not unfounded. The person who arranged Lancaster's invitation to Caracas, for instance, frankly explained to Lancaster that he hoped that the system could rid South America of its Catholic traditions. As he wrote from Quito, Ecuador, he hoped that Lancaster's system would "teach these poor ignorant sons of the Andes, that there is but one God whom we have to worship—that the Priests are but sinful mortals like themselves, and that their idols are composed of the same perishable materials with the hands that made them—[Lancaster should] come here and dispel the clouds of ignorance in which we are enveloped."[27] In addition, one of Lancaster's Quaker relatives wrote to him from London to say that she hoped he might cure South American Catholics of their sin of "Bow[ing] down to gravein [sic] images."[28]

In the Americas, at least, the themes of anti-Catholicism were often bound up with ideas of modernity and modern republican citizenship. In newly independent Haiti, for instance, Lancasterian schools were seen as key to creating "an independent national identity."[29] In South America, too, some reformers envisioned Lancasterian schooling as the key to joining the modern, liberated world.[30] As one Peruvian enthusiast put it, "It is not yet possible to calculate the revolution which will be produced by this system of mutual instruction." Like the champions of Lancaster in the United States, South American reformers believed that the schools would put an end to "ignorance." Unlike US elites, however, the Peruvian saw this dreamed-of transformation as a key part of joining "the civilized world."[31]

Alas, in Peru as in Pennsylvania, Lancasterian promises never came true. Yet throughout the world in the 1810s and 1820s, the name of Lancaster and the idea of a modern, scientific Lancasterian system were seen as key to establishing new cities and new nations. Unfortunately for the Colombians who worked with Lancaster himself in the 1820s, he quickly taught them the same lessons he had taught reformers in Europe and the United States.

Poor Indeed

Yet Lancaster himself never learned his lesson. Lancaster had moved to Caracas to cash in on an entirely imaginary cash promise. He seemed to have finally publicized his true intentions, his belief that an enormous financial bonanza would eventually solve all his problems at once. Throughout his stay, he seemed really to believe that it had been promised to him, and he spent the money several times over, in his imagination. Instead of teaching at the model school, Lancaster spent his time trying to convince various financial agents in London that he had received a line of credit from the Bolivarian government to the tune of $20,000. When he was refused the full amount, he tried to get a cash payout of only half that amount. Not surprisingly, none of the hard-nosed accountants in London agreed to front Lancaster such an enormous sum based on such flimsy imagined credit.[32]

Simon Bolivar was not the only world leader Lancaster harassed. Before he fled Caracas in the summer of 1827 to return to Philadelphia, he wrote a pleading letter to King George IV, reminding the king that Lancaster was "well known to thyself and to Mankind as having been the means of educating many thousands and tens of thousands of British Subjects." Lancaster's only reward to date, he told the king, was the loss of his youth, his health, and his future financial security. He had "enriched and exalted the minds of my countrymen in Knowledge and benevolence leaving myself and family in pecuniary circumstances—poor indeed." Luckily for the king, Lancaster knew of a solution to this vast injustice. Lancaster proposed a generous annuity for himself from the royal coffers. Upon receipt, Lancaster—desperate and poor in Caracas—was willing to return to London to lend his prestige to the support of the Crown.[33]

Unsurprisingly, Lancaster never received a response, so he returned to Philadelphia and importuned Roberts Vaux for money. He asked for forty dollars here, fifteen dollars there, always with a vague complaint about his "peculiar circumstances" and even vaguer promises to pay Vaux back, maybe "from the produce of any lectures on the way."[34] As he told Vaux, he had "been unable to do any thing to create an income" since he left Caracas, but he never abandoned hope that his genius would eventually receive its due.[35]

It didn't, but it wasn't for a lack of trying. Lancaster wrote to the governor of New York.[36] He wrote to the president of the United States. As he pleaded with President Andrew Jackson in 1829, Lancaster had "published [his] inventions to mankind when I could by taking a patent have enriched myself." He had been cruelly misled in South America. Could the president see fit to help him out?[37]

Lancaster never received any response or encouragement from President Jackson, but he never abandoned his quest for payouts, even when those requests provoked only puzzlement and confusion. For example, the mayor of Albany declined Lancaster's odd request for a community subscription in Lancaster's honor. The mayor tried to explain to Lancaster that they simply did not do that kind of thing. The mayor added that even if the city circulated Lancaster's unprecedented call for donations, "you may possibly find very few that would feel willing to contribute."[38] The leaders of New Haven were equally perplexed by Lancaster's requests. They could "deeply sympathize" with Lancaster in his "distress," they wrote in the summer of 1829, but they did not understand why Lancaster thought they would raise money to pay off his debts and support him in his planned move back to England.[39]

In his endless financial desperation, Lancaster moved to Montreal in 1829, where he experienced only another round of humiliation.[40] Out of options, out of money, out of friends, even out of distant admirers of his once-heralded system, Lancaster returned in 1833 to Philadelphia. To the public, who remained uninterested, Lancaster described a new experimental educational system in what he hoped were intriguing terms. It was a difficult task, because by that point reformers had moved on. Yet Lancaster didn't give up; he promised that his new system derived its "immense power" from secret modifications to the monitorial approach.[41] As he had in Montreal, Lancaster refused to describe his new plan before he received an adequate financial reward, but he trumpeted his new system's amazing results. As in Montreal, Lancaster claimed to have used his new system on a group of test subjects. These twenty children, Lancaster assured Philadelphians, were no paragons of learning when Lancaster started. One was blind in one eye, yet he still learned basic reading, writing, and arithmetic in only two months. Another, "who appeared as an idiot, and almost as hopeless," still learned to read and write in record-breaking time. Similarly, a child of only four years of age made such rapid educational progress under Lancaster's superior tutelage that the youngster "astonished the examiners &c."[42]

Unfortunately for Lancaster, these publicity statements were almost entirely fictional, and Lancaster's falsehoods alienated even his firmest and longest supporters. For example, Lancaster told Philadelphia that Roberts Vaux had vouched for his new program.[43] Lancaster had indeed tried to get Vaux to come and inspect his new experimental school,[44] but Vaux had refused.[45] After Lancaster heedlessly told the public that Vaux had examined the children in Lancaster's new school and found them amazingly proficient, Vaux finally stopped answering Lancaster's letters. When Lancaster came around to Vaux's house, Vaux was pointedly not at home.[46]

It was in this state, then—physically depleted, utterly alone, ignored even by his most ardent former admirers—that Joseph Lancaster traveled to New

York City in 1838 to plead for attention and money from the leaders of that city's Public School Society.

Echoes

Twenty years earlier, Lancaster had been embraced by urban reformers in the United States because they thought he could solve their "urchin" problem. In the first years of the 1800s, city leaders such as De Witt Clinton and Roberts Vaux looked with alarm at the crowds of low-income children thronging their streets. Though they usually talked about the lack of education for these street children, what they truly worried about was something else. They did not fear a lack of education, but rather the far more alluring kind of education on offer in the city's streets and alleys. Instead of going to school to learn to read, write, and pray, elites fretted, low-income children in the 1810s were hitting the streets to learn to be thieves and prostitutes.

Long after Lancaster's gruesome, lonely death in 1838, urban elites continued to worry. As one New Yorker warned in the mid-1850s, tens of thousands of urban children were out of school and in the street, "being educated . . . in habits of idleness, and a knowledge of vice." These hordes of hapless street children, this writer warned, would soon "graduate" from their infernal street lessons and "enter upon careers of debauchery and crime."[47]

Elite New Yorkers were just as terrified of their city's low-income children in the 1850s as an earlier generation had been in the 1810s. Their newspapers were full of dire warnings about children of the streets, whom they called "'gamins,' 'Arabs,' 'urchins,' 'gutter-snipes,' and 'street rats.'"[48] One grand jury reported that fully 80 percent of New York's felony indictments in 1854 were against minors.[49] Elites in the middle of the 1800s looked out their windows and recoiled in terror at the dangers they thought they faced from the lack of proper schools for poor children.

In other cities, too, reformers warned about the "education of the streets" and its dangers for both children and their eventual elite victims.[50] In the booming industrial town of Lowell, Massachusetts, elites warned in 1846 that up to a third of school aged children were not in any school.[51] These poor children would live "in constant exposure" to all the "corrupting scenes" of city life.[52] Just as they had done in the 1810s and the 1820s, education reformers tried to terrify their fellow elites with these kinds of statistics. If more children were not provided with healthy Christian educations, the

Lowell School Committee explained, "no language of ours can convey too strongly our sense of the dangers which await us from this source."[53]

Though these warnings tell us more about the political strategies of school reformers than they do about the children themselves, those children also tended to repeat some of the patterns of the earlier generation. The most striking example is that urban youth tended to use the "truant plan" in spite of all the changes and improvements in urban public schools. When public schools did not meet families' needs, children stayed home. In Philadelphia, for example, students responded to poor school conditions by staying away. By 1853, conditions in some of the city's segregated Black-only schools were atrocious. At West Philadelphia School, for instance, students had to climb over and under the jumbled furniture in order to get to their seats in the classroom. The building itself was "dilapidated," and in the winter the broken windows made the room impossible to keep warm.[54] As a result, reformers of the 1850s worried just as much as reformers of the 1820s about the "irregular attendance of scholars."[55]

In New York, too, low-income families continued to avoid public schools when conditions were unsatisfactory. And just as reformers did in the 1820s, in the next generation elites tried everything they could think of to compel students to attend. Seemingly unaware of the failures of the earlier generation, in the 1840s the New York Public School Society again attempted to send elite "visitors" to low-income families' homes to convince them to attend school. As one visitor reported breathlessly, she had been "searching for children for Public School" when she came across the following distressing scene: The "Mother" had reported herself a widow, but the visitor found the "Father" also at home. He "had been let out from State Prison the day before." The mother had not been expecting him—or the visitor—and she was "intoxicated, quite unable to attend to her Children" at nine in the morning. The surprise meeting of father and mother was "followed by blows and tumultuous noise." The visitor fled, "with my mind made up that there are multitudes of children in this City who never will be benifitted by Education unless they can be rescued from such an influence."[56] By 1842, the Public School Society canceled its visitors program, deciding that the problem might just be more complicated than they had originally thought.[57]

Elite reformers in New York and Philadelphia were not the only ones who seemed to ignore the obvious lessons of the Lancasterian movement. Even as Lancasterian methods had fallen out of favor in bigger cities, western US cities and states still rushed to implement them. At the very end of the 1820s, for example, even after most Lancasterian reformers had soured on Lancaster's inflated promises, reformers in Kentucky were repeating the pattern. In 1829, Louisville established its first "public monitorial school."[58] They even hired a veteran of the first failures of Lancasterian reform, Ed Baker, one of Lancaster's original apprentices in London. He had made a career for himself teaching in Lancasterian schools in Albany and Philadelphia. By the end of the 1820s, as prospects for Lancasterian reform dimmed on the East Coast, Baker migrated west to try it again.[59] Kentuckians had high hopes they could use Lancaster's failed methods to "extend the means of popular instruction" in their state, apparently unaware of the lessons from Philadelphia and New York.[60]

As late as 1837, when Lancaster's ideas had been roundly and officially rejected in Philadelphia and New York, some westerners thought they might work elsewhere. Two ambitious reformers hoped to introduce "the Lancasterian system" into Illinois, Michigan, Indiana, and Missouri. As far as they could tell, those "Western states" had perfect conditions for a dramatic Lancasterian success.[61] Unfortunately for the would-be western reformers, the system's internal contradictions and half-baked plans did not work any better in the 1830s than they had in the 1820s, and they did not work in the West any better than they had worked everywhere else.

Taxes and Rates

By the time those westerners considered a Lancasterian solution to their problems, Lancasterians elsewhere had moved on. By the end of the 1830s, the tweaks and adjustments that reformers had been making to their Lancasterian schools were generally recognized as something more than just tweaks and adjustments. Leaders in cities such as Baltimore, Boston, and Philadelphia no longer pretended to run modified Lancasterian schools. Instead, they recognized the system's vast failures and focused on other ways to improve their city schools. In New York, school leaders held on to Lancasterian labels a little longer, even though they had long since lost their original meanings.

Perhaps the most significant change by 1838 was that urban reformers no longer expected charity schools to be run as private philanthropies. If the trials of the 1810s and 1820s had taught them anything, it was that traditional benevolent subscriptions were not nearly adequate for a modern urban public school system. It was a slow-moving development, but it was a revolutionary one nonetheless. One of the reasons for Lancaster's sudden fame in the early 1800s, after all, had been his promise that his schools could provide universal basic education without changing the old philanthropic system. He had promised that elites in any city could cough up enough of their excess wealth to cover the miniscule costs of a Lancasterian school. For ardent urban reformers in the early 1800s, those promises made sense. They could not and did not imagine that governments would be expected to guarantee basic education for all citizens, paid for with reliable streams of tax funding. More importantly, they assumed that they would remain the people to make decisions about schools for poor children. By the time of Lancaster's death, however, reformers realized the truth: government funding from taxes would have to play a big role in public school budgets, and that funding came with more stringent demands for professional, accountable oversight.

This shift in reformers' assumptions has been hard for historians to trace and for contemporaries to notice, because it wholly lacked the dramatic changes of Lancaster's initial schemes. There was never a single, headline-grabbing decision to shift school funding to taxes. Instead, the changes came in dribs and drabs throughout the early decades of the 1800s as reformers tried and failed to patch the holes in Lancaster's delusionary promises. As historians such as Carl F. Kaestle and Nancy Beadie have charted, by the 1840s those piecemeal changes had added up to a remarkable change. By that time, public schools balanced—and expected to balance—their costs against a range of income, including income from government funding. In most places, the revolutionary nature of this change was muffled by the fact that it happened in fits and starts here and there. In New York City, all public schools were tuition-free by 1832.[62] In most places, however, families that could afford to pay tuition for their children did so for far longer. In the rest of New York, for example, parents continued to pay "rate bills" at public schools until after the Civil War.[63] In other states, the mix of tax-funded and family-funded public schooling changed only slowly, without a single dramatic transformation.[64] As long as some families continued to pay for schooling out of their own pockets, it was difficult to notice that all children could go to public schools whether they could afford the tuition or not.

A Classroom of Their Own

A time traveler from 1800 who landed in 1838 would be far more likely to notice a different change in reformers' attitudes. By the time of Lancaster's death, his empty promise of a free labor force of untrained child-teachers had been thoroughly discredited. The next generation of reformers looked instead to the challenge of training enough adult teachers to make the dream of universal public education come true. As the most famous reformer of the next generation, Horace Mann, put it, Lancaster's system relied foolishly on the "hampering, blinding, misleading instruction given by an inexperienced child." If the public wanted public schools to thrive, Mann lectured in 1843, they needed to rely on a new kind of hero, the "accomplished teacher."[65]

At least partly in response, one focus of the next generation of reformers was the establishment of teacher-training schools, called "normal schools." As one group of DC-based reformers assumed in 1857, their only hope to improve schools for African Americans was to train more Black teachers. After all, they reasoned, white teachers would never be allowed to teach Black students in the South, where most African Americans lived at the time. Their solution was not to rely on untrained children—monitors—to solve the dilemma, but rather to recruit "the more intelligent daughters of this people," give them a thorough education in the liberal arts, and then send them back to the South as professional teachers, to "extend ... the blessings of knowledge and religion."[66]

The dramatic shift away from unpaid child-monitors to paid, trained, adult teachers was the kind of change people noticed. They couldn't help it; the changes were reflected in literal brick-and-mortar restructuring, as well as the hefty price tag that went with those changes. Perhaps the architectural changes in Philadelphia best capture this shift. In 1818, just as Lancaster arrived in the United States and cities such as Philadelphia eagerly anticipated the revolutionary improvements his system would bring, the state built its Model School on Chestnut Street to Lancaster's specific architectural recommendations. It wasn't cheap. Including building lot and school furniture, the school was a significant investment for the state and city. Yet by the time of Lancaster's death, the city had to shell out once again for another expensive building project. To mark the decisive shift away from Lancasterian teaching, the model school was cut into ten separate classrooms, each to be taught by a separate trained, adult teacher. It had cost about $15,000 to build it to Lancasterian specifications in 1818. Remodeling it in 1837 for post-Lancasterian realities cost another $10,000.[67] It had taken years for Philadelphia's school leaders to admit it, but by the time they had exhausted their belief in Lancaster's promises they were willing to pay another hefty price tag to repurpose their Lancasterian building.

By that relatively late date, the physical changes in school buildings were merely an official, expensive recognition of the changes that had been going on for years. Soon, post-Lancasterian public school buildings became the norm. Near Boston, for example, in 1847 a new generation of reformers built a new kind of school from the ground up, one with separate classrooms for each teacher.[68] The new kind of school expected to need several trained adult teachers, each leading their own classroom.[69]

In New York, too, new ways of thinking about public education had become the norm. New York had already made drastic changes in order to fix the problems with Lancaster's system. In the mid-1820s, the Free School Society had changed its name to the Public School Society. By the early 1830s, they had added a broader variety of curricula and welcomed both rich and poor. They had first tried charging everyone tuition and then switched to charging no one. In addition, in 1834 the Manumission Society handed over control of its segregated African Free Schools to the Public School Society.[70] By that date, the assumptions of an earlier generation no longer made sense. For the elites who had founded groups such as the Manumission Society and the Free School Society, public schools were presumed to be charities, run by elites for other people's children. By the middle of the 1830s, that was not how people thought about public schools. Though they were still segregated by race, the public schools had become the city's schools, run by government as a public service for all, instead of by elites as a benevolent enterprise for the unfortunate.

As it made all its changes, New York's school leaders often kept the old names long after they had lost their original meaning. As early as 1836, for example, the Public School Society had established, in effect, a normal school, a separate institution that it used to train the paid, adult teachers it used in its system. However, in 1836 the New Yorkers still called their normal school a "School for Monitors." Teachers at the "School for Monitors" were often themselves called monitors, yet they were paid a regular salary and were expected to train young adults in the art and science of teaching. Their expectations were worlds away frozm those of Lancaster's manuals, in which teaching was presumed to be a simple task requiring no special education. A "monitor" in Lancaster's Borough Road School in 1805 was totally different from a "monitor" in New York's normal school in 1836, yet the name remained.[71]

"Extraneous Manouevres"

In Baltimore, the changes were more dramatic, perhaps because the city's leaders had less investment in Lancasterian ideas. As far back as 1819, the city's leaders had invited Lancaster to come to their city to establish Lancasterian schools, but Lancaster ruined his chances there, as he had in every other city.[72] With Lancaster himself removed from the process, the city's leaders—at least one faction of them—kept trying to establish a successful Lancasterian public school system. They tried and failed to cram a public school law through the state assembly in 1825, but they finally succeeded in 1826.[73] Even with the law in place, it wasn't easy for city leaders to get schools up and running. The Lancasterian schools did not actually open until 1829, and it was not until 1830 that the city opened its first specially built Lancasterian school building.[74]

Just as in London, Philadelphia, and New York, Baltimore's investment in Lancasterian schooling was significant. But also like every other city, the system immediately proved itself impractical. By 1829, one Baltimore teacher reported that he had never followed the instructions in Lancaster's manuals; he considered Lancaster's "extraneous manouevres" unnecessary and unhelpful.[75] By 1831, another teacher explained that Lancaster's system was "but little used" in Baltimore's public schools, even though the schools were officially Lancasterian.[76] In 1836, the lead teacher in the city's first public school pushed the city school committee to abandon the monitorial approach. It just didn't work.[77]

By the time of Lancaster's grisly death in 1838, the leaders of Baltimore's public school committee listened. As they noted in 1838, "In a short time . . . the public became dissatisfied with the mechanical methods and unprofitable manoeuvres of the Lancastrian [sic] schools and with the very limited range of instruction they afford."[78] Like school leaders in other cities, the leaders of Baltimore's fledgling public schools decided that they would no longer be using monitors. Paid, trained teachers, they explained, would be "far more satisfactory to the parents."[79]

Though teachers in Baltimore's supposedly Lancasterian schools had ditched Lancasterian methods long before, it was not until the end of the 1830s that those changes were reflected in official policies. In 1839, for example, the city's public schools doubled the number of teachers they hired, from eight to sixteen.[80] In 1840, they constructed a new building with separate classrooms in which those trained, adult teachers could work.[81] As always, the evidence of the failure of Lancasterian methods was provided most dramatically by families' responses. In Baltimore, as in other cities, families had kept their children out of the monitorial schools. But attendance shot up after the school committee made its changes, from 675 students in 1838 to 1,126 in 1839. Ten years later, those numbers had continued to climb, reaching 7,093 students by 1850.[82]

Repealed

In Philadelphia, the Lancasterian dream died with a whimper instead of a bang. Back in 1818 Pennsylvania had embraced the Lancasterian promise with remarkable vim, passing a law that required the use of the "Lancasterian system of education" in its new public schools. In contrast, the city's abandonment of Lancasterian methods staggered along uncertainly for years. In 1836, the state officially repealed its Lancasterian requirement, recognizing the changes that had gone on long before.[83] The Lancasterian system, the state's lawmakers agreed in 1836, did not meet the needs of a modern city like Philadelphia. Instead, the city's school leaders were encouraged to offer more advanced academic subjects. They were required to maintain public schools that no longer catered only to low-income families, welcoming all white children above the age of four.[84]

The official, legislatively mandated shift away from Lancasterian methods left Philadelphia's school leaders searching for a new way to organize their public schools. In 1836, they announced that they were considering "numerous suggestions" for non-Lancasterian public schools, even as they maintained the Lancasterian system in some schools.[85] They sent emissaries to Boston and New York to ask about the changes those cities had made to their formerly Lancasterian schools.[86] By 1837, the city's school leaders were not exactly sure what they wanted, but they knew the Lancasterian system had failed. They tried to find a new way to organize their schools now that they had officially recognized the fact that "juvenile monitors" only offered "imperfect aid."[87]

In some Philadelphia public schools, Lancasterian methods persisted even after the city's leaders had recognized their ineffectiveness. At the segregated school for African American students on Lombard Street, for example, a lack of funding meant that the school employed only one adult teacher for almost two hundred boys and only two teachers for 251 girls.[88] Even as late as 1838, that classroom crunch forced the district to maintain Lancasterian methods at Lombard Street, long after schools for white students had been offering smaller, separate teacher-led classrooms. It was only at the end of 1838 that the Lombard Street school building was cut up into separate classrooms to try for something better than vast Lancasterian failures.[89]

Fizzle

In Philadelphia, the earnest and legally binding embrace of Lancaster's delusions in 1818 was never matched by an equally dramatic new solution in 1838, or at any other moment. Certainly, by 1838 there had been huge changes. School buildings were repurposed at great expense. Adult teachers were trained and hired, at even greater costs. Governance had changed—a professional, tax-funded bureaucracy was established to handle the money. But the shifts away from Lancasterian promises never made the same splash as had the initial embrace. Perhaps not surprisingly, ambitious city politicians did not rush to publicize the evidences of their failure. There was no grand announcement of the city's repeal of its Lancasterian enthusiasm, perhaps because it was not entirely clear what would replace it.

In every city, the recognition of the abject failures of the Lancasterian promise came in bits and pieces, without fanfare. The changes were real and dramatic, but they were not anything school leaders wanted to brag about. Perhaps for that reason, new generations of school reformers stumbled into similar mistakes. When they noticed the throngs of children from lower-income families in their streets instead of their schools, they tended not to ask the children why they used the "truant plan." Instead, they cast about for another dramatic solution to their perceived problems. They looked to Prussia, or to a new set of normal schools, as the next big thing. They searched for a new system to impose on their city's children, instead of becoming skeptical of cheap and easy answers to complex urban problems.

This deeply unsatisfying and anticlimactic end to the tumultuous career of Lancaster's overhyped system has led both historians and contemporaries to misunderstand the meaning and importance of the Lancasterian movement. It has been tempting to dismiss the Lancasterian era as a mere mistake, an unfortunate delusion. It has been easy for commentators to ignore the changes that went on during the hectic 1820s, to begin the story of urban public education at a much later date. Without a sudden, dramatic replacement for the Lancasterian system, it has been all too easy for observers to downplay the significance of the revolutionary changes that were masked by the awkward failure of the Lancasterian system.

It is easy to ignore the changes that went on in urban school systems during Lancaster's career because they were often done unofficially and unobtrusively. There was no great public debate, but rather a quiet series of last-minute patches and adjustments. By setting the stage for those piecemeal modifications, the Lancasterian system unintentionally became the vital evolutionary staging ground for modern urban public school systems.

Conclusion

In the end, the importance of the Lancasterian movement in the United States had little to do with Lancaster himself and everything to do with the sweeping changes that were engulfing American cities in the first decades of the 1800s. At the moment Lancaster offered his supposedly miraculous cure for urban poverty, urban elites were roiled with fear of their fellow city dwellers. Leaders like De Witt Clinton and Roberts Vaux were looking for some way to corral and control their less elite neighbors without spending too much money. They assumed that they were the proper people to decide what was best for their cities. They thought of the public good as a question of elite benevolence, of elite decisions in the best interests of their poor neighbors. The failure of their Lancasterian fantasies illuminates the lingering, bitter death of their presumptions. It demonstrates the complicated ways in which elites' definition of the public good evolved into a more modern vision, one in which the public good was defined by the broader public and paid for from public funds.

That wasn't how it started. Lancaster promised that his system could provide basic schooling for all, all within the comfortable confines of traditional charity schooling. Reformers were transfixed by the empty promises of Lancasterianism: it was modern, it was urban, it was high-tech; it was all the things they assumed their solutions would need to be. They didn't look elsewhere, closer to home, to see that other kinds of public schools were succeeding and had been for a while. If they had, they might have discovered the achingly obvious key to public school reform with less heartache, less acrimony, and less expense—namely, public schools needed adequate resources, and they needed to respond to community needs.

That lesson is obvious in retrospect, but at the time Lancaster's promises made perfect sense. They matched the world-changing accomplishments of other modern marvels. De Witt Clinton was just as enthusiastic about his hugely successful Erie Canal as he was about his hugely unsuccessful Lancasterian schools. It's easy to criticize enthusiasts like Clinton for backing Lancaster's empty promises, but sometimes a losing bet only appears to be a bad gamble after the race is run. Lancaster's manuals spoke the language that school reformers at the time longed to hear. Reformers pressed for evidence, but they accepted flimsy proof because they already assumed that Lancaster's ideas could be true. They assumed there was a solution like Lancaster's out there, a scientific system from a big city that could solve their problems. When Lancaster showed up with his inflated promises, reformers never poked or prodded them too strenuously.

When the system did not immediately deliver on its impossible promises, reformers were in a bind. They were committed to Lancaster's system—they were literally invested in it. When it didn't work as promised, they fixed and patched Lancaster's system to make it address the demands of families, and in doing so they created modern urban public school systems. This quiet and embarrassing process has always been difficult for reformers to talk about and therefore difficult for historians to uncover, yet this slow, uneven, unplanned, messy procedure carries the most important lessons of the Lancasterian movement. Families rejected Lancasterian schools—voting with their feet—and forced reformers to quietly modify Lancaster's original plans into something totally different. Families knew that public schools could be something different, something better. Outside of cities, towns and villages had been providing the kinds of public schools their communities wanted, as opposed to the kinds of public schools the Roberts Vauxes wanted them to want. It is easy enough to see the results in the vast empty Lancasterian schoolrooms of the 1820s, but it is not so easy to trace the way those schoolrooms changed into modern public schools. Unlike the reams of manuals and brochures describing the imaginary wonders of the Lancasterian system, the unspoken negotiations between parents and reformers only show up indirectly in the archives. Yet that process of give-and-take—of the truant plan and the resulting series of experiments both successful and unsuccessful—is key to understanding the significance of the Lancasterian movement. As in so many school reform plans, attention has been focused on Lancaster's showy declarations and overconfident explanations. The hard work of school reform happened in much less dramatic ways, in practical adjustments and temporary stopgaps. The creators of the public schools were not the Lancasters who trumpeted their impractical ideas to urban elites around the world, nor even the Clintons and Vauxes who prided themselves on creating modern public schools; rather, it was the parents, students, teachers, and administrators who transformed reformers' impractical ideas into practical classrooms that met the needs and desires of their communities.

Those needs and desires were not simply for village schools in their cities. Those village schools had their own problems. But post-Lancasterian urban public schools improved on the fundamental promise of the village model, the promise that schools would receive the funding they needed to meet community demands. In cities, those demands included more than the village norm: city families wanted trained adult teachers, longer school terms, and advanced specialized classes, including high schools. Those changes cost money, and reformers could not pay for their expanding schools using only traditional philanthropic donations, so they patched together new ramshackle funding systems, combining tax funding, tuition payments, and philanthropic donations into a rickety but functional system to pay for universal public education.

As public schools evolved and improved to meet the demands of lower-income parents, middle-class parents wanted in. Why, they asked, should their tax dollars pay for schools that their own children could not attend? And as public schools opened to all citizens, though still segregated by race, lower-income families embraced them more enthusiastically as well. If public schools were going to be something more than holding pens for the poor, then lower-income families gave them wholehearted support.

This messy process was never publicized in a single, distributable manual. It did not rocket any reform celebrities into grand careers as world-famous geniuses. It did not leave clear records in archives of each step in this off-the-books evolution. Yet in all its inelegance, in all its uncertainty and endless negotiation, this process heralded the creation of modern public school systems.

Discount Utopia

Digging into the history of the Lancasterian movement allows us to see more clearly the awkward evolution of cities and their public school systems. But the story also offers insights into perennial questions about schools and school reform. For example, one clear lesson of the Lancasterian "delusion" is that elite reformers had far more power than wisdom. Leaders such as Roberts Vaux in Philadelphia and De Witt Clinton in New York were not fools. They were not even really deluded. They demanded proof that Lancaster's promises would come true, but they lacked the experience to evaluate that proof. They had not worked in schools long enough to know what questions to ask. Clinton's experience in schools was limited to his own time as a student, attending the institutions that became Princeton and Columbia Universities. Vaux had volunteered briefly at a charity school,[1] but his time there had only given him a false confidence that he understood the challenges of urban education.

When Lancaster assured them that his methods held the key to miraculous improvements, reformers like Vaux and Clinton lacked the ability to ask the right questions. They did not know the ingredients needed for any successful school, so they had no ability to recognize the obvious flaws in Lancaster's recipe. Unfortunately for their entire generation, reformers like Vaux and Clinton did not notice that Lancaster was too blinded by his own vanity to explain the true sources of his early successes. Like Lancaster, the first generation of Lancasterian reformers believed that the secret to school success could be found in the perfect systematization of classroom methods. They truly believed they could create a one-size-fits-all manual, a set of fast solutions that they could package and ship to any city around the globe. They thought that their instruction manuals and guidebooks could capture the London magic of Lancaster's Borough Road School and replicate it quickly, easily, and cheaply in any school, anywhere. Their shortsighted focus only on classroom methods helps explain their obsessions; it helps explain why they were so intensely interested in the blueprints, sketches, and minute-by-minute lesson planning we saw in chapter 3. It helps explain why they drafted and revised their manuals in such painstaking detail, each new edition claiming to make the system ever more perfect.

With a little more experience, Lancasterian reformers might have seen through Lancaster's unintentional sleight of hand. They might have known at the outset that classroom methods are important, but there are more fundamental issues that Lancaster breezily and foolishly ignored. When those fundamental issues were addressed, when schools had enough funding and flexibility to incorporate community desires and demands—as at John Lovell's Lancasterian school in New Haven and William B. Fowle's Lancasterian school in Boston—Lancasterian methods worked fine. When they were not, no level of painstakingly detailed lesson planning could make Lancasterian schools work.

When the first generation of Lancasterian reformers saw Lancaster's supposed miracle at the Borough Road School, they naively believed Lancaster's inflated claims. They believed Lancaster's promises that his classroom methods had been the key to making his successful school. They did not know enough to peek behind the curtain, to ask about the fundamental supports of any successful school, the supports that Lancaster himself seemed unaware of. At Borough Road, for example, Lancaster's real success was not due to his use of monitors. It was not due to his ideas about new technology or proper school architecture. He said it was—and it seems likely that he really believed it himself—but the true reason Borough Road School briefly thrived was because it floated on huge hidden reservoirs of money and anxious energy. Lancaster poured vast financial resources into his school, borrowing and spending heedlessly yet keeping those enormous costs off the books. Lancaster's criminal slush fund was not the only hidden resource that made Borough Road a success. In its early years, the school benefitted from the untraceable investments Lancaster made in time and energy, as well as the enthusiastic support of its local community and the tireless, self-sacrificing dedication of the school's unpaid child-teachers, terrified by Lancaster's private abuses and putting on a bold public face.

In essence, what Lancaster created at his Borough Road School was a one-of-a-kind institution, reliant on fear and an intense investment of money, energy, time, and community support. But what Lancaster sold was the set of methods that he used at that institution, a set of methods that he promised could replicate the success of a high-resource school in any low-resource situation. It wasn't just a scam, at least not a simple one; Lancaster was foolish enough that he truly did not know how much money he was spending or how much suffering his apprentices were enduring to keep Borough Road humming along. He had no idea that his methods only worked because they were used at a well-supported school. He seemed honestly to believe that his methods had a kind of modern magic all their own, magic he could box up and sell to a desperate world.

The real tragedy of the Lancasterian movement was not that so much money and energy were wasted on a delusion but that the lessons of its failures have gone unheeded for so long. Instead of focusing on the fundamental reasons for school success, such as establishing schools that meet the needs of local communities and securing enough resources to make them thrive, reformers have tended to search for simplistic silver-bullet solutions, dramatic reforms that could deliver prefabricated successful schools to any community, whether or not those schools had the kinds of support all schools need.

For the Public Good

The details of the Lancasterian story also shed light on one of the oldest questions about the history of public schools: were those schools an elite scheme to control the poor, or were they a social benefit demanded by lower-income citizens? Beginning in the 1960s, scholars began arguing that public schools were originally a cynical tool to control the urban poor, to force students to be better citizens and more docile workers.[2] Yet as other scholars have pointed out, early public schools were not merely educational prisons; they were also demanded by lower-income citizens.[3] Far from being just an imposition of plotting elites, in this view, public schools in the United States were created as a benefit precisely for the people they were supposed to control.

A quick look at the history of the Lancasterian movement provides plenty of evidence for both sides. On the one hand, Lancaster's allies often dreamed of using his methods to impose better social controls on unruly workers. As Robert Owen wrote from his Lancasterian school in Scotland, the students at his school, culled from "the very lowest classes," were easily turned by Lancaster's plan into "by far the most valuable Servants."[4] In the United States, too, philanthropists such as Roberts Vaux thought that their new Lancasterian schools would be the best way to control the "vicious children" of "indolent and worthless parents."[5]

Yet, on the other hand, Lancasterian schools were often celebrated and demanded by those very children and their parents. In New York City, for example, as historians such as Carla L. Peterson and Leslie M. Harris have argued, the African Free Schools were more than just holding pens for Black children. In many cases, students, teachers, and families used the schools to create a nurturing path to professional success and community advancement.[6] White working-class families were not merely passive victims of elite schemes either. In schools as in other institutions at the time such as almshouses, the low-income urbanites who were pressed into labor could often exert their own leadership.⁷ For schools, the promise of the next generation often brought lower-income people into the public school camp. As we saw in chapter 6, working-class pundits insisted that decent public schools were nothing less than the most important "cause of the people."⁸

The birth of urban public schools, in other words, really was a plan by elites to control the poor. Yet it was also a plan by the poor to offer their children all the educational advantages they themselves had never had, to import the responsiveness of village schools into a new kind of public school for cities. If we were to only read the cruel, confident brochures of early elites and the stinging counter-rhetoric of African American journals and white working-class newspapers, we would never get a sense of how the two things came together. It was only behind the scenes, in the off-the-record, unspoken negotiations between parents, students, reformers, and teachers, that this chronic tension led to the creation of modern urban public school systems. The key, as we saw in chapter 6, was not in rhetoric but in attendance. As a rule, lower-income families wanted more education for their children, but not if it was coercive, humiliating, or a waste of children's valuable time.

Though elites would have probably liked to impose basic-only schooling on lower-income children, they were forced to improve and modify Lancaster's ideas in order to entice students to attend. Public schools, in the end, did not emerge in US cities merely as elite tools to control the poor. Nor were they created simply in response to working-class and African American demands. Rather, urban public schools evolved out of an extended and awkward indirect negotiation, a back-and-forth between frustrated elites and frustrated families.

Once that give-and-take led to a different kind of school, more families wanted in. The original schools Lancaster dreamed of—vast urban learning factories crammed with low-income children—were a bust. They could not attract enough students to justify their own existence. However, by adding more advanced academic offerings and replacing untrained, unpaid child-teachers with experienced, paid teachers, school leaders ended up creating a new kind of public school, one that middle-class families wanted too. Once the Lancasterian schools were seen as a free benefit rather than a harsh penalty, and once their leaders responded to community demands, they became more attractive to both working-class and middle-class families. As we saw in chapter 6, modern urban public schools that included both richer and poorer students—though always segregated by race—were the result of Lancasterian enthusiasm, but not the way Lancasterians imagined. Most Lancasterians wanted to create schools for just the poorest children, but the failure of those plans led instead to a different kind of American school, a public school that was open to all and paid for by all.

The Lure

Historians have avoided this mess. They have studied other urban institutions for the poor, particularly the way those institutions awkwardly modernized along with the explosive growth of their cities.[9] And they noticed the significance of the Lancasterian movement in the early 1800s (how could they not?), but they only noted the fact that the failure of Lancaster's ideas led somehow to the successes of early urban public school systems.[10] As the leading historian of early American public education put it, it was the Lancasterian movement that somehow begat modern public schools, "quite in contrast to the history which traces the genesis of the public school from the New England town grammar school."[11] Yet this urban origin story for modern public education leaves us with a seeming paradox: one of the greatest flops in US history produced one of its greatest, most revolutionary successes.

The key to understanding the connection between failure and success is not plainly evident in the archival record. That record is crystal clear about both halves of the puzzle. That is, there is plenty of proof about what Lancasterian schools were supposed to look like and plenty of proof about what came after. But the connections are murky. Joseph Lancaster and many of his followers cranked out reams of pamphlets, guidebooks, and instruction manuals. They described in lavish details their dreams for perfect schools full of perfect students, all moving toward perfect knowledge in perfectly choreographed movements. It is also clear from the record that Lancaster's ideas landed in fertile soil in the imaginations and fears of urban elites in the early 1800s. It made sense to leaders at the time to go all in on Lancaster's impractical system. In the cities of the Northeast, from Baltimore to Boston, New York to New Haven, and everywhere in between, city leaders invested in Lancasterian schoolhouses. They mandated Lancaster's ideas by law in places such as Philadelphia, Boston, and Baltimore. It is also perfectly clear from the archival record that their dreams failed, and failed hard. By the time of Lancaster's death in 1838, reformers had to recognize that their dream had been an illusion.

Similarly, the archival record offers plenty of proof that modern public school systems emerged from this failure. By 1838, the flawed assumptions of 1818 had been fixed. It was clear by 1838 that funding from elite subscriptions was never enough to provide schools for all children. It was clear by that time that good schools needed trained adult teachers, not just the free labor of untrained children. It was clear by 1838 that public schools needed to offer more advanced academic courses to all the children of the city, not just the basics to just the poor. And most importantly, by 1838 it seemed obvious that city governments would be responsible for providing modern public schools for citizens. A new era had dawned in America's cities, at least in the North. Schools were no longer seen as a purely private resource, offered by entrepreneurs for the children of the rich and by churches and philanthropists for the children of the poor. Instead, a new vision had become the norm in ways that elites in 1818 had never imagined and certainly never planned for. A new kind of public school had emerged, segregated by race but no longer segregated by family income level. It was a breathtaking development.

Historians and the general public have often assumed that the development of urban public schools followed Lancaster's death. They have avoided the tricky conundrum of Lancaster's failed success by jumping instead to the less tricky successes of the next generation. Antebellum leaders such as Horace Mann spread the solutions to Lancaster's failure to cities and villages alike in the 1840s. They sought to systematize the unsystematic patches and fixes that had turned Lancasterian schools into modern public schools. They took the piecemeal improvements made to urban public schools—better-trained teachers, expanded academic offerings, reliable tax funding—and made them into a plan instead of an accident. But leaders like Horace Mann were spreaders of the gospel of modern public education, not its creators. Yet the myth endures that Mann and his generation were the "fathers" of American public education. Outside the State House in Mann's home state of Massachusetts, for example, his statue calls Horace Mann the "Father of the American public school system" for his work in the 1840s. The credit given to midcentury common school reformers such as Horace Mann does not give enough weight to the work done by an earlier generation. It assumes that the big changes happened around 1840. It sidesteps the difficulty of explaining the Lancasterian paradox by starting after the dust had settled, instead of discovering what kicked up all the dust in the first place.

The most important changes, in fact, happened during Lancaster's time, not Horace Mann's. Without that missing link, the evolution of urban public education in the United States will always remain mysterious. The answers are not obvious, but they can be distilled from the full, messy story of the Lancasterian "delusion." The long-term significance of the Lancasterian movement does not lie in Lancaster's overly specific classroom methods. Those failed. In most cases, they were never really implemented at all, in spite of the fact that so many urban public schools called themselves "Lancasterian" for decades. Rather, the best way to understand how the failure of Lancaster's visions led to the success of urban public school systems is to see Lancaster's promises as a kind of bait, a lure that hooked urban elites on the possibility of providing schools for all the children in their cities.

After all, Lancaster achieved his worldwide fame because he offered city leaders around the globe an answer to a seemingly intractable problem. Using traditional educational methods, the kind commonly in place in England and the United States before the Lancasterian revolution, one teacher could reasonably educate a few dozen children at a time. By the early 1800s, urban elites confronted the utter inadequacy of this traditional system. With thousands upon thousands of low-income children in their streets, children whose families could not afford to hire a teacher on their own, it seemed impossible to provide teachers for them all. Yet without basic education in literacy and morals, elites were convinced that children could not grow into productive, law-abiding citizens.

Lancaster's system supposedly squared this circle. By using the free labor of the children themselves, Lancaster promised that his schools would allow city leaders to provide universal basic education on the cheap. Lancaster's delusional system dangled the promise of affordable universal schooling, and elites around the world took the bait. Once they had committed to providing schools for all, those elite reformers were forced to make the unworkable Lancasterian system work. Their efforts—their fixes, patches, adjustments, and practical compromises—created modern urban public school systems. It is hard to build a statue to a process like this. There was never one "father" to this kind of public school, but rather a drawn-out evolution, a string of piecemeal changes and unarticulated protests. Yet this elusive give-and-take created urban public schools in their modern form. It was this process that mattered, not any single leader's ambition.

City leaders would have never started that awkward evolutionary process if they had not first been lured by Lancasterian promises. Certainly, urban public schools would have happened somehow. After all, in rural areas and small towns the patterns of American public education had been established for decades. Common schools had been attracting more and more of the children of villages and small towns. Yet without the impossibly convenient solutions offered by Lancasterian manuals, city leaders did not think they could afford those common schools for the hordes of low-income children who haunted the streets of their modern cities. The false promises of Lancasterian reform were the bogus collateral that gave city leaders the confidence to offer schools for all.

Mr. Lancaster's system promised the modern answer to a modern problem, but in fact, it was an obsolete gimmick, an implausible charade that only seemed plausible to reformers who found comfort in its confidence, confirmation for their outmoded ideas. They did not expect to start down the path to a tax-funded school system run by elected bureaucrats. They did not expect to offer the children of the poor an education similar to that of their better-off neighbors. They did not expect that modernizing their cities would cost them their cherished role as the articulators of the public good. They embraced the delusions of Lancasterian reform because those reforms offered a vision of a modernity they could recognize, a modern city that left them firmly still in control. In the end, however, by promising school for all—even the stunted and inadequate schooling of the Lancasterian vision— elite reformers opened the door that led to modern public school systems.

Notes

Preface

1. See Adam Laats, "Betsy DeVos Wants to Resurrect an Old—and Failed—Model of Public Education," *Washington Post*, May 16, 2019, https://www.washingtonpost.com/out look/2019/05/16/betsy-devos-wants-resurrect-an-old-failed-model-public-education/?utm_term=.e153ee0ea215.

2. See Dale Russakoff, "Schooled," *New Yorker*, May 12, 2014, https://www.newyorker.com/magazine/2014/05/19/schooled.

3. Matt Stieb, "Eric Adams Criticized for Proposing 400-Kid Zoom Classes, Year-Round School," *Intelligencer, New York Magazine*, June 13, 2021, https://nymag.com/intelligencer/2021/06/eric-adams-criticized-for-proposing-400-kid-zoom-class-sizes.html.

Introduction

1. "Lecture on National Education," 1834. [Flyer in the collection of the Library Company of Philadelphia.] Emphasis in the original.

2. Joseph Lancaster, *The British System of Education: Being a Complete Epitome of the Improvements and Inventions Practised at the Royal Free Schools, Borough-Road, Southwark* (London: Royal Free School, 1810), front matter.

3. De Witt Clinton, *An Address, to the Benefactors and Friends of the Free School Society of New York, Delivered on the Opening of That Institution, in Their New and Spacious Building, on the Eleventh of the Twelfth Month (December) 1809* (New York: Collins & Perkins, 1810), 10.

4. *An Act to Provide for the Education of Children at Public Expense within the City and County of Philadelphia* (Harrisburg, PA: s.n., 1818).

5. *Niles' National Register* 10, no. 5 (November 3, 1838): 146.

6. John E. Lovell to Joseph Lancaster, February 14, 1823, box 2, folder 7, Lancaster Papers, American Antiquarian Society, Worcester, Massachusetts.

7. Michael B. Katz, *Reconstructing American Education* (Cambridge, MA: Harvard University Press, 1987), 25, 53.

8. Thomas Boese, *Public Education in the City of New York: Its History, Condition, and Statistics* (New York: Harper & Brothers, 1869), 27n2.

9. Boese, *Public Education*, 27.

10. As this book will explore in detail in chap. 5, the successful model for public schools came not from London but from American villages and small towns. See, e.g., Carl F. Kaestle and Maris A. Vinovskis, *Education and Social Change in Nineteenth-Century Massachusetts* (Cambridge: Cambridge University Press, 1980), 5, 24; Nancy Beadie, *Education and the Creation of Capital in the Early American Republic* (New York: Cambridge University Press, 2010), 147; Sun Go and Peter Lindert, "The Uneven Rise of American Public Schools to 1850," *Journal of Economic History* 70 (March 2010): 1–26; Johann Neem, "Path Dependence and

the Emergence of Common Schools: Ohio to 1853," *Journal of Policy History* 28, no. 1 (2016): 48–80.

11. Hilary Moss, "Race and Schooling in Early Republican Philadelphia," in *The Great Contest: The Founding Fathers, Education, and the American Philosophical Society*, ed. Benjamin Justice (New York: Palgrave Macmillan, 2013), 103–18; Erica Armstrong Dunbar, *A Fragile Freedom: African American Women and Emancipation in the Antebellum City* (New Haven, CT: Yale University Press, 2008), 19–34; Jane E. Dabel, *A Respectable Woman: The Public Roles of African American Women in 19th-Century New York* (New York: New York University Press, 2008), 44–45; Leslie M. Harris, *In the Shadow of Slavery: African Americans in New York City, 1626–1863* (Chicago: University of Chicago Press, 2003), 8; Sarah L. H. Gronningsater, "Practicing Formal Politics without the Vote: Black New Yorkers in the Aftermath of 1821," in *Revolutions and Reconstructions: Black Politics in the Long Nineteenth Century*, ed. Van Gosse and David Waldstreicher (Philadelphia: University of Pennsylvania Press, 2020), 116–38; Mark Boonshoft, "From Property to Education: Public Schooling, Race, and the Transformation of Suffrage in the Early National North," *Journal of the Early Republic* 41, no. 3 (Fall 2021): 1–36; Paul J. Polgar, "'Whenever They Judge it Expedient': The Politics of Partisanship and Free Black Voting Rights in Early National New York," *American Nineteenth Century History* 12, no. 1 (March 2011): 1–23.

12. Paul A. Gilje, *The Road to Mobocracy: Popular Disorder in New York City, 1763–1834* (Chapel Hill: University of North Carolina Press, 1987), 125; Robert E. Cray Jr., *Paupers and Poor Relief in New York City and Its Rural Environs, 1700–1830* (Philadelphia: Temple University Press, 1988), 105.

13. Susan B. Carter, Scott Sigmund Gartner, Michael R. Haines, Alan L. Olmstead, Richard Sutch, and Gavin Wright, eds., "Table Aa832-1033—Population of Cities with At Least 100,000 Population in 1990: 1790–1990," in *Historical Statistics of the United States: Millennial Edition* (New York: Cambridge University Press, 2006).

14. Thomas Bender, *Toward an Urban Vision: Ideas and Institutions in Nineteenth-Century America* (Lexington: University Press of Kentucky, 1975), 19–27.

15. Michael B. Katz, *In the Shadow of the Poorhouse: A Social History of Welfare in America* (New York: Basic Books, 1986), 11–12; David J. Rothman, *The Discovery of the Asylum: Social Order and Disorder in the New Republic* (Boston: Little, Brown, 1971), 58, 61; Raymond A. Mohl, *Poverty in New York, 1783–1825* (New York: Oxford University Press, 1971); Billy G. Smith, *The "Lower Sort": Philadelphia's Laboring People, 1750–1800* (Ithaca, NY: Cornell University Press, 1990); Michael Meranze, *Laboratories of Virtue: Punishment, Revolution, and Authority in Philadelphia, 1760–1835* (Chapel Hill: University of North Carolina Press, 1996); Gary B. Nash, *The Urban Crucible: Social Change, Political Consciousness, and the Origins of the American Revolution* (Cambridge, MA: Harvard University Press, 1979); Simon P. Newman, *Embodied History: The Lives of the Poor in Early Philadelphia* (Philadelphia: University of Pennsylvania Press, 2003), 9; Billy G. Smith, ed., *Down and Out in Early America* (University Park: Pennsylvania State University Press, 2004); Ruth Wallis Herndon, "Poor Women and the Boston Almshouse in the Early Republic," *Journal of the Early Republic* 21, no. 3 (Fall 2012): 349–81.

16. Newman, *Embodied History*, 2.

17. For the lingering power of the Horace Mann myth, see, e.g., Nomi M. Stolzenberg

and David N. Myers, "Private Schools Have Public Responsibilities Too," *Atlantic*, September 22, 2022; Anya Kamenetz, "School Is for Everyone," *New York Times*, September 1, 2022.

18. Lawrence A. Cremin, *American Education: The National Experience, 1783–1876* (New York: Harper & Row, 1980), 396.

19. Carl F. Kaestle, *Pillars of the Republic: Common Schools and American Society, 1780–1860* (New York: Hill & Wang, 1983), 41.

20. Kaestle, *Pillars of the Republic*, 59.

21. Carl F. Kaestle, ed., *Joseph Lancaster and the Monitorial School Movement: A Documentary History* (New York: Teachers College Press, 1973), 47. Kaestle made the argument for a much earlier starting point for public schools in many of his works. See, e.g., Carl F. Kaestle, "Common Schools before the 'Common School Revival': New York Schooling in the 1790s," *History of Education Quarterly* 12, no. 4 (Winter 1972): 466: "The most important turning point between the informal colonial mode of education and the nineteenth-century concept of a consolidated system was not, in New York City at least, in the 1830s and 1840s, but around the turn of the century." For more recent mentions of the earlier roots of modern American public school systems, see also Benjamin Justice, *The War That Wasn't: Religious Conflict and Compromise in the Common Schools of New York State, 1865–1900* (Albany: State University of New York Press, 2005), 18, 25; David Komline, *The Common School Awakening: Religion and the Transatlantic Roots of American Public Education* (New York: Oxford University Press, 2020), 3, 13.

22. Mora Dickson, *Teacher Extraordinary: Joseph Lancaster, 1778–1838* (Sussex, UK: Book Guild Limited, 1986); Joyce Taylor, *Joseph Lancaster: The Poor Child's Friend; Educating the Poor in the Early Nineteenth Century* (Kent, UK: Campanile, 1996).

23. Komline, *Common School Awakening*, 19–29.

24. Kaestle, *Pillars of the Republic*, 76–103; Carl F. Kaestle, *The Evolution of an Urban School System: New York City, 1750–1850* (Cambridge, MA: Harvard University Press, 1973), 145–57; James W. Fraser, *Between Church and State: Religion and Public Education in a Multicultural America*, 2nd ed. (Baltimore: Johns Hopkins University Press, 2016), 22–64; Steven K. Green, *The Bible, the Schools, and the Constitution: The Clash That Shaped Modern Church-State Doctrine* (New York: Oxford University Press, 2012), 18–19; Justice, *War That Wasn't*, 37; Komline, *Common School Awakening*, 9, 16–17; R. Laurence Moore, "Bible Reading and Nonsectarian Schooling: The Failure of Religious Instruction in Nineteenth-Century Public Education," *Journal of American History* 86, no. 4 (2000): 1588; Noah Feldman, "Nonsectarianism Reconsidered," *Journal of Law and Politics* 18 (2002): 66.

25. Kaestle, *Pillars of the Republic*, 56–57, 192–217.

26. Kaestle, *Joseph Lancaster*, 46–49.

27. Marcelo Caruso and Eugenia Roldan Vera, "Pluralizing Meanings: The Monitorial System of Education in Latin America in the Early Nineteenth Century," *Paedagogica Historica* 41, no. 6 (December 2005): 645. See also Komline, *Common School Awakening*.

Chapter 1. Borough Road

1. Edward Flavin Wall Jr., "Joseph Lancaster and the Origins of the British and Foreign School Society" (PhD diss., Columbia University, 1966), 38.

2. "A Short Account," 1802, box 15, folder 1, Lancaster Papers, American Antiquarian

Society, Worcester, Massachusetts (hereafter cited as "LP"); Joseph Lancaster to the Duchess of York, 1804, box 1, folder 1, LP.

3. Mora Dickson, *Teacher Extraordinary: Joseph Lancaster 1778–1838* (Sussex, UK: Book Guild Limited, 1986), 5–15.

4. Wall, "Joseph Lancaster," 24–29. See also David Komline, *The Common School Awakening: Religion and the Transatlantic Roots of American Public Education* (New York: Oxford University Press, 2020).

5. "A Short Account," 1802, box 15, folder 1, LP.

6. See Komline, *Common School Awakening*, 19–24; see also Wall, "Joseph Lancaster," 53.

7. Wall, "Joseph Lancaster," 46.

8. "Education Society," box 4, vol. First Folio, LP.

9. Joseph Lancaster, *The British System of Education: Being a Complete Epitome of the Improvements and Inventions Practised at the Royal Free Schools, Borough-Road, Southwark* (London: Royal Free School, 1810), 45.

10. Jonathan Walken Phipps to Joseph Lancaster, 1806, box 1, folder 4, letter 1, LP; Phipps to Lancaster, 1806, box 1, folder 4, letter 2, LP.

11. Joseph Lancaster to the Duchess of York, 1804, box 1, folder 1, LP; Duke of Bedford to Joseph Lancaster, September 8, 1805, box 1, folder 4, LP.

12. Wall, "Joseph Lancaster," 48–51.

13. "Proceedings of a Meeting Held on 2nd Day Monday 7 of 1st Mo 1804, at the Schoolhouse Borough Road—Georges Fields," box 15, folder 1, LP.

14. "Act Incorporating the Free School Society, Passed April 9, 1805," New York Free Society Trustees Meeting Minutes, New-York Historical Society, New York, New York; see also *An Account of the Free-School Society of New-York* (New York: Collins, 1814), 5–8.

15. Marcelo Caruso and Eugenia Roldan Vera, "Pluralizing Meanings: The Monitorial System of Education in Latin America in the Early Nineteenth Century," *Paedagogica Historica* 41, no. 6 (December 2005): 651.

16. Joseph Foster to Joseph Lancaster, September 2, 1813, box 12, folder 1, LP; "Minister of Denmark" to Joseph Lancaster, April 27, 1813, box 1, folder 5, LP.

17. *Letters Written from London, Descriptive of Various Scenes and Occurrences Frequently Met with in the Metropolis and Its Vicinity. For the Amusement of Children. Illustrated by Plates* (Philadelphia: Jacob Johnson, 1808), 13.

18. Wall, "Joseph Lancaster," 132.

19. Catherine Maria Sedgwick, *The Deformed Boy* (Boston: Munroe & Francis, 1826), 23.

20. Anonymous, *Little John, the Farmer's Boy* (New Haven, CT: S. Babcock, 1832), 3.

21. "Account of money collected by Joseph Lancaster for Free School, between April 20, 1800 and March 22, 1801," box 3, folder 5, LP.

22. See, e.g., David Barclay to Joseph Lancaster, February 9, 1805, box 164, folder 2, LP, Gratz Collection, Historical Society of Pennsylvania, Philadelphia (hereafter cited as "GC"). This entire folder is full of similar letters, asking for copies of pamphlets and enclosing money.

23. Charles Pickton to Robert Ould, June 10, 1814, box 12, folder 4, LP.

24. Charles Pickton to Robert Ould, June 10, 1814, box 12, folder 4, LP.

25. Thomas Noon Talfourd, "Addressed to Mr. Joseph Lancaster on his Plans for the Education of the Poor" (Reading: Theodore Page, May 28, 1810), box 14, folder 6, LP.
26. Wall, "Joseph Lancaster," 115.
27. Charles Pickton to Robert Ould, June 10, 1814, box 12, folder 4, LP.
28. Wall, "Joseph Lancaster," 86.
29. Thomas Sturge to Joseph Lancaster, July 28, 1809, box 164, folder 8, GC.
30. The collection of Lancaster's papers at the American Antiquarian Society includes the records of these disputes. See esp. box 1, folder 1, and box 2, folder 2, LP. See also Wall, "Joseph Lancaster," 89–185.
31. See, e.g., Robert Owen to Joseph Lancaster, 1813, box 2, folder 1, LP. In this letter, the famous social reformer tried to talk Lancaster into accepting the guidance of the committee. Lancaster's original letter that prompted this reply is lost, but Lancaster was clearly complaining unfairly. As Owen wrote, Lancaster must be "deceived with regard to the committee—they have your interest and comfort very much at heart."
32. Joseph Lancaster to William Allen and Joseph Fox, April 29, 1814, box 2, folder 2, LP.
33. Joseph Lancaster, memorandum, December 4, 1813, box 2, folder 2, LP.
34. Francis Place Papers, British Library, London (hereafter cited as "FPP"), Add. MSS 27, 823, fol. 25.
35. FPP, Add. MSS 27, 823, fol. 25.
36. FPP, Add. MSS 27, 823, fol. 26.
37. FPP, Add. MSS 27, 823, fol. 26.
38. FPP, Add. MSS 27, 823, fol. 26.
39. FPP, Add. MSS 27, 823, fol. 26.

Chapter 2. Children of the City

1. Vaux was part of every reform movement in Philadelphia for decades. See "Public offices and Societies in which Roberts Vaux has served," manuscript, n.d., box 5, folder 19: Miscellaneous—Charitable organizations, Vaux Family Papers, 1739–1923, Collection 684, Historical Society of Pennsylvania, Philadelphia. Vaux was Philadelphia's exemplar of changing ideas among urban elites about helping and controlling their poor neighbors. On Vaux, see Michael Meranze, *Laboratories of Virtue: Punishment, Revolution, and Authority in Philadelphia, 1760–1835* (Chapel Hill: University of North Carolina Press, 1996), 1; Roderick Naylor Ryon, "Roberts Vaux: A Biography of a Reformer" (PhD diss., Pennsylvania State University, 1966), 31. On changing ideas about benevolence, see Michael B. Katz, *In the Shadow of the Poorhouse: A Social History of Welfare in America* (New York: Basic Books, 1986), 11–12; David J. Rothman, *The Discovery of the Asylum: Social Order and Disorder in the New Republic* (New York: Little, Brown, 1971), 94, 137, 188; Robert E. Cray Jr., *Paupers and Poor Relief in New York City and Its Rural Environs, 1700–1830* (Philadelphia: Temple University Press, 1988); Monique Bourque, "Poor Relief 'Without Violating the Rights of Humanity': Almshouse Administration in the Philadelphia Region, 1790–1860," in *Down and Out in Early America*, ed. Billy G. Smith (University Park: Pennsylvania State University Press, 2004), 190.

2. Jean Barth Toll and Mildred S. Gillam, eds., *Invisible Philadelphia: Community through Voluntary Organizations* (Philadelphia: Atwater Kent Museum, 1995), 695.

3. Roberts Vaux, *Eighth Annual Report of the Controllers of the Public Schools of the First School District of the State of Pennsylvania; With Their Accounts* (Philadelphia: Printed by Order of the Board of Control, 1826), 6.

4. Pennsylvania Society for the Promotion of Public Economy, *Report of the Committee on Public School to the Pennsylvania Society for the Promotion of Public Economy* (Philadelphia: SPPE, 1817), 6–8.

5. *Manual of the System of Teaching Reading, Writing, Arithmetic, and Needle-Work, in the Elementary Schools of the British and Foreign School Society*, 1st American ed. (Philadelphia: Philadelphia Society for the Establishment and Support of Charity Schools, published by Benjamin Warner, printed by William Fry, 1817), xii.

6. De Witt Clinton, *An Address, to the Benefactors and Friends of the Free School Society of New York, Delivered on the Opening of That Institution, in Their New and Spacious Building, on the Eleventh of the Twelfth Month (December) 1809* (New York: Collins & Perkins, 1810), 9, preface.

7. Clinton, *Address*, 7.

8. Clinton, *Address*, 7.

9. *Some Very Gentle Touches to Some Very Gentle-Men/by a Humble Country Cousin of Peter Pindar Esq.; Dedicated to All the Little Girls & Boys, of the City of New York* (New York[?]: n.p., 1806). [Handmade book in the collections of the American Antiquarian Society, Worcester, Massachusetts.] In Philadelphia, too, white elites mused about the dangers of city streets filled with "children, dogs and hogs." See Simon P. Newman, *Embodied History: The Lives of the Poor in Early Philadelphia* (Philadelphia: University of Pennsylvania Press, 2003), 1.

10. Thomas Bender, *Toward an Urban Vision: Ideas and Institutions in Nineteenth-Century America* (Lexington: University Press of Kentucky, 1975), 3.

11. Susan B. Carter, Scott Sigmund Gartner, Michael R. Haines, Alan L. Olmstead, Richard Sutch, and Gavin Wright, eds., *Historical Statistics of the United States: Millennial Edition* (New York: Cambridge University Press, 2006).

12. Andrew Lees, *Cities Perceived: Urban Society in European and American Thought, 1820–1940* (New York: Columbia University Press, 1985), 9.

13. Paul A. Gilje, *The Road to Mobocracy: Popular Disorder in New York City, 1763–1834* (Chapel Hill: University of North Carolina Press, 1987), 133.

14. Gilje, *Road to Mobocracy*, 133.

15. Cray, *Paupers and Poor Relief*, 116.

16. Timothy J. Gilfoyle, *City of Eros: New York City, Prostitution, and the Commercialization of Sex, 1790–1920* (New York: Norton, 1992), 31.

17. Raymond A. Mohl, "Education as Social Control in New York City, 1784–1825," *New York History* 51, no. 3 (April 1970): 221.

18. From an address by the American Society for the Encouragement of Domestic Manufactures, quoted in Bender, *Toward an Urban Vision*, 19.

19. *An Account of the Free-School Society of New-York* (New York: Collins, 1814), 4.

20. De Witt Clinton, *Twelfth Annual Report of the Free-School Society of New York* (New York: Collins, 1817), n.p.

21. *An Account of the Origin and Progress of the Savannah Free-School Society, Instituted in the Year 1816* (New York: Day & Turner, 1819), front matter.

22. Tina H. Sheller, "The Origins of Public Education in Baltimore, 1825–1829," *History of Education Quarterly* 22, no. 1 (Spring 1982): 35.

23. Joseph Lancaster, *Improvements in Education, as It Respects the Industrious Classes of the Community: Containing, among Other Important Particulars, an Account of the Institution for the Education of One Thousand Poor Children, Borough Road, Southwark; and of the New System of Education on Which It Is Conducted*, 3rd ed. (New York: Collins & Perkins, 1807), vi.

24. Pennsylvania Society for the Promotion of Public Economy, *Report of the Committee on Public School*, 8.

25. Clinton, *Address*, 7.

26. Gilfoyle, *City of Eros*, 63.

27. Gilje, *Road to Mobocracy*, 263.

28. Carl F. Kaestle, *Pillars of the Republic: Common Schools and American Society, 1780–1860* (New York: Hill & Wang, 1983), 30–31.

29. *Manual of the System*, B [front matter paginated by letter].

30. Lancaster, *Improvements in Education*, vii–ix.

31. *An Account of the Female Association for the Relief of the Sick Poor, and for the Education for Such Female Children as Do Not Belong to, or Are Not Provided for, by Any Religious Society* (New York: Collins, 1814), 5.

32. John C. Van Horne, "The Education of African Americans in Benjamin Franklin's Philadelphia," in *"The Good Education of Youth": Worlds of Learning in the Age of Franklin*, ed. John H. Pollack (New Castle, DE: Oak Knoll, 2009), 92.

33. Erica Armstrong Dunbar, *A Fragile Freedom: African American Women and Emancipation in the Antebellum City* (New Haven, CT: Yale University Press, 2008), 56–57.

34. Leslie M. Harris, *In the Shadow of Slavery: African Americans in New York City, 1626–1863* (Chicago: University of Chicago Press, 2003), 86.

35. Carla L. Peterson, *Black Gotham: A Family History of African Americans in Nineteenth-Century New York City* (New Haven, CT: Yale University Press, 2011), 65–69.

36. Jon Teaford, "The Transformation of Massachusetts Education, 1670–1780," *History of Education Quarterly* 10, no. 3 (Autumn 1970): 290.

37. Stanley K. Schultz, *The Culture Factory: Boston Public Schools, 1789–1860* (New York: Oxford University Press, 1973), 11–23; William J. Reese, *The Origins of the American High School* (New Haven, CT: Yale University Press, 1995), 7; William Michael Weber, "Before Horace Mann: Elites and Boston Public Schools, 1800–1812" (EdD diss., Harvard University, 1974), 54.

38. Nancy Beadie, "'Encouraging Useful Knowledge' in the Early Republic: The Roles of State Governments and Voluntary Organizations," in *The Founding Fathers, Education, and "The Great Contest": The American Philosophical Society Prize of 1797*, ed. Benjamin Justice (New York: Palgrave Macmillan, 2013), 87.

39. *An Act for the Encouragement of Schools, Passed at the Eighteenth Session of the Legislature of the State of Newyork and of the Independence of the United States the Nineteenth 1795*, 9, Collections of the Library Company, Philadelphia.

40. Toll and Gillam, *Invisible Philadelphia*, 695.

41. Harry S. Silcox, "Delay and Neglect: Negro Public Education in Antebellum Philadelphia, 1800–1860," *Pennsylvania Magazine of History and Biography* 97 (October 1973): 444.

42. *Arthur Donaldson, Has Established a School Back of No. 88, North Front Street, Philadelphia, for the Tuition of Children of Colour of Both Sexes, in Reading, Writing, and Arithmetic*, Collections of the Library Company, Philadelphia.

43. Weber, "Before Horace Mann," 45.

44. Sharon Braslaw Sundue, "Confining the Poor to Ignorance? Eighteenth-Century American Experiments with Charity Education," *History of Education Quarterly* 47, no. 2 (May 2007): 123–48.

45. Sundue, "Confining the Poor to Ignorance?," 134.

46. Peterson, *Black Gotham*, 69; Harris, *In the Shadow of Slavery*, 64.

47. Kaestle, *Pillars of the Republic*, 38; Van Horne, "Education of African Americans," 88.

48. Kaestle, *Pillars of the Republic*, 31.

49. *Manual of the System*, B.

50. Toll and Gillam, *Invisible Philadelphia*, 695.

51. Hilary J. Moss, "Race and Schooling in Early Republican Philadelphia," in *The Founding Fathers, Education, and "The Great Contest": The American Philosophical Society Prize of 1797*, ed. Benjamin Justice (New York: Palgrave Macmillan, 2013), 111.

52. Weber, "Before Horace Mann," 94.

53. *Act for the Encouragement of Schools*.

54. *Account of the Female Association*, 5.

55. *A Sketch of the Origin and Progress of the Adelphi School in the Northern Liberties, Established under the Direction of the Philadelphia Association of Friends for the Instruction of Poor Children* (Philadelphia: Meyer & Jones, 1810), 17.

56. Rothman, *Discovery of the Asylum*, 66.

57. "Education Society," box 4, vol. First Folio, Lancaster Papers, American Antiquarian Society, Worcester, Massachusetts.

58. Clinton, *Address*, 7.

59. *Fifth Annual Report of the Controllers of the Public Schools of the First School District of the State of Pennsylvania; With Their Accounts* (Philadelphia: Printed by Order of the Board of Control, 1823), 8.

60. *The Cries of Philadelphia: Ornamented with Elegant Wood Cuts* (Philadelphia: Johnson & Warner, 1810), 21–22.

61. *Cries of Philadelphia*, 9–10.

62. William J. Reese, "The Origins of Progressive Education," *History of Education Quarterly* 41, no. 1 (Spring 2001): 6.

63. See Steven Mintz, *Huck's Raft: A History of American Childhood* (Cambridge, MA: Harvard University Press, 2006), 52; Paula S. Fass, *Children of a New World: Society, Culture, and Globalization* (New York: New York University Press, 2007), 2–5; Karen Sànchez-Eppler, *Dependent States: The Child's Part in Nineteenth-Century American Culture* (Chicago: University of Chicago Press, 2005); Michael Grossberg, "Child Welfare in the United States, 1820–1935," in *American Public Life and the Historical Imagination*, ed. Wendy Gamber, Michael Grossberg, and Hendrik Hartog (Notre Dame, IN: University of Notre Dame Press, 2003), 3–41. For broader examinations of the role of childhood in the nineteenth-century United

States, see also Sarah Maza, "The Kids Aren't All Right: Historians and the Problem of Childhood," *American Historical Review* 125, no. 4 (October 2020): 1261–85; Corinne T. Field and Nicholas L. Syrett, eds., *Age in America: The Colonial Era to the Present* (New York: Oxford University Press, 2015); Anna Mae Duane, ed., *The Children's Table: Childhood Studies and the Humanities* (Athens: University of Georgia Press, 2013); Sally Shuttleworth, *The Mind of the Child: Child Development in Literature, Science, and Medicine, 1840–1900* (New York: Oxford University Press, 2010); Anna Mae Duane, ed., *Child Slavery before and after Emancipation: An Argument for a Child-Centered Slavery Studies* (New York: Cambridge University Press, 2017); Ruth Wallis Herndon and John E. Murray, eds., *Children Bound to Labor: The Pauper Apprentice System in Early America* (Ithaca, NY: Cornell University Press, 2009).

64. Mintz, *Huck's Raft*, 59; Gillian Brown, *The Consent of the Governed: The Lockean Legacy in Early American Culture* (Cambridge, MA: Harvard University Press, 2001), 17–23.

65. Holly Brewer, *By Birth or Consent: Children, Law, and the Anglo-American Revolution in Authority* (Chapel Hill: University of North Carolina Press, 2005), 1. See also Courtney Weikle-Mills, *Imaginary Citizens: Child Readers and the Limits of American Independence* (Baltimore: Johns Hopkins University Press, 2013), 11.

66. Patricia Crain, *Reading Children: Literacy, Property, and the Dilemmas of Childhood in Nineteenth-Century America* (Philadelphia: University of Pennsylvania Press, 2016), 7.

67. Benjamin Justice, introduction to *The Founding Fathers, Education, and "The Great Contest": The American Philosophical Society Prize of 1797*, ed. Benjamin Justice (New York: Palgrave Macmillan, 2013), 2.

Chapter 3. Mr. Lancaster's System

1. Thomas Allis to Joseph Lancaster, October 4, 1810, box 2, folder 1, Lancaster Papers, American Antiquarian Society, Worcester, Massachusetts (hereafter cited as "LP").

2. Notebook, box 14, folder 1, LP.

3. "Rules for Admission of Scholars to the Royal Free School Borough Road," box 14, folder 1, LP.

4. "Rules for Admission of Scholars to the Royal Free School Borough Road," box 14, folder 1, LP.

5. "Rules for Admission of Scholars to the Royal Free School Borough Road," box 14, folder 1, LP.

6. "Rules for Admission of Scholars to the Royal Free School Borough Road," box 14, folder 1, LP.

7. "Duty of the Principal Monitor," box 14, folder 1, LP.

8. *Manual of the System of Teaching Reading, Writing, Arithmetic, and Needle-Work, in the Elementary Schools of the British and Foreign School Society*, 1st American ed. (Philadelphia: Philadelphia Society for the Establishment and Support of Charity Schools, published by Benjamin Warner, printed by William Fry, 1817), 14.

9. *Manual of the System*, 17.

10. *Manual of the System*, 15.

11. *Manual of the System*, 15.

12. *Manual of the System*, 17.

13. *Manual of the System*, 36.

14. William A. Tweed Dale, *Manual of the Albany Lancaster School; or, The System of Mutual Instruction Simplified, Improved and Adapted to the United States* (Albany, NY: Websters & Skinners, 1820), 3.

15. Dale, *Manual*, 22.

16. William Bentley Fowle, *The True English Grammar: Being an Attempt to Form a Grammar of the English Language, Not Modeled upon Those of the Latin, Greek, and Other Foreign Languages* (Boston: Munroe & Francis, 1827), 12.

17. Fowle, *True English Grammar*, 12.

18. William Russell, *Manual of Mutual Instruction; Consisting of Mr. Fowle's Directions for Introducing in Common Schools the Improved System Adopted in the Monitorial School, Boston. With an Appendix, Containing Some Consideration in Favor of the Monitorial Method, and a Sketch of Its Progress, Embracing a View of Its Adaptation to Instruction in Academies, Preparatory Seminaries, and Colleges* (Boston: Wait, Greene, 1826), 16.

19. Russell, *Manual of Mutual Instruction*, 16.

20. Russell, *Manual of Mutual Instruction*, 16.

21. Joseph Lancaster, *The British System of Education: Being a Complete Epitome of the Improvements and Inventions Practised at the Royal Free Schools, Borough-Road, Southwark* (London: Royal Free School, 1810), 38.

22. Dale, *Manual*, 67.

23. Russell, *Manual of Mutual Instruction*, 29.

24. Lancaster, *British System* (1810), 29.

25. Lancaster, *British System* (1810), 32.

26. J. M. Opal, "Exciting Emulation: Academies and the Transformation of the Rural North, 1780s–1820s," *Journal of American History* 91, no. 2 (September 2004): 447; see also William J. Reese, *America's Public Schools: From the Common School to "No Child Left Behind"* (Baltimore: Johns Hopkins University Press, 2005), 41.

27. Lancaster, *British System* (1810), 34; emphasis in the original.

28. Lancaster, *British System* (1810), 35.

29. Lancaster, *British System* (1810), 35; emphasis in the original.

30. Lancaster, *British System* (1810), 34.

31. Lancaster, *British System* (1810), 45; emphasis in the original.

32. *Manual of the System*, 61.

33. *Manual of the System*, 66; emphasis in the original.

34. *Manual of the System*, 9.

35. *Manual of the System*, 45.

36. Report from the Committee on Rewards, New York Free School Society Trustees Meeting Minutes, January 2, 1818, New-York Historical Society, New York, New York (hereafter cited as "NYHS").

37. Report from the Committee on Rewards, New York Free School Society Trustees Meeting Minutes, January 2, 1818, NYHS.

38. Report from the Committee on Rewards, New York Free School Society Trustees Meeting Minutes, January 2, 1818, NYHS; emphasis in the original.

39. William J. Reese, *The Origins of the American High School* (New Haven, CT: Yale University Press, 1995), 84.

40. *The British System of Education: Being a Complete Epitome of the Improvements and Inventions Practised by Joseph Lancaster: To Which Is Added, a Report of the Trustees of the Lancaster School at Georgetown, Col.* (Washington, DC: Joseph Milligan, 1812), 2.

41. *British System* (1812), 3.

42. *Manual of the System*, 2–3.

43. *Manual of the Lancasterian System of Teaching Reading, Writing, Arithmetic, and Needle-work, as Practised in the Schools of the Free-School Society of New-York* (New York: Free-School Society, Samuel Wood & Sons, 1820), 16.

44. Russell, *Manual of Mutual Instruction*, 5.

45. Russell, *Manual of Mutual Instruction*, 8.

46. Russell, *Manual of Mutual Instruction*, 12.

47. Notebook, box 4, "No 1 or Manuel," LP.

48. Lancaster, *British System* (1810), 12.

49. Lancaster, *British System* (1810), 24–25.

50. *Manual of the Lancasterian System* (1820), 9.

51. Dale, *Manual*, 12,

52. John Griscom, *Monitorial Instruction. Address, Pronounced at the Opening of the New-York High-School, with Notes and Illustrations* (New York: Mahlon Day, 1825), 46.

53. Account sheet, 1800–1801, box 15, folder 1, LP.

54. Lancaster, *British System* (1810), 39.

55. New York Free School Society, preface to *Improvements in Education, as It Respects the Industrious Classes of the Community: Containing, among Other Important Particulars, an Account of the Institution for the Education of One Thousand Poor Children, Borough Road, Southwark; and of the New System of Education on Which It Is Conducted*, 3rd ed., by Joseph Lancaster (New York: Collins & Perkins, 1807), xxx.

56. John Preston, *Every Man His Own Teacher; or, Lancaster's Theory of Education, Practically Displayed, Being an Introduction to Arithmetic, Written in Thirteen Parts. To Which Are Annexed Thirty-Two Cards of Lessons, to Be Suspended in the School-Room Conformably to the Lancaster Plan. The Whole Is Calculated for the Use of Families Destitute of a School, for School-Masters, and for the Amusement of Private Gentlemen* (Albany: self-pub., 1817), preface.

57. Benjamin Shaw to the Controllers of the Public Schools, April 16, 1818, box 1, folder 15: Roberts Vaux Correspondence Jan–July 1818, Vaux Family Papers, 1739–1923, Collection 684, Historical Society of Pennsylvania, Philadelphia.

58. Edward Baker, *A Brief Sketch of the Lancasterian System, Intended as a Companion in Visiting a Lancasterian School, with Advice to Committees on the Establishment, Management and Examination of Such Schools* (Troy, NY: F. Adancourt, 1816), 21.

59. Carl F. Kaestle, *Pillars of the Republic: Common Schools and American Society, 1780–1860* (New York: Hill & Wang, 1983), 42.

60. Russell, *Manual of Mutual Instruction*, 104.

61. Pennsylvania Society for the Promotion of Public Economy, *Report of the Committee on Public School to the Pennsylvania Society for the Promotion of Public Economy* (Philadelphia: SPPE, 1817), 5–6.

62. *Manual of the System*, ix.

63. Lancaster, *Improvements in Education*, 72; emphasis in the original.

64. *Manual of the System*, x.
65. *Report on the Subject of Education, Read in the Senate of Pennsylvania, March 1, 1822* (Harrisburg, PA: C. Mowry, 1822), 23.
66. Dale, *Manual*, 76–80.
67. Dale, *Manual*, 76.
68. Russell, *Manual of Mutual Instruction*, 20.
69. Box 4, vol. "Jos. Lancaster's First lecture ever given with notes—Gloucester 1808," LP.
70. Russell, *Manual of Mutual Instruction*, 27.

Chapter 4. A Numbers Game

1. De Witt Clinton, *An Address, to the Benefactors and Friends of the Free School Society of New York, Delivered on the Opening of That Institution, in Their New and Spacious Building, on the Eleventh of the Twelfth Month (December) 1809* (New York: Collins & Perkins, 1810), 10.

2. Edward Flavin Wall Jr., "Joseph Lancaster and the Origins of the British and Foreign School Society" (PhD diss., Columbia University, 1966), 132.

3. See, e.g., the edition of Lancaster's early manual, with which Clinton would have been familiar: Joseph Lancaster, *Improvements in Education, as It Respects the Industrious Classes of the Community: Containing, among Other Important Particulars, an Account of the Institution for the Education of One Thousand Poor Children, Borough Road, Southwark; and of the New System of Education on Which It Is Conducted*, 3rd ed. (New York: Collins & Perkins, 1807).

4. Clinton, *Address*, 10.

5. Clinton, *Address*, 9.

6. Joseph Lancaster to Elizabeth Lancaster (senior), September 3, 1818, box 2, folder 3, Lancaster Papers, American Antiquarian Society, Worcester, Massachusetts (hereafter cited as "LP"); Lancaster travel diary, box 15, folder 6, LP.

7. Joseph Lancaster to Elizabeth Lancaster (senior), September 3, 1818, box 2, folder 3, LP.

8. Joseph Lancaster to Roberts Vaux, January 27, 1819, box 2, folder 1: Roberts Vaux Correspondence Jan–Feb 1819, Vaux Family Papers, 1739–1923, Collection 684, Historical Society of Pennsylvania, Philadelphia (hereafter cited as "VFP").

9. Joseph Lancaster to Roberts Vaux, January 27, 1819, box 2, folder 1: Roberts Vaux Correspondence Jan–Feb 1819, VFP.

10. Joseph Lancaster to Roberts Vaux, January 27, 1819, box 2, folder 1: Roberts Vaux Correspondence Jan–Feb 1819, VFP; see also Joseph Lancaster to Elizabeth (Betsy) Lancaster (junior), January 23, 1819, box 2, folder 3, LP.

11. John Preston, *Every Man His Own Teacher; or, Lancaster's Theory of Education, Practically Displayed, Being an Introduction to Arithmetic, Written in Thirteen Parts. To Which Are Annexed Thirty-Two Cards of Lessons, to Be Suspended in the School-Room Conformably to the Lancaster Plan. The Whole Is Calculated for the Use of Families Destitute of a School, for School-Masters, and for the Amusement of Private Gentlemen* (Albany: self-pub., 1817), preface.

12. John Murray, *Fourteenth Annual Report of the Free-School Society* (New York: Collins, 1819), n.p.

13. J. DeWitt to Joseph Lancaster, 1818, box 3, folder 1, LP.

14. Joseph Lancaster to Roberts Vaux, November 30, 1819, box 2, folder 1: Roberts Vaux Correspondence Jan–Feb 1819, VFP.

15. William Thurston to Joseph Lancaster, October 11, 1819, box 3, folder 1, LP.

16. Joseph Bringhurst to Joseph Lancaster, April 13, 1819, box 3, folder 1, LP.

17. Joseph C. Cabell to Joseph Lancaster, July 1, 1819, box 3, folder 1, LP.

18. Joshua Abbott to Joseph Lancaster, August 5, 1819, box 3, folder 1, LP.

19. Ezekiel Clarke to Joseph Lancaster, April 19, 1821, box 13, folder 4, LP.

20. John C. Calhoun to Joseph Lancaster, March 13, 1820, box 3, folder 1, LP.

21. Joseph Lancaster to Elizabeth Lancaster (senior), September 9, 1818, box 2, folder 3, LP.

22. Joseph Lancaster to Elizabeth (Betsy) Lancaster (junior), January 16, 1819, box 2, folder 3, LP. See also Joseph Lancaster to Roberts Vaux, January 23, 1819, box 2, folder 1: Roberts Vaux Correspondence Jan–Feb 1819, VFP.

23. Lancaster travel diary, started June 15, 1818, box 15, folder 6, LP.

24. Joseph Lancaster, "PROPOSALS for a Publication to Diffuse a Correct Knowledge of the Lancasterian System throughout the United States of America," 1819, box 2, folder 5, LP.

25. Henry Ould to Joseph Lancaster, February 26, 1819, box 3, folder 1, LP.

26. Joseph Lancaster to Roberts Vaux, January 23, 1819, box 2, folder 1: Roberts Vaux Correspondence Jan–Feb 1819, VFP.

27. Benjamin Shaw to Roberts Vaux, August 4, 1818, box 1, folder 16: Roberts Vaux Correspondence Aug–Dec 1818, VFP.

28. Lancaster, *Improvements in Education*, xxv.

29. Mora Dickson, *Teacher Extraordinary: Joseph Lancaster 1778–1838* (Sussex, UK: Book Guild Limited, 1986), 110.

30. *Manual of the System of Teaching Reading, Writing, Arithmetic, and Needle-Work, in the Elementary Schools of the British and Foreign School Society*, 1st American ed. (Philadelphia: Philadelphia Society for the Establishment and Support of Charity Schools, published by Benjamin Warner, printed by William Fry, 1817), ix.

31. New York Free School Society Trustees Meeting Minutes, August 1, 1817, New-York Historical Society, New York, New York (hereafter cited as "NYHS").

32. Washington L. Lane to Roberts Vaux, July 9, 1827, box 3, folder 5: Roberts Vaux Correspondence July–Dec 1827, VFP.

33. Benjamin Shaw to Roberts Vaux, August 4, 1818, box 1, folder 16: Roberts Vaux Correspondence Aug–Dec 1818, VFP.

34. Patriot, letter to the editor, *American Monthly Magazine and Critical Review*, November 1817, 47–48. The letter was copied by a student at the African Free School and included in the New York African Free School Records, vol. 3, NYHS.

35. William J. Reese, *Testing Wars in the Public Schools: A Forgotten History* (Cambridge, MA: Harvard University Press, 2013), 8–37.

36. Isaiah G. Degrass, "Essay," *Freedom's Journal*, March 14, 1828, 1.

37. George R. Allen, "Essay," *Freedom's Journal*, March 14, 1828, 1.

38. Letter to the editor, *Belfast Chronicle*, January 2, 1815, clipping in box 4, vol. "First Folio," LP.

39. David Hoffman, "To the Washington Society of Alexandra," *Alexandria Gazette*, February 27, 1813, clipping in box 4, folder 14, LP.

40. *Report of a Committee Appointed by the High School Society of New-York, to Prepare a Plan of Instruction to Be Pursued in the High School* (New York: J. Seymour, 1824), 5.

41. T., letter to the editor, *Mechanics Free Press*, December 13, 1828, 2.

42. Daniel Walker Howe, *What Hath God Wrought: The Transformation of America, 1815–1848* (New York: Oxford University Press, 2007), 270.

43. Howe, *What Hath God Wrought*, 294.

44. Benjamin Justice, introduction to *The Founding Fathers, Education, and "The Great Contest": The American Philosophical Society Prize of 1797*, ed. Benjamin Justice (New York: Palgrave Macmillan, 2013), 1.

45. Justice, introduction to *Founding Fathers*, 4.

46. Richard H. Gassan, "Fear, Commercialism, Reform, and Antebellum Tourism to New York City," *Journal of Urban History* 41, no. 6 (November 2015): 1079.

47. Rush quoted in Julie Flavell, *When London Was Capital of America* (New Haven, CT: Yale University Press, 2010), 1.

48. Carl F. Kaestle, *The Evolution of an Urban School System: New York City, 1750–1850* (Cambridge, MA: Harvard University Press, 1973), 10.

49. Lisa Krissoff Boehm and Steven H. Corey, *America's Urban History* (New York: Routledge, 2015), 141.

50. Lancaster, *Improvements in Education*, xxxi.

51. Robert Owen to Joseph Lancaster, June 19, 1812, box 2, folder 1, LP; emphasis in the original.

52. Clinton, *Address*, 9.

53. Joseph Palethorpe to Joseph Lancaster, September 16, 1811, box 2, folder 1, LP.

54. *Prospectus of a New School for Young Ladies; Embracing the Modern Improvements of the British and Swiss Systems* (Boston: n.p., 1823), 7.

55. Joseph Lancaster, *Letters on National Subjects, Auxiliary to Universal Education, and Scientific Knowledge; Addressed to Burwell Bassett, Late a Member of the House of Representatives; Henry Clay, Speaker of the House of Representatives, and James Monroe, President of the United States of America* (Washington City: Jacob Gideon Jr., 1820), 52.

56. Lancaster, *Letters on National Subjects*, 46.

57. Howe, *What Hath God Wrought*, 117.

58. Nathaniel Hawthorne, "The Canal Boat," *New-England Magazine* 9 (December 1835): 398.

59. *Fourth Annual Report of the Controllers of the Public Schools of the First School District of the State of Pennsylvania; With Their Accounts* (Philadelphia: Printed by Order of the Board of Control, 1822), 3.

60. *Report on the Subject of Education, Read in the Senate of Pennsylvania, March 1, 1822* (Harrisburg, PA: C. Mowry, 1822), 22.

61. Lancaster, *Improvements in Education*, xxii.

62. *An Account of the Free-School Society of New-York* (New York: Collins, 1814), 14.
63. New York Free School Society Trustees Meeting Minutes, May 1, 1818, NYHS; Murray, *Fourteenth Annual Report*.
64. *Sixteenth Annual Report of the Free-School Society* (New York: Collins, 1821), n.p.
65. *Twentieth Annual Report of the Trustees of the Free-School Society of New-York* (New York: Samuel Wood & Sons, 1825), 12.
66. New York Free School Society Trustees Meeting Minutes, January 4, 1822, NYHS.
67. Carla L. Peterson, *Black Gotham: A Family History of African Americans in Nineteenth-Century New York City* (New Haven, CT: Yale University Press, 2011), 69.
68. New York African Free School Records, vol. 1: Regulations, By-laws and Reports, 1817–1832, NYHS.
69. New York African Free School Records, vol. 2: Reports of the Visiting Committee, 1820–1831, NYHS.
70. New York African Free School Records, vol. 2: Reports of the Visiting Committee, 1820–1831, NYHS.
71. William Michael Weber, "Before Horace Mann: Elites and Boston Public Schools, 1800–1812" (EdD diss., Harvard University, 1974), 94; William J. Reese, *The Origins of the American High School* (New Haven, CT: Yale University Press, 1995), 11; Stanley K. Schultz, *The Culture Factory: Boston Public Schools, 1789–1860* (New York: Oxford University Press, 1973), 264, 266.
72. Tina H. Sheller, "The Origins of Public Education in Baltimore, 1825–1829," *History of Education Quarterly* 22, no. 1 (Spring 1982): 36, 38.
73. Mary C. Taylor to Board of Trustees, July 29, 1817, New York Free School Society Trustees Meeting Minutes, NYHS; New York Free School Society Trustees Meeting Minutes, October 2, 1818, NYHS; *An Account of the Origin and Progress of the Savannah Free-School Society, Instituted in the Year 1816* (New York: Day & Turner, 1819); Tim Lockley, "Survival Strategies of Poor White Women in Savannah, 1800–1860," *Journal of the Early Republic* 32, no. 3 (Fall 2012): 415–35.
74. Carl F. Kaestle, *Pillars of the Republic: Common Schools and American Society, 1780–1860* (New York: Hill & Wang, 1983), 42.
75. For more on Lancasterianism specifically in Philadelphia, see David Hogan, "The Market Revolution and Disciplinary Power: Joseph Lancaster and the Psychology of the Early Classroom System," *History of Education Quarterly* 29, no. 3 (Autumn 1989): 381–417; David Hogan, "Examinations, Merit, and Morals: The Market Revolution and Disciplinary Power in Philadelphia's Public Schools, 1838–1868," *Historical Studies in Education/Revue d'Histoire de l'Education* 4, no. 1 (1992): 31–78; William C. Kashatus III, "The Inner Light and Popular Enlightenment: Philadelphia Quakers and Charity Schooling, 1790–1820," *Pennsylvania Magazine of History and Biography* 118, no. 1/2 (January–April 1994): 87–116.
76. John C. Van Horne, "The Education of African Americans in Benjamin Franklin's Philadelphia," in *"The Good Education of Youth": Worlds of Learning in the Age of Franklin*, ed. John H. Pollack (New Castle, DE: Oak Knoll, 2009), 92; Jean Barth Toll and Mildred S. Gillam, eds., *Invisible Philadelphia: Community through Voluntary Organizations* (Philadelphia: Atwater Kent Museum, 1995), 695.
77. Kaestle, *Pillars of the Republic*, 31.

78. *Manual of the System*, ix–x.

79. *An Act to Provide for the Education of Children at Public Expense within the City and County of Philadelphia* (Harrisburg, PA: s.n., 1818). [Copy at the Historical Society of Pennsylvania, Philadelphia.]

80. Franklin Davenport Edmunds, *The Public School Buildings of the City of Philadelphia from 1745 to 1845* (Philadelphia: self-pub., 1913), 53.

81. Given that a male teacher in those years would often earn a $600 annual salary, if a teacher today might earn $75,000, the equivalent would put the cost of the Philadelphia school at roughly $1,887,625 in 2020 dollars. Of course, a $600 salary was considered very high in 1818 (at least by the trustees of New York's Free School Society), so this estimate is likely on the low side.

82. *Eighth Annual Report of the Controllers of the Public Schools of the First School District of the State of Pennsylvania; With Their Accounts* (Philadelphia: Printed by Order of the Board of Control, 1826). The numbers here come from the series of annual reports collected at the archives of the Historical Society of Pennsylvania.

Chapter 5. A Growing Disorder

1. De Witt Clinton, *An Address, to the Benefactors and Friends of the Free School Society of New York, Delivered on the Opening of That Institution, in Their New and Spacious Building, on the Eleventh of the Twelfth Month (December) 1809* (New York: Collins & Perkins, 1810), 10.

2. Mora Dickson, *Teacher Extraordinary: Joseph Lancaster 1778–1838* (Sussex, UK: Book Guild Limited, 1986), 88.

3. John Mackellen to Joseph Lancaster, February 15, 1811, box 10, folder 1, Lancaster Papers, American Antiquarian Society, Worcester, Massachusetts (hereafter cited as "LP").

4. William B. Fowle, "July 1, Visited the Adams School, Writing Department," n.d., box 2, folder: undated letter drafts, William B. Fowle Papers, Massachusetts Historical Society, Boston, Massachusetts.

5. *First Annual Report of the Trustees of the High-School Society. In the City of New-York* (New York: Mahlon Day, 1825), 4.

6. Mann Butler, *Report on Monitorial Education; to the Hon. Mayor and Council, of Louisville* (Louisville, KY: S. Penn Jr., 1829), 4.

7. Butler, *Report on Monitorial Education*, 4.

8. *A Sketch of the Origin and Progress of the Adelphi School in the Northern Liberties, Established under the Direction of the Philadelphia Association of Friends for the Instruction of Poor Children* (Philadelphia: Meyer & Jones, 1810), 13.

9. *Second Annual Report of the Controllers of the Public Schools of the First School District of the State of Pennsylvania; With Their Accounts. Also, an Abstract of the Law of March 6th, 1818, Providing for Public Education, and a List of the Controllers and Directors Elected for the Year 1820* (Philadelphia: Printed by Order of the Board of Control, 1820), 3.

10. Joseph J. McCadden, "Joseph Lancaster and the Philadelphia Schools," *Pennsylvania History* 3, no. 4 (October 1936): 229–37.

11. Joseph Lancaster to Roberts Vaux, November 20, 1818, box 1, folder 16: Roberts Vaux Correspondence Aug–Dec 1818, Vaux Family Papers, 1739–1923, Collection 684, Historical Society of Pennsylvania, Philadelphia (hereafter cited as "VFP").

12. New York Free School Society Trustees Meeting Minutes, May 5, 1817, New-York Historical Society, New York, New York (hereafter cited as "NYHS").
13. New York Free School Society Trustees Meeting Minutes, January 15, 1819, NYHS.
14. New York Free School Society Trustees Meeting Minutes, July 2, 1819, NYHS.
15. Betsy Lancaster on behalf of Joseph Lancaster to Roberts Vaux, August 2, 1819, box 2, folder 1: Roberts Vaux Correspondence Jan–Feb 1819, VFP.
16. Joseph Lancaster to Roberts Vaux, November 4, 1819, box 2, folder 1: Roberts Vaux Correspondence Jan–Feb 1819, VFP.
17. Joseph Lancaster to Roberts Vaux, November 20, 1818, box 1, folder 16: Roberts Vaux Correspondence Aug–Dec 1818, VFP.
18. Joseph Lancaster to Roberts Vaux, November 20, 1818 [second letter that day], box 1, folder 16: Roberts Vaux Correspondence Aug–Dec 1818, VFP; Joseph Lancaster to Roberts Vaux, November 28, 1818, box 1, folder 16: Roberts Vaux Correspondence Aug–Dec 1818, VFP.
19. Joseph Lancaster to Roberts Vaux, November 28, 1818, box 1, folder 16: Roberts Vaux Correspondence Aug–Dec 1818, VFP.
20. Joseph Lancaster to Betsy Lancaster, September 18, 1819, box 163, folder 16: Lancaster, Joseph (1819), Lancaster Papers, Gratz Collection, Historical Society of Pennsylvania, Philadelphia; emphasis in the original.
21. Dickson, *Teacher Extraordinary*, 201.
22. Joseph Lancaster to Roberts Vaux, January 17, 1822, box 2, folder 10: Correspondence, Jan–Mar 1822, VFP.
23. Joseph Lancaster to Roberts Vaux, March 3, 1819, box 2, folder 2: Roberts Vaux Correspondence Mar–July 1819, VFP.
24. Joseph Lancaster to Roberts Vaux, March 3, 1819, box 2, folder 2: Roberts Vaux Correspondence Mar–July 1819, VFP.
25. McCadden, "Joseph Lancaster," 237.
26. New York Free School Society Trustees Meeting Minutes, August 1, 1817, NYHS.
27. New York Free School Society Trustees Meeting Minutes, January 15, 1819, NYHS.
28. Account sheet, 1800–1801, box 15, folder 1, LP.
29. New York Free School Society Trustees Meeting Minutes, January 15, 1819, NYHS.
30. New York Free School Society Trustees Meeting Minutes, June 2, 1820, NYHS; New York Free School Society Trustees Meeting Minutes, February 2, 1821, NYHS.
31. New York Free School Society Trustees Meeting Minutes, June 2, 1820, NYHS.
32. Michael B. Katz, *Reconstructing American Education* (Cambridge, MA: Harvard University Press, 1987), 25–28. See also David J. Rothman, *The Discovery of the Asylum: Social Order and Disorder in the New Republic* (Boston: Little, Brown, 1971); Robert E. Cray Jr., *Paupers and Poor Relief in New York City and Its Rural Environs, 1700–1830* (Philadelphia: Temple University Press, 1988); Monique Bourque, "Poor Relief 'Without Violating the Rights of Humanity': Almshouse Administration in the Philadelphia Region, 1790–1860," in *Down and Out in Early America*, ed. Billy G. Smith (University Park, PA: Pennsylvania State University Press, 2004), 189–212.
33. "Public offices and Societies in which Roberts Vaux has served," manuscript, n.d., box 5, folder 19: Miscellaneous—Charitable organizations, n.d., VFP.

34. *Manual of the System of Teaching Reading, Writing, Arithmetic, and Needle-Work, in the Elementary Schools of the British and Foreign School Society*, 1st American ed. (Philadelphia: Philadelphia Society for the Establishment and Support of Charity Schools, published by Benjamin Warner, printed by William Fry, 1817), B [front matter paginated by letter].

35. *The Constitution of the Society for the Free Instruction of the Black People Formed in the Year 1789* (Philadelphia: W. Brown, 1813), 7.

36. *Constitution and By-Laws of the Orphan Society of Philadelphia Instituted December 20th 1814* (Philadelphia: William Fry, 1815).

37. See, e.g., *An Account of the Female Association for the Relief of the Sick Poor, and for the Education for Such Female Children as Do Not Belong to, or Are Not Provided for, by Any Religious Society* (New York: Collins, 1814), 5; see also Joseph Lancaster, *Improvements in Education, as It Respects the Industrious Classes of the Community: Containing, among Other Important Particulars, an Account of the Institution for the Education of One Thousand Poor Children, Borough Road, Southwark; and of the New System of Education on Which It Is Conducted*, 3rd ed. (New York: Collins & Perkins, 1807), vi.

38. *Sketch of the Origin*, 24–29.

39. *Manual of the System*, vi.

40. *Manual of the System*, vii.

41. Fifteenth Annual Report, New York Free School Society, manuscript in New York Free School Society Trustees Meeting Minutes, April 25, 1820, NYHS.

42. New York Free School Society Trustees Meeting Minutes, June 6, 1817, NYHS.

43. New York Free School Society Trustees Meeting Minutes, November 7, 1817, NYHS.

44. *Subscriptions to New York Free School No. 3*, box 2, New York Free School Society Papers, NYHS.

45. New York Free School Society Trustees Meeting Minutes, January 15, 1819, NYHS.

46. New York Free School Society Trustees Meeting Minutes, September 3, 1819, NYHS.

47. New York Free School Society Trustees Meeting Minutes, January 19, 1819, NYHS.

48. New York Free School Society Trustees Meeting Minutes, March 5, 1819, NYHS.

49. New York Free School Society Trustees Meeting Minutes, March 18, 1819, NYHS.

50. New York Free School Society Trustees Meeting Minutes, April 9, 1819, NYHS.

51. New York Free School Society Trustees Meeting Minutes, March 18, 1819, NYHS.

52. New York Free School Society Trustees Meeting Minutes, July 2, 1819, NYHS.

53. New York Free School Society Trustees Meeting Minutes, August 6, 1819, NYHS.

54. New York Free School Society Trustees Meeting Minutes, May 5, 1817, NYHS; New York Free School Society Trustees Meeting Minutes, May 7, 1819, NYHS.

55. Edward Baker, *A Brief Sketch of the Lancasterian System, Intended as a Companion in Visiting a Lancasterian School, with Advice to Committees on the Establishment, Management and Examination of Such Schools* (Troy, NY: F. Adancourt, 1816); *Eleventh Annual Report of the Free-School Society of New York* (New York: Collins, 1816); McCadden, "Joseph Lancaster," 227–31.

56. *Ninth Annual Report of the Trustees of the Free-School Society of New York* (New York: n.p., 1814); *Eleventh Annual Report*; *Twelfth Annual Report of the Free-School Society of New York* (New York: Collins, 1817).

57. New York Free School Society Trustees Meeting Minutes, July 2, 1819, NYHS.

58. Pay slip for Elizabeth C. Darracott, box 6, folder Dodd Family, Apr.–Jun. 1828, Dodd Family Papers, 1769–1839, Massachusetts Historical Society, Boston, Massachusetts (hereafter cited as "DFP").

59. See school records of student Caroline Dodd, ending January 1, 1828, box 6, folder Dodd Family, Apr.–Jun. 1828, DFP. Her teacher was originally expected to be Maria Hall, but Hall left and was replaced at the last minute by Elizabeth Darracott.

60. New York Free School Society Trustees Meeting Minutes, April 25, 1820, NYHS.

61. New York Free School Society Trustees Meeting Minutes, March 1, 1822, NYHS.

62. George Fowle to Proprietors of N. Boston Monitorial School, October 6, 1829, box 6, folder Dodd Family, Aug.–Oct. 1829, DFP.

63. New York African Free School Records, vol. 2: Reports of the Visiting Committee, 1820–1831, NYHS.

64. Lancaster, *Improvements in Education*, 9.

65. Robert Ould to Joseph Lancaster, February 5, 1812, box 1, folder 1, LP.

66. See, e.g., John Fell to Joseph Lancaster, January 4, 1813, and J. W. Waddington to Joseph Lancaster, February 12, 1813, box 12, folder 1, LP.

67. Mary C. Taylor to Board of Trustees, July 19, 1817, New York Free School Society Trustees Meeting Minutes, NYHS.

68. Mary C. Taylor to Board of Trustees, July 19, 1817, New York Free School Society Trustees Meeting Minutes, NYHS.

69. Joseph Boringhurst to Joseph Lancaster, March 5, 1819, box 3, folder 1, LP.

70. New York Free School Society Trustees Meeting Minutes, November 6, 1818, NYHS.

71. *By-Laws of the Free School Society, of New York, as Revised and Adopted by the Trustees, 12th Month (December) 1818* (New York: W. Treadwell, 1819), 8.

72. Baker, *Brief Sketch*, front matter.

73. Josiah L. Hearn to Joseph Lancaster, April 28, 1824, box 3, folder 2, LP.

74. Joseph Lancaster to Roberts Vaux, November 26, 1818, box 1, folder 16: Roberts Vaux Correspondence Aug–Dec 1818, VFP.

75. Joseph Lancaster to Roberts Vaux, March 3, 1819, box 2, folder 2: Roberts Vaux Correspondence Mar–July 1819, VFP.

76. New York Free School Society Trustees Meeting Minutes, October 1, 1817, NYHS.

77. New York Free School Society Trustees Meeting Minutes, October 1, 1817, NYHS.

78. Joseph Fox to Joseph Lancaster, November 25, 1813, box 1, folder 1, LP.

79. John Walker, Esq. to Joseph Lancaster, July 4, 1813, box 12, folder 3, LP.

80. The literature on changing labor patterns in the early United States is vast. Some representative works include Kenneth Morgan, *Slavery and Servitude in Colonial North America: A Short History* (New York: New York University Press, 2001); and Christopher Tomlins, "Reconsidering Indentured Servitude: European Migration and the Early American Labor Force, 1600–1775," *Labor History* 42, no. 1 (2001): 5–43.

81. See W. J. Rorabaugh, *The Craft Apprentice: From Franklin to the Machine Age* (New York: Oxford University Press, 1986), 57–75; Ruth Wallis Herndon and John E. Murray, eds., *Children Bound to Labor: The Pauper Apprentice System in Early America* (Ithaca, NY: Cornell University Press, 2009).

82. Thomas Sullivan to Joseph Lancaster, December 1, 1813, box 12, folder 3, LP.

83. New York Free School Society Trustees Meeting Minutes, August 7, 1818, NYHS.
84. New York Free School Society Trustees Meeting Minutes, October 2, 1818, NYHS.
85. New York Free School Society Trustees Meeting Minutes, November 6, 1818, NYHS.
86. New York Free School Society Trustees Meeting Minutes, March 5, 1819, NYHS.
87. New York Free School Society Trustees Meeting Minutes, October 1, 1817, NYHS.
88. New York Free School Society Trustees Meeting Minutes, December 10, 1818, NYHS.
89. New York Free School Society Trustees Meeting Minutes, April 2, 1819, NYHS.
90. New York Free School Society Trustees Meeting Minutes, June 2, 1820, NYHS.
91. New York Free School Society Trustees Meeting Minutes, February 2, 1821, NYHS.
92. New York Free School Society Trustees Meeting Minutes, February 2, 1821, NYHS.
93. Benjamin F. Hart to Trustees, November 12, 1821, box 1, unlabeled folder, New York Free School Society Papers, NYHS.

Chapter 6. The Truant Plan

1. Joseph Lancaster, *The British System of Education: Being a Complete Epitome of the Improvements and Inventions Practised at the Royal Free Schools, Borough-Road, Southwark* (London: Royal Free School, 1810), 38.

2. Monique Bourque, "Poor Relief 'Without Violating the Rights of Humanity': Almshouse Administration in the Philadelphia Region, 1790–1860," in *Down and Out in Early America*, ed. Billy G. Smith (University Park: Pennsylvania State University Press, 2004), 198; Ruth Wallis Herndon, "Poor Women and the Boston Almshouse in the Early Republic," *Journal of the Early Republic* 21, no. 3 (Fall 2012): 349–81.

3. Lancaster, *British System of Education* (1810), 38; emphasis in the original.

4. James Jacklin, "Poem Read at Annual Examination," April 4, 1819, New York African Free School Records, vol. 3, New-York Historical Society, New York, New York (hereafter cited as "NYHS").

5. John L. Rury, "Philanthropy, Self Help, and Social Control: The New York Manumission Society and Free Black, 1785–1810," *Phylon* 46, no. 3 (1985): 235.

6. See, e.g., David Gellman, *Emancipating New York: The Politics of Slavery and Freedom, 1777–1827* (Baton Rouge: Louisiana State University Pres, 2006); Leslie M. Harris, *In the Shadow of Slavery: African Americans in New York City, 1626–1863* (Chicago: University of Chicago Press, 2003); John Wood Sweet, *Bodies Politic: Negotiating Race in the American North, 1730–1830* (Baltimore: Johns Hopkins University Press, 2003); Joshua R. Greenberg, *Advocating the Man: Masculinity, Organized Labor, and the Household in New York, 1800–1840* (New York: Columbia University Press, 2008); Joshua A. Lynn and Harry L. Watson, "Introduction: Race, Politics, and Culture in the Age of Jacksonian 'Democracy,'" *Journal of the Early Republic* 39, no. 1 (Spring 2019): 81–87; Paul J. Polgar, "'Whenever They Judge it Expedient': The Politics of Partisanship and Free Black Voting Rights in Early National New York," *American Nineteenth Century History* 12, no. 1 (March 2011): 1–23; Sean Wilentz, *Chants Democratic: New York City and the Rise of the American Working Class, 1788–1850*, 20th anniv. ed. (New York: Oxford University Press, 2004); Sarah L. H. Gronningsater, "Practicing Formal Politics without the Vote: Black New Yorkers in the Aftermath of 1821," in *Revolutions and Reconstructions: Black Politics in the Long Nineteenth Century*, ed. Van Gosse and David Waldstreicher (Philadelphia: University of Pennsylvania Press, 2020), 116–38; Mark Boon-

shoft, "From Property to Education: Public Schooling, Race, and the Transformation of Suffrage in the Early National North," *Journal of the Early Republic* 41, no. 3 (Fall 2021): 1–36.

7. Bourque, "Poor Relief," 190.

8. Daniel Walker Howe, *What Hath God Wrought: The Transformation of America, 1815–1848* (New York: Oxford University Press, 2007), 3.

9. Mark Boonshoft, *Aristocratic Education and the Making of the American Republic* (Chapel Hill: University of North Carolina Press, 2020), 168.

10. "Education," *New York Mirror* 6 (May 9, 1830): 351, quoted in William J. Reese, *The Origins of the American High School* (New Haven, CT: Yale University Press, 1995), 16.

11. Arthur Meier Schlesinger, *The Rise of the City, 1878–1898* (New York: Macmillan, 1933), 53.

12. Roberta Balstad Miller, *City and Hinterland: A Case Study of Urban Growth and Regional Development* (Westport, CT: Greenwood, 1979); Diana Lindstrom, *Economic Development in the Philadelphia Region, 1810–1850* (New York: Columbia University Press, 1978), 93; Allan Pred, *Urban Growth and City-Systems in the U.S., 1840–1860* (Cambridge, MA: Harvard University Press, 1980); David Goldfield, *Cottonfields and Skyscrapers: Southern City and Region, 1607–1980* (Baton Rouge: Louisiana State University Press, 1982); Carl Abbott, "Dimensions of Regional Change in Washington, D.C.," *American Historical Review* 95 (1990): 1367–93; Charles Tilly, "What Good Is Urban History?," *Journal of Urban History* 22, no. 6 (September 1996): 702–19; Raymond A. Mohl, "City and Region: The Missing Dimension in U.S. Urban History," *Journal of Urban History* 25, no. 1 (November 1998): 3–21; Timothy J. Gilfoyle, "Michael Katz on Place and Space in Urban History," *Journal of Urban History* 41, no. 4 (July 2015): 572–84.

13. Thomas Dublin, ed., *Farm to Factory: Women's Letters, 1830–1860*, 2nd ed. (New York: Columbia University Press, 1993), 30. See also Miller, *City and Hinterland*, 5, 20; Gary B. Nash, "The Social Evolution of Preindustrial Cities, 1700–1820: Reflections and New Directions," *Journal of Urban History* 13 (February 1987): 120; Robert E. Cray Jr., *Paupers and Poor Relief in New York City and Its Rural Environs, 1700–1830* (Philadelphia: Temple University Press, 1988), 110. As Monique Bourque has found, even when administrators tried to keep low-income inmates of almshouses separate and isolated, inmates were in constant contact with the outside. See Bourque, "Poor Relief," 190.

14. Carl F. Kaestle and Maris A. Vinovskis, *Education and Social Change in Nineteenth-Century Massachusetts* (Cambridge: Cambridge University Press, 1980), 15.

15. Nancy Beadie, *Education and the Creation of Capital in the Early American Republic* (New York: Cambridge University Press, 2010), 147. A separate but relevant body of literature uses information from the 1860 census to determine school attendance for a later generation. See Lee Soltow and Edward Stevens, "Economic Aspects of School Participation in Mid-Nineteenth-Century United States," *Journal of Interdisciplinary History* 8, no. 2 (Autumn 1977): 221–43; David Galenson, "Determinants of the School Attendance of Boys in Early Chicago," *History of Education Quarterly* 35 (Winter 1995): 371–400; Donald H. Parkerson and Jo Ann Parkerson, *The Emergence of the Common School in the US Countryside* (Lewiston, NY: Edwin Mellen, 1998).

16. Carl F. Kaestle and Maris A. Vinovskis, *Education and Social Change in Nineteenth-Century Massachusetts* (Cambridge: Cambridge University Press, 1980), 18.

17. Kaestle and Vinovskis, *Education and Social Change*, 21.

18. Kaestle and Vinovskis, *Education and Social Change*, 24.

19. Carl F. Kaestle, *Pillars of the Republic: Common Schools and American Society, 1780–1860* (New York: Hill & Wang, 1983), 20–21. A huge body of memoirs generally agrees on the point: rural and village schools were tied tightly to their communities, but the quality of instruction was often low and the teachers were often minimally qualified. See, e.g., Orville Taylor, *The District School* (New York: Harper, 1834), 40–41; William Burton, *The District School as It Was*, rev. ed. (Boston: Philips, Samson, 1850), 43; Horace Greeley, *Recollections of a Busy Life* (New York: J. B. Ford, 1869), 42–47; William A. Mowry, *Recollections of a New England Educator* (New York: Silver, Burdett, 1908), 33–57.

20. Carl F. Kaestle, ed., *Joseph Lancaster and the Monitorial School Movement: A Documentary History* (New York: Teachers College Press, 1973), 46–49.

21. Sun Go and Peter Lindert, "The Uneven Rise of American Public Schools to 1850," *Journal of Economic History* 70 (March 2010): 13.

22. Benjamin Justice, *The War That Wasn't: Religious Conflict and Compromise in the Common Schools of New York State, 1865–1900* (Albany: State University of New York Press, 2005), 29–34, quotation on 29.

23. Johann Neem, "Path Dependence and the Emergence of Common Schools: Ohio to 1853," *Journal of Policy History* 28, no. 1 (2016): 48–80.

24. New York Free School Society Trustees Meeting Minutes, December 10, 1818, NYHS.

25. *Sixteenth Annual Report of the Free-School Society* (New York: Collins, 1821), n.p.

26. Robert Ould to Joseph Lancaster, February 15, 1819, box 3, folder 1, Lancaster Papers, American Antiquarian Society, Worcester, Massachusetts.

27. *Third Annual Report of the Controllers of the Public Schools of the First School District of the State of Pennsylvania; With Their Accounts* (Philadelphia: Printed by Order of the Board of Control, 1821), 4.

28. Visitors' reports, July 28, 1818, New York African Free School Records, vol. 1: Regulations, By-laws and Reports, 1817–1832, NYHS.

29. Visitors' reports, March 9, 1821, New York African Free School Records, vol. 1: Regulations, By-laws and Reports, 1817–1832, NYHS.

30. Visitors' reports, April 6, 1821, New York African Free School Records, vol. 1: Regulations, By-laws and Reports, 1817–1832, NYHS.

31. Visitors' reports, April 13, 1821, New York African Free School Records, vol. 1: Regulations, By-laws and Reports, 1817–1832, NYHS.

32. Visitors' reports, School Number Two, April 20, 1821, New York African Free School Records, vol. 2: Reports of the Visiting Committee, 1820–1831, NYHS.

33. Clipping from the *American Sentinel*, Philadelphia, February 23, 1822, box 2, folder 10: Correspondence Jan–Mar 1822, Vaux Family Papers, 1739–1923, Collection 684, Historical Society of Pennsylvania, Philadelphia (hereafter cited as "VFP").

34. *Fifth Annual Report of the Controllers of the Public Schools of the First School District of the State of Pennsylvania; With Their Accounts* (Philadelphia: Printed by Order of the Board of Control, 1823), 8–9.

35. *Sixth Annual Report of the Controllers of the Public Schools of the First School District*

of the State of Pennsylvania; With Their Accounts (Philadelphia: Printed by Order of the Board of Control, 1824), 4.

36. *Seventh Annual Report of the Controllers of the Public Schools of the First School District of the State of Pennsylvania; With Their Accounts* (Philadelphia: Printed by Order of the Board of Control, 1825), 6.

37. *Eighth Annual Report of the Controllers of the Public Schools of the First School District of the State of Pennsylvania; With Their Accounts* (Philadelphia: Printed by Order of the Board of Control, 1826), 6.

38. *Eleventh Annual Report of the Controllers of the Public Schools of the First School District of the State of Pennsylvania; With Their Accounts* (Philadelphia: Printed by Order of the Board of Control, 1829), 8.

39. James Ronaldson to Roberts Vaux, August 27, no year, box 5, folder 1: Correspondence n.d. O-R, VFP.

40. James Ronaldson to Roberts Vaux, December 10, no year, box 5, folder 1: Correspondence n.d. O-R, VFP.

41. R. A. Foakes, "'Thriving Prisoners': Coleridge, Wordsworth, and the Child at School," *Studies in Romanticism* 28, no. 2 (Summer 1989): 194. I am grateful to Dr. Campbell Scribner for this reference.

42. New York Free School Society Trustees Meeting Minutes, October 5, 1821, NYHS.

43. Lancaster, *British System of Education* (1810), 37.

44. *Manual of the System of Teaching Reading, Writing, Arithmetic, and Needle-Work, in the Elementary Schools of the British and Foreign School Society*, 1st American ed. (Philadelphia: Philadelphia Society for the Establishment and Support of Charity Schools, published by Benjamin Warner, printed by William Fry, 1817), 66. See also *Manual of the Lancasterian System of Teaching Reading, Writing, Arithmetic, and Needle-work, as Practised in the Schools of the Free-School Society of New-York* (New York: Free-School Society, Samuel Wood & Sons, 1820); William A. Tweed Dale, *Manual of the Albany Lancaster School; or, The System of Mutual Instruction Simplified, Improved and Adapted to the United States* (Albany, NY: Websters & Skinners, 1820); J. L. Rhees, *A Pocket Manual of the Lancasterian System of Education in Its Most Improved State: As Practised in the Model School, First School District, Pennsylvania* (Philadelphia: School District of Philadelphia, 1827).

45. James Jacklin, "Poem Read at Annual Examination," April 4, 1819, New York African Free School Records, vol. 3, NYHS.

46. Visitors' reports, February 21, 1827, New York African Free School Records, vol. 1: Regulations, By-laws and Reports, 1817–1832, NYHS.

47. Visitors' reports, March 16, 1827, and April 5, 1827, New York African Free School Records, vol. 1: Regulations, By-laws and Reports, 1817–1832, NYHS.

48. Visitors' reports, School Number Two, June 18, 1821, New York African Free School Records, vol. 2: Reports of the Visiting Committee, 1820–1831, NYHS.

49. "A Dialogue, Spoken by Jack Smith and William Hill at a public exam, 1822. Written for the occasion by C. C. A. [Charles Andrews] Teacher," New York African Free School Records, vol. 3, 46, NYHS; see also Anna Mae Duane, "'Like a Motherless Child': Racial Education at the New York African Free School and in *My Bondage and My Freedom*," *American Literature* 82, no. 3 (2010): 469–71.

50. "A Dialogue, Spoken by Jack Smith and William Hill at a public exam, 1822. Written for the occasion by C. C. A. [Charles Andrews] Teacher," New York African Free School Records, vol. 3, 47, NYHS.

51. New York Free School Society Trustees Meeting Minutes, January 2, 1818, NYHS; emphasis in the original.

52. New York Free School Society Trustees Meeting Minutes, November 6, 1818, NYHS.

53. The number of expulsions during this period can be gleaned from the minutes of the trustees of the (white) New York Free Schools and the (Black) African Free Schools. Between May 1817 and November 1822, six students were expelled from the white schools and nine from the Black ones. The enrollment records are not complete but suggestive. Enrollments varied, from 1,218 at the white schools in October 1817, to 1,151 in August 1818, to 1,250 in May 1819. At the Black schools, enrollment varied from 186 in July 1818 (before the second Black school was opened), to 425 in January 1822, to 414 in February 1822.

54. New York Free School Society Trustees Meeting Minutes, February 6, 1818, NYHS.

55. *Fifth Annual Report*, 4.

56. Visitors' reports, June 8, 1819, New York African Free School Records, vol. 1: Regulations, By-laws and Reports, 1817–1832, NYHS.

57. Visitors' reports, School Number Two, June 2, 1823, and June 18, 1824, New York African Free School Records, vol. 2: Reports of the Visiting Committee, 1820–1831, NYHS.

58. "City African Free Schools," *Freedom's Journal*, December 21, 1827, 3.

59. "School Meeting," *Freedom's Journal*, January 11, 1828, 2; on Cornish's background, see Michael Hines, "Learning Freedom: Education, Elevation, and New York's African-American Community, 1827–1829," *History of Education Quarterly* 56, no. 4 (November 2016): 627.

60. "School Meeting," *Freedom's Journal*, January 11, 1828, 2; "City Free Schools," *Freedom's Journal*, January 11, 1828, 3.

61. Visitors' reports, School Number Two, March 7, 1829, New York African Free School Records, vol. 2: Reports of the Visiting Committee, 1820–1831, NYHS. See also Visitors' reports, April 17, 1828, and November 11, 1828, New York African Free School Records, vol. 2: Reports of the Visiting Committee, 1820–1831, NYHS.

62. *A Sketch of the Origin and Progress of the Adelphi School in the Northern Liberties, Established under the Direction of the Philadelphia Association of Friends for the Instruction of Poor Children* (Philadelphia: Meyer & Jones, 1810), 17.

63. New York Free School Society Trustees Meeting Minutes, November 6, 1818, NYHS.

64. New York Free School Society Trustees Meeting Minutes, April 2, 1819, NYHS. This letter addressed white mothers; insulting the parenting skills of Black mothers was also an established tradition. See Anna Mae Duane, "'Like a Motherless Child,'" 467.

65. *Second Annual Report of the Controllers of the Public Schools of the First School District of the State of Pennsylvania; With Their Accounts. Also, an Abstract of the Law of March 6th, 1818, Providing for Public Education, and a List of the Controllers and Directors Elected for the Year 1820* (Philadelphia: Printed by Order of the Board of Control, 1820), 7.

66. *Third Annual Report*, 4.

67. *Sixteenth Annual Report*, n.p.; emphasis added.

68. Stanley K. Schultz, *The Culture Factory: Boston Public Schools, 1789–1860* (New York: Oxford University Press, 1973), 36.

69. *Fourth Annual Report of the Controllers of the Public Schools of the First School District of the State of Pennsylvania; With Their Accounts* (Philadelphia: Printed by Order of the Board of Control, 1822), 4.

70. *Eighth Annual Report*, 6; Robert Forster to John Sergeant, January 15, 1827, box 3, folder 3: Correspondence Jan–April 1827, VFP. On Houses of Refuge in the 1820s, see David J. Rothman, *The Discovery of the Asylum: Social Order and Disorder in the New Republic* (Boston: Little, Brown, 1971), 209–21.

71. *Eighth Annual Report*, 6.

72. *Fourth Annual Report*, 5.

73. *Eighth Annual Report*, 6.

74. *Eleventh Annual Report*, 8.

75. Jane E. Dabel, "Education's Unfulfilled Promise: The Politics of Schooling for African American Children in Nineteenth Century New York City," *Journal for the History of Children and Youth* 5, no. 2 (Spring 2012): 202.

76. Harris, *In the Shadow of Slavery*, 130.

77. *The Cries of New-York* (New York: S. Wood ["at the Juvenile Books-store"], 1808), 40.

78. *The Cries of Philadelphia: Ornamented with Elegant Wood Cuts* (Philadelphia: Johnson & Warner, 1810); *Cries of New-York*.

79. *Cries of New-York*, 22.

80. *Cries of New-York*, 22.

81. Robert Cornell, March 9, 1821, Visitors' reports, School Number Two, New York African Free School Records, vol. 2: Reports of the Visiting Committee, 1820–1831, NYHS.

82. Elizabeth Blackmar, *Manhattan for Rent, 1785–1850* (Ithaca, NY: Cornell University Press, 1989), 213–16.

83. Robert Hicks, April 30, 1821, Visitors' reports, School Number Two, New York African Free School Records, vol. 2: Reports of the Visiting Committee, 1820–1831, NYHS. See also Gilbert Hicks, May 2, 1823, Visitors' reports, School Number Two, New York African Free School Records, vol. 2: Reports of the Visiting Committee, 1820–1831, NYHS.

84. *Fourth Annual Report*, 6.

85. *Fifth Annual Report*, 6.

86. *Eighth Annual Report*, 6.

87. *Tenth Annual Report of the Controllers of the Public Schools of the First School District of the State of Pennsylvania; With Their Accounts* (Philadelphia: Printed by Order of the Board of Control, 1828), 8.

88. See Frederick Cooper, "Elevating the Race: The Social Thought of Black Leaders, 1827–50," *American Quarterly* 24, no. 5 (December 1972): 608, 611–13; Hilary J. Moss, *Schooling Citizens: The Struggle for African American Education in Antebellum America* (Chicago: University of Chicago Press, 2009), 29–31.

89. "Evening Schools," *Freedom's Journal*, November 23, 1827, 3.

90. Tunde Adeleke, "Afro-Americans and Moral Suasion: The Debate in the 1830's," *Journal of Negro History* 83 (Spring 1998): 128; Patrick Rael, *Black Identity and Black Protest*

in the Antebellum North (Chapel Hill: University of North Carolina Press, 2002), 119–20, 128–29, 143–46.

91. Philanthropos, "For the Freedom's Journal Education," *Freedom's Journal*, March 30, 1827, 2.

92. Amicus, "For the Freedom's Journal. Koxciusko School. No. II," *Freedom's Journal*, June 15, 1827, 3.

93. Matilda, "For the Freedom's Journal," *Freedom's Journal*, August 10, 1827, 2.

94. William Michael Weber, "Before Horace Mann: Elites and Boston Public Schools, 1800–1812" (EdD diss., Harvard University, 1974), 34, 50.

95. An Act for the Encouragement of Schools, Passed at the Eighteenth Session of the Legislature of the State of Newyork and of the Independence of the United States the Nineteenth 1795, 9. [Copy in the collections of the Library Company of Philadelphia.]

96. Harry S. Silcox, "Delay and Neglect: Negro Public Education in Antebellum Philadelphia, 1800–1860," *Pennsylvania Magazine of History and Biography* 97 (October 1973): 444.

97. Silcox, "Delay and Neglect," 449.

98. Kabria Baumgartner, *In Pursuit of Knowledge: Black Women and Educational Activism in Antebellum America* (New York: New York University Press, 2019), 223.

99. *Short History of the African Union Meeting and School-House, Erected in Providence (R.I.) in the Years 1819, '20, '21; with Rules for Its Future Government* (Providence, RI: Brown & Danforth, 1821), 5.

100. *Short History*, 10.

101. Lewis Woodson and William Dailey, "From the Genius of Universal Emancipation," *Freedom's Journal*, April 6, 1827, 1.

102. "Notice," *Freedom's Journal*, September 14, 1827, 4; "Notice," *Freedom's Journal*, October 5, 1827, 3; "African Infant Schools," *Freedom's Journal*, December 21, 1827, 3.

103. Gronningsater, "Practicing Formal Politics," 121–22.

104. "The Academy," *Freedom's Journal*, September 2, 1828, 5.

105. Visitors' reports, December 24, 1821, New York African Free School Records, vol. 1: Regulations, By-laws and Reports, 1817–1832, NYHS. As Margaret A. Nash has pointed out, at the time the word "ornamental" could mean "anything beyond basic literacy." See Margaret A. Nash, "'Cultivating the Powers of *Human Beings*': Gendered Perspectives on Curricula and Pedagogy in Academies of the New Republic," *History of Education Quarterly* 41, no. 2 (Summer 2001): 249–50.

106. Editors, "African Free Schools in the United States," *Freedom's Journal*, June 1, 1827, 3.

107. "The Academy," *Freedom's Journal*, October 17, 1828, 7.

108. "Education in Philadelphia," *Freedom's Journal*, October 10, 1828, 2.

109. Robert J. Swan, "John Teasman: African American Educator and the Emergence of Community in Early Black New York City, 1785–1815," *Journal of the Early Republic* 12 (Autumn 1992): 348.

110. Editors, "African Free Schools in the United States," *Freedom's Journal*, June 1, 1827, 3; emphasis in the original.

111. Rury, "Philanthropy, Self Help," 236–37.

112. Swan, "John Teasman," 349.

113. Rael, *Black Identity*, 125. See also Harris, *In the Shadow of Slavery*, 122–25.
114. Hines, "Learning Freedom," 625.
115. Editors, "African Free Schools in the United States," *Freedom's Journal*, May 18, 1827, 2–3.
116. Editors, "Propriety of Conduct," *Freedom's Journal*, July 20, 1827, 3[?].
117. Philanthropos, "Original Communications for the Freedom's Journal. Education. No. II," *Freedom's Journal*, April 6, 1827, 2.
118. Rael, *Black Identity*, 146–47.
119. Rev. Peter Williams, "Education," *Freedom's Journal*, June 13, 1828, 3.
120. Williams, "Education," 3.
121. "Coloured Free Schools," *Freedom's Journal*, September 12, 1828, 2.
122. Jane E. Dabel, *A Respectable Woman: The Public Roles of African American Women in 19th-Century New York* (New York: New York University Press, 2008), 48, 72.
123. Dabel, *Respectable Woman*, 44.
124. Dabel, *Respectable Woman*, 49.
125. Dabel, *Respectable Woman*, 45.
126. "Duties of Wives," *Freedom's Journal*, February 21, 1829, 367.
127. Warren Star, "Let Every Man Mind His Own Business," *Freedom's Journal*, August 3, 1827, 1.
128. Member, "Female Dorcas Society," *Freedom's Journal*, September 26, 1828, 6.
129. Rael, *Black Identity*; Paul J. Polgar, "'To Raise Them to an Equal Participation': Early National Abolitionism, Gradual Emancipation, and the Promise of African American Citizenship," *Journal of the Early Republic* 31, no. 2 (Summer 2011): 237.
130. Visitors' reports, School Number Two, Edmund Haviland, n.d. but in context, late July or early August 1829, New York African Free School Records, vol. 2: Reports of the Visiting Committee, 1820–1831, NYHS.
131. John L. Rury, "The New York African Free School, 1827–1836: Conflict over Community Control of Black Education," *Phylon* 44, no. 3 (1983): 192.
132. See Rael, *Black Identity*, 150–51; Polgar, "'To Raise Them,'" 229–58.
133. Hilary Moss, "Race and Schooling in Early Republican Philadelphia," in *The Great Contest: The Founding Fathers, Education, and the American Philosophical Society*, ed. Benjamin Justice (New York: Palgrave Macmillan, 2013), 105.
134. Boonshoft, "From Property to Education," 438–39.
135. Rury, "New York African Free School," 192.
136. "Communipaw" [James McCune Smith], *Frederick Douglass' Paper*, April 15, 1852, 3.
137. Carla L. Peterson, *Black Gotham: A Family History of African Americans in Nineteenth-Century New York City* (New Haven, CT: Yale University Press, 2011), 77.
138. Charles C. Andrews, *The History of the New-York African Free-Schools, From Their Establishment in 1787 to the Present Time* (New York: Mahlon Day, 1830), 30.
139. Peterson, *Black Gotham*, 4.
140. Peterson, *Black Gotham*, 5.
141. Andrews, *History*, 46.
142. Andrews, *History*, 45.
143. Dabel, *Respectable Woman*, 26.

144. George G. Foster, *New York by Gas-Light and Other Urban Sketches*, ed. Stuart M. Blumin (1850; repr., Berkeley: University of California Press, 1990), 101.

145. Foster, *New York by Gas-Light*, 100.

146. Dabel, *Respectable Woman*, 28.

147. Visitors' reports, School Number Two, January 11, 1822, March 12, 1824, June 19, 1826, April 5, 1827, New York African Free School Records, vol. 2: Reports of the Visiting Committee, 1820–1831, NYHS.

148. Rury, "New York African Free School," 192; Hines, "Learning Freedom," 637.

149. Peterson, *Black Gotham*, 78; Harris, *In the Shadow of Slavery*, 134, 142–43.

150. Rury, "New York African Free School," 193.

151. Rury, "New York African Free School," 196; Gronningsater, "Practicing Formal Politics," 122.

152. See, e.g., Mary H. Blewett, *Men, Women, and Work: Class, Gender, and Protest in the New England Shoe Industry, 1780–1910* (Champaign: University of Illinois Press, 1988); Alan Dawley, *Class and Community: The Industrial Revolution in Lynn*, 25th anniv. ed. (Cambridge, MA: Harvard University Press, 2000); Thomas L. Dublin, *Women at Work: The Transformation of Work and Community in Lowell, Massachusetts, 1826–1860* (New York: Columbia University Press, 1964); Bruce Laurie, *Artisans into Workers: Labor in Nineteenth-Century America* (Champaign: University of Illinois Press, 1997); David Montgomery, *Citizen Worker: The Experience of Workers in the United States with Democracy and the Free Market during the Nineteenth Century* (New York: Cambridge University Press, 1993); Christopher L. Tomlins, *Law, Labor, and Ideology in the Early Republic* (New York: Cambridge University Press, 1993); Wilentz, *Chants Democratic*.

153. "Address of the County Delegates to Their Constituents," *Mechanics Free Press*, September 27, 1828, 1.

154. T., letter to the editor, *Mechanics Free Press*, December 13, 1828, 2.

155. "A Well Educated Village Tends to Purify the Government under Which It Exists," *Mechanics Free Press*, December 27, 1828, 1.

156. "EDUCATION," *Mechanics Free Press*, November 21, 1829, 3.

157. R.D.O., "Cause of the People," *Mechanics Free Press*, September 26, 1829, 1.

158. Editors, "School Bill," *Mechanics Free Press*, February 28, 1829, 3.

159. "A Friend of Equality," letter to the editor, *Mechanics Free Press*, June 27, 1829, 2; emphasis in the original.

160. "Address," *Mechanics Free Press*, July 10, 1830, 1.

161. Joseph C. Hart, "Address," *Mechanics Free Press*, July 31, 1830, 2.

162. Joseph Lancaster, *The British System of Education Being a Complete Epitome of the Improvements and Inventions Practised at the Royal Free Schools, Borough-Road, Southwark* (Georgetown: William Cooper, 1812), 122.

163. *Manual of the System*, ix; emphasis in the original.

164. *Report of the Committee Appointed at a Meeting of the Several School Committees, and Other Citizens of Portsmouth, to Consider the Expediency of Introducing the Lancastrian System of Education, into This Town, and to Report Thereupon, at the Ensuing Annual Town Meeting* (Portsmouth, NH: S. Whidden, March 25, 1818), 6.

165. *Report of the Committee*, 10.

166. Boonshoft, *Aristocratic Education*, 153.
167. Paul, "On the Proposed System of State Education, Addressed to the General Committee of Working Men, of the City and County of Philadelphia," *Mechanics Free Press*, October 3, 1829, 1.
168. "Working Men," *Mechanics Free Press*, October 10, 1829, 2.
169. "Address," *Mechanics Free Press*, July 10, 1830, 1.
170. "Address of the County Delegates," 1.
171. Paul, "On the Proposed System," 1.
172. Paul, "On the Proposed System," 1.
173. Mallet, "Republican Education," *Mechanics Free Press*, October 3, 1829, 2.
174. "Public Education, Essay III," *Mechanics Free Press*, May 1, 1830, 1.
175. Yorick, "Loose Thoughts—No. II," *Mechanics Free Press*, November 21, 1829, 2.
176. Paul, "On the Proposed System," 1.

Chapter 7. Public School Society

1. Anonymous "Friend of Lancaster" to Joseph Lancaster, August 26, 1818, box 3, folder 1, Lancaster Papers, American Antiquarian Society, Worcester, Massachusetts (hereafter cited as "LP"); emphasis in the original.

2. *On the Establishment of Public Schools in the City of New-York* (New York: Mahlon Day, 1825), 4.

3. Kim Tolley, "Music Teachers in the North Carolina Education Market, 1800–1840: How Mrs. Sambourne Earned a Comfortable Living for Herself and Her Children," *Social Science History* 32, no. 1 (Spring 2008): 76.

4. W. Thompson to Joseph Lancaster, March 15, 1824, box 3, folder 2, LP.

5. William J. Reese, *Testing Wars in the Public Schools: A Forgotten History* (Cambridge, MA: Harvard University Press, 2013), 41; Kim Tolley and Nancy Beadie, "Socioeconomic Incentives to Teach in New York and North Carolina: Toward a More Complex Model of Teacher Labor Markets, 1800–1850," *History of Education Quarterly* 46 (2006): 36–72; Carl F. Kaestle, *The Evolution of an Urban School System: New York City, 1750–1850* (Cambridge, MA: Harvard University Press, 1973), 37–41. As Kaestle found, teachers in New York City had a range of earnings in the years before the Lancasterian revolution. At the bottom were teachers such as Daniel Smith, who claimed an income of £46 in 1795–96. At the top were teachers such as Stanton Latham and Donald Fraser, who reported in 1796 annual incomes of £200 and £208, respectively. Kaestle uncovered the reported earnings of eighteen teachers in the city that year, with an average annual income of £122. That average, according to Kaestle, was roughly comparable to what a skilled craftsperson would earn at the time, but teachers also often received additional compensation in the form of fuel, food, and lodging. Avaricious and confident young people like Joseph Lancaster likely set their sights on the top of the scale, dreaming of salaries much higher than the average, a life of comfort and surplus.

6. Notebook, box 4, vol. "First Folio," LP.

7. Robert and Henry Ould to Joseph Lancaster, April 23, 1812, box 1, folder 1, LP.

8. Joseph Lancaster to Elizabeth (Betsy) Lancaster, September 27, 1819, box 2, folder 3, LP. Lancaster sometimes referred to both his wife Elizabeth and daughter Elizabeth as

"Eliza," or "Eliza.," and sometimes he called his daughter "Betsy." For clarity's sake, these notes will call the mother Elizabeth and the daughter Betsy.

9. Joseph Lancaster to Betsy Lancaster, June 10, 1819, box 2, folder 3, LP; emphasis in the original.

10. Joseph Lancaster to Betsy Lancaster, July 14, 1819, box 2, folder 3, LP; emphasis in the original.

11. Joseph Lancaster to Betsy Lancaster, July 26, 1819, box 2, folder 3, LP.

12. See, e.g., Joseph Lancaster to Betsy Lancaster, July 19, 1819, box 2, folder 3, LP. He repeated this fantastical figure throughout the summer of 1819 in his correspondence with his daughter.

13. Joseph J. McCadden, "Joseph Lancaster and the Philadelphia Schools," *Pennsylvania History* 3, no. 4 (October 1936): 229; Joseph Lancaster to Roberts Vaux, January 22, 1822, box 2, folder 10: Roberts Vaux Correspondence Jan–Mar 1822, Vaux Family Papers, 1739–1923, Collection 684, Historical Society of Pennsylvania, Philadelphia (hereafter cited as "VFP"); New York Free School Society Trustees Meeting Minutes, May 5, 1817, New-York Historical Society, New York, New York (hereafter cited as "NYHS").

14. Joseph Lancaster to Roberts Vaux, April 9, 1821, box 2, folder 8: Roberts Vaux Correspondence Jan–April 1821, VFP.

15. Joseph Lancaster to Betsy Lancaster, September 18, 1819, box 163, folder 16: Lancaster, Joseph (1819), Lancaster Papers, Gratz Collection, Historical Society of Pennsylvania, Philadelphia (hereafter cited as "GC"); emphasis in the original.

16. Joseph Lancaster to Elizabeth Lancaster, September 3, 1818, box 2, folder 3, LP.

17. Joseph Lancaster to Betsy Lancaster, January 16, 1819, box 2, folder 3, LP; Joseph Lancaster to Betsy Lancaster, June 21, 1819, box 2, folder 3, LP.

18. Edward Flavin Wall Jr., "Joseph Lancaster and the Origins of the British and Foreign School Society" (PhD diss., Columbia University, 1966), 197; John E. Lovell to Joseph Lancaster, December 27, 1819, box 2, folder 7, LP; John E. Lovell to Joseph Lancaster, February 1, 1820, box 2, folder 3, LP; Richard M. Jones to Joseph Lancaster, February 4, 1820, box 2, folder 5, LP; Joseph Lancaster to Betsy Lancaster, February 23, 1820, box 2, folder 7, LP.

19. Websters and Skinners to Joseph Lancaster, February 23, 1819, box 3, folder 1, LP; Isaac T. Hopper to Joseph Lancaster, February 4, 1820, box 3, folder 1, LP; Thomas Dobsonthon to Joseph Lancaster, December 27, 1820, box 3, folder 1, LP.

20. Betsy Lancaster to Joseph Lancaster, July 21, 1819, box 163, folder 15: Lancaster, Joseph, GC.

21. John E. Lovell to Joseph Lancaster, September 24, 1819, box 2, folder 7, LP.

22. Joseph Lancaster to Betsy Lancaster, February 23, 1820, box 2, folder 3, LP.

23. A. L. Boggs to Joseph Lancaster, February 6, 1822, box 3, folder 1, LP.

24. William Gwynn to Joseph Lancaster, February 5, 1822, box 3, folder 1, LP.

25. See, e.g., Isaac Hopper to Joseph Lancaster, March 4, 1820, box 3, folder 1, LP. Hopper was a clothing merchant in Philadelphia to whom Lancaster owed money. In this letter, Hopper notes that Lancaster sent him a partial payment, so Hopper agreed to "stay proceedings" against Lancaster in court. But Hopper still demanded immediate repayment of the full debt.

26. Thomas Dobsonthon to Joseph Lancaster, December 27, 1821, box 3, folder 1, LP.

27. John Lambert to Joseph Lancaster, September 30, 1818, box 3, folder 1, LP.

28. Betsy Lancaster to Joseph Lancaster, July 21, 1819, box 163, folder 15: Lancaster, Joseph, GC.

29. Betsy Lancaster to Joseph Lancaster, June 21, 1819, box 163, folder 15: Lancaster, Joseph, GC.

30. Betsy Lancaster to Joseph Lancaster, July 21, 1819, box 163, folder 15: Lancaster, Joseph, GC.

31. John E. Lovell to Joseph Lancaster, September 24, 1819, box 2, folder 7, LP.

32. John E. Lovell to Joseph Lancaster, September 24, 1819, box 2, folder 7, LP; John E. Lovell to Joseph Lancaster, October 28, 1819, box 2, folder 7, LP.

33. John E. Lovell to Joseph Lancaster, September 24, 1819, box 2, folder 7, LP.

34. John E. Lovell to Joseph Lancaster, February 1, 1820, box 2, folder 7, LP.

35. John E. Lovell to Joseph Lancaster, August 15, 1820, box 2, folder 7, LP.

36. John E. Lovell to Joseph Lancaster, August 22, 1820, box 2, folder 7, LP.

37. John E. Lovell to Joseph Lancaster, December 27, 1819, box 2, folder 7, LP.

38. Betsy Lancaster to Joseph Lancaster, June 21, 1819, box 3, folder 1, LP.

39. Joseph Lancaster to Betsy Lancaster, July 18, 1819, box 2, folder 3, LP; emphasis in the original.

40. John E. Lovell to Joseph Lancaster, December 19, 1822, box 2, folder 7, LP.

41. Circular letter, "Distress of Joseph Lancaster," 1818[?; year written in pencil on manuscript], box 15, folder 10, LP.

42. Joseph Lancaster to Betsy Lancaster, January 23, 1819, box 2, folder 3, LP.

43. "Sir Thomas Barnard's Reports of Joseph Lancaster's domestic affliction," manuscript, n.d. but likely 1830 or 1831, box 15, folder 5, LP.

44. "Sir Thomas Barnard's Reports of Joseph Lancaster's domestic affliction," manuscript, n.d. but likely 1830 or 1831, box 15, folder 5, LP.

45. "Sir Thomas Barnard's Reports of Joseph Lancaster's domestic affliction," manuscript, n.d. but likely 1830 or 1831, box 15, folder 5, LP.

46. "Sir Thomas Barnard's Reports of Joseph Lancaster's domestic affliction," manuscript, n.d. but likely 1830 or 1831, box 15, folder 5, LP.

47. John E. Lovell to Joseph Lancaster, December 27, 1819, box 2, folder 7, LP.

48. Joseph Lancaster to Betsy Lancaster, August 24, 1819, box 2, folder 3, LP.

49. Joseph Lancaster to Elizabeth Lancaster, February 17, 1820, box 2, folder 3, LP.

50. Elizabeth Lancaster to Joseph Lancaster, 1820, box 163, folder 17: Lancaster, Joseph (1820), GC.

51. Joseph Lancaster to Betsy Lancaster, July 10, 1819, box 2, folder 3, LP.

52. Richard M. Jones to Joseph Lancaster, February 4, 1820, box 2, folder 5, LP; emphasis in the original.

53. New York Free School Society Trustees Meeting Minutes, January 15, 1819, NYHS.

54. Elizabeth Hamilton, *Hints Addressed to the Patrons and Directors of Schools; Principally Intended to Shew, That the Benefits Derived from the New Modes of Teaching May Be Increased by a Partial Adoption of the Plan of Pestalozzi* (London: Longman, Hurst, Rees, Orme, & Brown, 1815), 32.

55. Hamilton, *Hints Addressed*, 33.

56. Edward Baker, *A Brief Sketch of the Lancasterian System, Intended as a Companion in Visiting a Lancasterian School, with Advice to Committees on the Establishment, Management and Examination of Such Schools* (Troy, NY: F. Adancourt, 1816), front matter.

57. Baker, *Brief Sketch*, 24.

58. Deblieux to Joseph Lancaster, December 24, 1818, box 3, folder 1, LP.

59. Joseph Lancaster, *Letters on National Subjects, Auxiliary to Universal Education, and Scientific Knowledge; Addressed to Burwell Bassett, Late a Member of the House of Representatives; Henry Clay, Speaker of the House of Representatives, and James Monroe, President of the United States of America* (Washington City: Jacob Gideon Jr., 1820), 49.

60. Joseph Lancaster, *True Friend* 1, no. 1 (July 1829): 1.

61. Visitors' reports, July 28, 1818, New York African Free School Records, vol. 1: Regulations, By-laws and Reports, 1817–1832.

62. New York Free School Society Trustees Meeting Minutes, March 25, 1819, NYHS.

63. *First Annual Report of the Controllers of the Public Schools of the First School District of the State of Pennsylvania; With Their Accounts. Also, an Abstract of the Law of March 6th, 1818, Providing for Public Education, and a List of the Controllers and Directors Constituted under the Act, &c., &c.* (Philadelphia: Printed by Order of the Board of Control, 1819), 6.

64. *Second Annual Report of the Controllers of the Public Schools of the First School District of the State of Pennsylvania; With Their Accounts. Also, an Abstract of the Law of March 6th, 1818, Providing for Public Education, and a List of the Controllers and Directors Elected for the Year 1820* (Philadelphia: Printed by Order of the Board of Control, 1820), 5.

65. *Fifth Annual Report of the Controllers of the Public Schools of the First School District of the State of Pennsylvania; With Their Accounts* (Philadelphia: Printed by Order of the Board of Control, 1823), 8.

66. Timothy Dwight to Joseph Lancaster, May 30, 1822, box 3, folder 1, LP.

67. Timothy Dwight to Joseph Lancaster, November 12, 1827, box 3, folder 3, LP; Timothy Dwight to Joseph Lancaster, May 13, 1828, box 3, folder 3, LP; Aldis S. Allen to Joseph Lancaster, June 3, 1828, box 3, folder 3, LP; Aldis S. Allen to Joseph Lancaster, January 17, 1830, box 3, folder 3, LP; John E. Lovell to Joseph Lancaster, April 24, 1829, box 2, folder 7, LP; John E. Lovell to Joseph Lancaster, January 23, 1831, box 2, folder 7, LP.

68. John E. Lovell to C. J. Gayler, October 30, 1838, box 2, folder 7, LP.

69. John E. Lovell to Joseph Lancaster, December 2, 1822, box 2, folder 7, LP.

70. John E. Lovell to Joseph Lancaster, February 14, 1823, box 2, folder 7, LP.

71. John E. Lovell to Joseph Lancaster, January 21, 1823, box 2, folder 7, LP.

72. John E. Lovell to Joseph Lancaster, July 18, 1824, box 2, folder 7, LP.

73. John E. Lovell to Joseph Lancaster, November 20, 1827, box 2, folder 7, LP.

74. John E. Lovell to Joseph Lancaster, November 20, 1827, box 2, folder 7, LP; emphasis in the original.

75. John E. Lovell to Joseph Lancaster, May 28, 1826, box 2, folder 7, LP.

76. "New Year, 1833," box 1, folder: Lectures, 1833, William Bentley Fowle Papers, Massachusetts Historical Society, Boston, Massachusetts (hereafter cited as "WBFP"); "Announcement," box 4, folder: 1821–1825, WBFP.

77. "Address delivered in Feb. 1824," box 1, folder: Lectures, 1824, WBFP.

78. "Address delivered May 1824," box 1, folder: Lectures, 1824, WBFP.

79. "Address delivered May 1824," box 1, folder: Lectures, 1824, WBFP.
80. *Second Report of the Instructer of the Monitorial School, Boston* (Boston: Munroe & Francis, 1828), 16.
81. "Address delivered in Feb. 1824," box 1, folder: Lectures, 1824, WBFP.
82. *First Biennial Report of the Trustees and Instructer of the Monitorial School, Boston* (Boston: Thomas B. Wait & Son, 1826), 15–16.
83. Undated address, box 2, folder: Undated Letter Drafts, WBFP.
84. Carla L. Peterson, *Black Gotham: A Family History of African Americans in Nineteenth-Century New York City* (New Haven, CT: Yale University Press, 2011), 77.
85. *Report of the Committee Appointed at a Meeting of the Several School Committees, and Other Citizens of Portsmouth, to Consider the Expediency of Introducing the Lancastrian System of Education, into This Town, and to Report Thereupon, at the Ensuing Annual Town Meeting* (Portsmouth, NH: S. Whidden, March 25, 1818), 18.
86. William J. Reese, *The Origins of the American High School* (New Haven, CT: Yale University Press, 1995), 19.
87. *Report of a Committee Appointed by the High School Society of New-York, to Prepare a Plan of Instruction to Be Pursued in the High School* (New York: J. Seymour, 1824), 4.
88. William Russell, *Manual of Mutual Instruction; Consisting of Mr. Fowle's Directions for Introducing in Common Schools the Improved System Adopted in the Monitorial School, Boston. With an Appendix, Containing Some Consideration in Favor of the Monitorial Method, and a Sketch of Its Progress, Embracing a View of Its Adaptation to Instruction in Academies, Preparatory Seminaries, and Colleges* (Boston: Wait, Greene, 1826), 107.
89. *First Annual Report of the Trustees of the High-School Society. In the City of New-York* (New York: Mahlon Day, 1825), 4.
90. *First Annual Report of the Trustees*, 6.
91. *First Annual Report of the Trustees*, 7.
92. Mann Butler, *Report on Monitorial Education; to the Hon. Mayor and Council, of Louisville* (Louisville, KY: S. Penn Jr., 1829), 8.
93. *Annual Report of the Trustees of the High School Society of New-York, Made on Monday, November 13, 1826. Pursuant to the Act of Incorporation* (New York: William A. Mercein, 1826), 7.
94. Joseph Lancaster, *Improvements in Education, as It Respects the Industrious Classes of the Community: Containing, among Other Important Particulars, an Account of the Institution for the Education of One Thousand Poor Children, Borough Road, Southwark; and of the New System of Education on Which It Is Conducted*, 3rd ed. (New York: Collins & Perkins, 1807).
95. New York Free School Society Trustees Meeting Minutes, February 2, 1821, NYHS.
96. Stephen Marbrouch[?] to committee on monitors, May 29, 1827, box 1, folder: "Letters related to teachers," New York Free School Society Papers, New-York Historical Society, New York, New York (hereafter cited as "FSSP").
97. Paybill for "African Section NO. 1," February 22, 1836, box 3, folder: Hester Miller Teacher; Public School Society: Teachers and Monitors Bills, May, Nov 1835–Jan 1836, MS 500, FSSP.
98. Paybill for January 31, 1836, box 3, folder: Hester Miller Teacher; Public School Society: Teachers and Monitors Bills, May, Nov 1835–Jan 1836, MS 500, FSSP.

99. Paybill for January 31, 1836, box 3, folder: Hester Miller Teacher; Public School Society: Teachers and Monitors Bills, May, Nov 1835–Jan 1836, MS 500, FSSP.

100. Paybill for October 31, 1840, box 6, folder: "Coloured Schools," FSSP.

101. *Tenth Annual Report of the Controllers of the Public Schools of the First School District of the State of Pennsylvania; With Their Accounts* (Philadelphia: Printed by Order of the Board of Control, 1828), 7.

102. *Nineteenth Annual Report of the Controllers of the Public Schools for the City and County of Philadelphia, Composing the First School District of the State of Pennsylvania; With Their Accounts* (Philadelphia: Printed by Order of the Board of Control, 1837), 7.

103. Carl F. Kaestle, *Pillars of the Republic: Common Schools and American Society, 1780–1860* (New York: Hill & Wang, 1983), 56–61.

104. Nancy Beadie, "Education and the Creation of Capital: Or What I Have Learned from Following the Money," *History of Education Quarterly* 48, no. 1 (February 2008): 8.

105. *Report of the Committee on Education of the House of Representatives of Kentucky, on So Much of the Governor's Message as Relates to Schools and Seminaries of Learning* (Lexington, KY: Joseph G. Norwood, 1830), 11.

106. *An Act for the Encouragement of Schools, Passed at the Eighteenth Session of the Legislature of the State of Newyork and of the Independence of the United States the Nineteenth 1795*. [MS copy in the collections of the Library Company of Philadelphia.]

107. Kaestle, *Evolution of an Urban School System*, 65–71, 86.

108. *An Account of the Free-School Society of New-York* (New York: Collins, 1814), 9.

109. New York Free School Society Trustees Meeting Minutes, March 13, 1822, NYHS.

110. New York Free School Society Trustees Meeting Minutes, March 18, 1822, NYHS.

111. *Report of the Committee on Education Read in the Senate, January 18, 1828* (Harrisburg, PA: S. C. Stambaugh, 1828), 4.

112. *Report of the Committee on Education. Read in the House of Representatives, January 27, 1831* (Harrisburg, PA: Henry Welsh, 1831), 7–8.

113. Butler, *Report on Monitorial Education*, 6.

114. *An Account of the Louisville City School, Together with the Ordinances of the City Council, and the Regulations of the Board of Trustees for the Government of the Institution* (Louisville, KY: Norwood & Palmer, 1830), 5.

115. *Report of the Committee on Education* (1830), 4.

116. *Report of the Committee on Education* (1830), 7.

117. Act Incorporating the Free School Society, April 9, 1805, in New York Free School Society Trustees Meeting Minutes, front cover, NYHS.

118. De Witt Clinton, *An Address, to the Benefactors and Friends of the Free School Society of New York, Delivered on the Opening of That Institution, in Their New and Spacious Building, on the Eleventh of the Twelfth Month (December) 1809* (New York: Collins & Perkins, 1810), 14.

119. *Manual of the System of Teaching Reading, Writing, Arithmetic, and Needle-Work, in the Elementary Schools of the British and Foreign School Society*, 1st American ed. (Philadelphia: Philadelphia Society for the Establishment and Support of Charity Schools, published by Benjamin Warner, printed by William Fry, 1817), B.

120. *Manual of the System*, X.

121. *Account of the Free-School Society*, 8.
122. *An Act to Provide for the Education of Children at Public Expense within the City and County of Philadelphia* (Harrisburg, PA: s.n., 1818), 8. [Copy at the Historical Society of Pennsylvania, Philadelphia.]
123. *Report of a Committee Appointed*, 4.
124. *Twentieth Annual Report of the Trustees of the Free-School Society of New-York* (New York: Samuel Wood & Sons, 1825), 7.
125. *A Sketch of the Origin and Progress of the Adelphi School in the Northern Liberties, Established under the Direction of the Philadelphia Association of Friends for the Instruction of Poor Children* (Philadelphia: Meyer & Jones, 1810), 11.
126. Elisha Wales to Joseph Lancaster, March 8, 1821, box 3, folder 1, LP.
127. Joseph Lancaster, "Proposals for Lancasterian Schools in Boston," n.d. [broadside in the collections of the American Antiquarian Society, Worcester, Massachusetts].
128. J. L. Williams to Joseph Lancaster, November 15, 1822, box 3, folder 1, LP.
129. *Act for the Encouragement of Schools*; Kaestle, *Evolution of an Urban School System*, 65–71.
130. New York Free School Society Trustees Meeting Minutes, February 2, 1822, NYHS.
131. New York Free School Society Trustees Meeting Minutes, March 1, 1822, NYHS.
132. James Ronaldson to Roberts Vaux, August 27, no year, box 5, folder 1: Correspondence n.d. O-R, VFP.
133. New York Free School Society Trustees Meeting Minutes, April 2, 1819, NYHS.
134. *Nineteenth Annual Report of the Trustees of the Free-School Society of New York; With an Appendix: Containing, Memorials and Certificates relative to the School Fund Law, and to the Bethel Baptist Schools, &c. &c.* (New York: Samuel Wood & Sons, 1824), 3.
135. *On the Establishment of Public Schools*, 4.
136. *On the Establishment of Public Schools*, 3.
137. *On the Establishment of Public Schools*, 5.
138. *On the Establishment of Public Schools*, 9.
139. Kaestle, *Evolution of an Urban School System*, 87.
140. Kaestle, *Evolution of an Urban School System*, 88.
141. Kaestle, *Evolution of an Urban School System*, 88.
142. William Oland Bourne, *History of the Public School Society of the City of New York: With Portraits of the Presidents of the Society* (New York: W. Wood, 1870), 150.
143. *Report of the Committee on Education* (1828), 4.
144. *Report of the Committee on Education* (1831), 5.
145. *Report of the Committee on Education* (1831), 6.
146. See, e.g., David Hogan, "The Market Revolution and Disciplinary Power: Joseph Lancaster and the Psychology of the Early Classroom System," *History of Education Quarterly* 29, no. 3 (Autumn 1989): 386–88.

Chapter 8. The Next Big Thing

1. *Report of the Committee on Education, on So Much of the Governor's Message as Relates to the School Fund* (n.p., March 5, 1835), 8. On the antebellum reformers' fascination with the "Prussian model," see also Carl F. Kaestle, *Pillars of the Republic: Common Schools and*

American Society, 1780–1860 (New York: Hill & Wang, 1983), 73; Jonathan Messerli, *Horace Mann: A Biography* (New York: Knopf, 1972), 392–407; David Komline, *The Common School Awakening: Religion and the Transatlantic Roots of American Public Education* (New York: Oxford University Press, 2020), 102–21.

2. J. P. Lalsey to Joseph Lancaster, October 19, 1838, box 13, folder 8, Lancaster Papers, American Antiquarian Society, Worcester, Massachusetts (hereafter cited as "LP").

3. John W. Francis, *Old New York, or, Reminiscences of the Past Sixty Years* (New York: W. J. Widdleton, 1866), 187.

4. Robert K. Lowry to Joseph Lancaster, February 27, 1824, box 3, folder 2, LP.

5. For more about Lancaster and Lancasterian education in South America, see Karen Racine, "Monitors and Moralists: The Lancasterian System of Mutual Education and the Vision of a New Moral Order in Spanish America, 1818–1831," *History of Education* 49, no. 2 (2020): 143–59; Marcelo Caruso and Eugenia Roldan Vera, "Pluralizing Meanings: The Monitorial System of Education in Latin America in the Early Nineteenth Century," *Paedagogica Historica* 41, no. 6 (December 2005): 645–56; Marcelo Caruso, "The Persistence of Educational Semantics: Patterns of Variation in Monitorial Schooling in Colombia (1821–1844)," *Paedagogica Historica* 41, no. 6 (December 2005): 721–44; Eudenia Roldan Vera, "Order in the Classroom: The Spanish American Appropriation of the Monitorial System of Education," *Paedagogica Historica* 41, no. 6 (December 2005): 655–75. See also Everett Figueroa Peralta, "The English Legacy of Joseph Lancaster to the Mexican Philosophy of Education: 1825 to 1925" (EdD diss., Arizona State University, 2005).

6. Notice, September 19, 1825, box 163, folder 18: Lancaster, Joseph, Lancaster Papers, Gratz Collection, Historical Society of Pennsylvania, Philadelphia (hereafter cited as "GC").

7. Joseph Lancaster to Simon Bolivar, February 7, 1826, box 13, folder 7, LP.

8. Mora Dickson, *Teacher Extraordinary: Joseph Lancaster, 1778–1838* (Sussex, UK: Book Guild Limited, 1986), 226.

9. Racine, "Monitors and Moralists," 155.

10. Peralta, "English Legacy of Joseph Lancaster," 52.

11. Vera, "Order in the Classroom," 655.

12. Peralta, "English Legacy of Joseph Lancaster," 54.

13. Dickson, *Teacher Extraordinary*, 230.

14. Richard M. Jones to Joseph Lancaster, March 14, 1827, box 2, folder 4, LP.

15. Dickson, *Teacher Extraordinary*, 235–36.

16. Caruso and Vera, "Pluralizing Meanings," 651.

17. Racine, "Monitors and Moralists," 147–48.

18. British and Foreign School Society, *Proceedings of the British and Foreign School Society* (London: n.p., 1819), 2–3.

19. British and Foreign School Society, *Proceedings at the Nineteenth Anniversary Meeting of the British and Foreign School Society held at Freemasons' Tavern* (London: Richard Taylor, 1824), 4.

20. British and Foreign School Society, *Proceedings at the Nineteenth Anniversary Meeting*, 4.

21. "Original Communications," *Freedom's Journal*, October 12, 1827, 2; clipping from *Morning Palladium*, December 24, 1833, box 13, folder 8, LP; Ladies' Society for Promoting

the Early Education and Improvement of the Children of Negroes and of People of Color in the British West Indies, *The First Annual Report of the Ladies' Society for Promoting the Early Education and Improvement of the Children of Negroes and of People of Color in the British West Indies, with a List of Subscribers* (London: W. Marchant, 1826), 19; "Moral Improvement in the West Indies," *Freedom's Journal*, January 31, 1829, 1–2.

22. John Griscom, *Monitorial Instruction. Address, Pronounced at the Opening of the New-York High-School, with Notes and Illustrations* (New York: Mahlon Day, 1825), 34.

23. British and Foreign School Society, *Proceedings at the Nineteenth Anniversary Meeting*, 4.

24. Caruso and Vera, "Pluralizing Meanings," 651; Caruso, "Persistence of Educational Semantics," 722.

25. Bruce Curtis, "Joseph Lancaster in Montreal (bis): Monitorial Schooling and Politics in a Colonial Context," *Historical Studies in Education* 17, no. 1 (Spring 2005): 6.

26. British and Foreign School Society, *Nineteenth Report of the British and Foreign School Society, to the General Meeting, May 10, 1824* (London, Richard Taylor, 1824), 27.

27. Brooke Young to Joseph Lancaster, August 20, 1825, box 3, folder 2, LP.

28. Sarah Lancaster to Joseph Lancaster, August 2, 1825, box 163, folder 18: Lancaster, Joseph, GC.

29. Laura Michel, "Joseph Lancaster, Philanthropy, and Reform" (paper presented at the History of Education Society Annual Meeting, Columbus, Ohio, November 2, 2019), 6.

30. Caruso, "Persistence of Educational Semantics," 725.

31. Don Bernardo Monteagudo, *Peruvian Pamphlet; Being an Exposition of the Administrative Labours of the Peruvian Government, from the Time of Its Formation, till the 15th of July, 1822; Presented to the Council by the Minister of State and Foreign Relations* (London: A. Applegath, 1823), 86.

32. R. Ackermann to Joseph Lancaster, November 3, 1825, box 3, folder 2, LP; S. C. Powles to Joseph Lancaster, December 24, 1825, box 3, folder 2, LP; R. Ackermann to Joseph Lancaster, February 11, 1826, box 3, folder 2, LP; R. Ackermann to Joseph Lancaster, October 4, 1826, box 3, folder 2, LP.

33. Joseph Lancaster to King George IV, February 5, 1825, box 163, folder 18: Lancaster, Joseph, GC; emphasis in the original.

34. Joseph Lancaster to Roberts Vaux, July 11, 1827, box 3, folder 5: Roberts Vaux Correspondence July–Dec 1827, Vaux Family Papers, 1739–1923, Collection 684, Historical Society of Pennsylvania, Philadelphia (hereafter cited as "VFP"); see also Roberts Vaux to Joseph Lancaster, June 12, 1827, box 3, folder 3, LP.

35. Joseph Lancaster to Roberts Vaux, October 2, 1827, box 3, folder 5: Correspondence July–Dec 1827, VFP.

36. Joseph Lancaster to Martin Van Buren, February 25, 1828, box 163, folder 21: Lancaster, Joseph, GC.

37. Joseph Lancaster to Andrew Jackson, 1829, box 163, folder 22: Lancaster, Joseph, GC.

38. John Townsend to Joseph Lancaster, April 21, 1829, box 3, folder 3, LP.

39. James Brewster to Joseph Lancaster, July 8, 1829, box 3, folder 3, LP.

40. For the story of Lancaster's time in Montreal, see Curtis, "Joseph Lancaster in Montreal," 1–27.

41. *Lancasterian Institute, Haines' Street, in North Sixth Street, between Arch and Race, Philadelphia* (1837). [Flyer in the collection of the Library Company of Philadelphia.]

42. *Report of Progress of the Improvements Made in the Lancasterian Institute, in Haines Street, Near North Sixth Street, between Cherry and Race Streets* (Philadelphia: n.p., August 20, 1836). [Flyer in the collection of the Library Company of Philadelphia.]

43. *Report of Progress.*

44. Joseph Lancaster to Roberts Vaux, October 18, 1834, box 4, folder 10: Correspondence Oct–Dec 1834, VFP.

45. Roberts Vaux to Joseph Lancaster, October 21, 1834, box 3, folder 3, LP.

46. Joseph Lancaster to Roberts Vaux, March 20, 1835, box 4, folder 12: Correspondence May–June 1835, VFP.

47. Quoted in Carl F. Kaestle, *The Evolution of an Urban School System: New York City, 1750–1850* (Cambridge, MA: Harvard University Press, 1973), 115.

48. Timothy J. Gilfoyle, *A Pickpocket's Tale: The Underworld of Nineteenth-Century New York* (New York: Norton, 2006), 23.

49. Gilfoyle, *Pickpocket's Tale*, 25.

50. Thomas Bender, *Toward an Urban Vision: Ideas and Institutions in Nineteenth-Century America* (Lexington: University Press of Kentucky, 1975), 120.

51. Bender, *Toward an Urban Vision*, 124.

52. Bender, *Toward an Urban Vision*, 119.

53. Bender, *Toward an Urban Vision*, 124.

54. Benjamin C. Bacon, *Colored School Statistics* (Philadelphia: Board of Education, 1853), 1.

55. Bacon, *Colored School Statistics*, 4.

56. Quoted in Kaestle, *Evolution of an Urban School System*, 119.

57. Kaestle, *Evolution of an Urban School System*, 120.

58. *An Account of the Louisville City School, Together with the Ordinances of the City Council, and the Regulations of the Board of Trustees for the Government of the Institution* (Louisville, KY: Norwood & Palmer, 1830), 5.

59. *Account of the Louisville City School*, 6.

60. *Report of the Committee on Education of the House of Representatives of Kentucky, on So Much of the Governor's Message as Relates to Schools and Seminaries of Learning* (Lexington, KY: Joseph G. Norwood, 1830), 10.

61. Heman Howlett and James G. Guthrie to Joseph Lancaster, January 24, 1837, box 13, folder 8, LP.

62. Kaestle, *Evolution of an Urban School System*, 88.

63. Nancy Beadie, "Tuition Funding for Common Schools: Education Markets and Market Regulation in Rural New York, 1815–1850," *Social Science History* 32, no. 1 (Spring 2008): 108–9.

64. Kaestle, *Pillars of the Republic*, 149–51.

65. Horace Mann, "Seventh Annual Report (1843)," in *Life and Works of Horace Mann* (Boston: Lee & Shepard, 1891), 3:279.

66. Washington Association for the Education of Free Colored Youth, *Normal School for Colored Girls, Washington, D.C.* (Washington, DC: n.p., 1857), 3.

67. Franklin Davenport Edmunds, *The Public School Buildings of the City of Philadelphia from 1745 to 1845* (Philadelphia: self-pub., 1913), 53.

68. Rachel Regina Remmel, "The Origins of the American School Building: Boston Public School Architecture, 1800–1860" (PhD diss., University of Chicago, 2006), xiii.

69. William J. Reese, *Testing Wars in the Public Schools: A Forgotten History* (Cambridge, MA: Harvard University Press, 2013), 147.

70. John L. Rury, "The New York African Free School, 1827–1836: Conflict over Community Control of Black Education," *Phylon* 44, no. 3 (1983): 196.

71. Paybill for January 31, 1836, box 3, folder: Hester Miller Teacher; Public School Society: Teachers and Monitors Bills, May, Nov 1835–Jan 1836, MS 500, New York Free School Society Papers, New-York Historical Society, New York, New York.

72. Joseph Lancaster to Roberts Vaux, November 30, 1819, box 2, folder 1: Correspondence Jan–Feb 1819, VFP.

73. Tina H. Sheller, "The Origins of Public Education in Baltimore, 1825–1829," *History of Education Quarterly* 22, no. 1 (Spring 1982): 36–37.

74. Peter E. Kurtze, "'A School House Well Arranged': Baltimore Public School Buildings on the Lancasterian Plan, 1829–1839," *Perspectives in Vernacular Architecture* 5 (1995): 73.

75. William R. Johnson, "'Chanting Choristers': Simultaneous Recitation in Baltimore's Nineteenth-Century Primary Schools," *History of Education Quarterly* 34 (Spring 1994): 10.

76. Johnson, "'Chanting Choristers,'" 10.

77. Kurtze, "'A School House Well Arranged,'" 75.

78. Johnson, "'Chanting Choristers,'" 11.

79. Johnson, "'Chanting Choristers,'" 11.

80. Johnson, "'Chanting Choristers,'" 16.

81. Johnson, "'Chanting Choristers,'" 11.

82. Johnson, "'Chanting Choristers,'" 16.

83. *A Digest of the Acts of Assembly Relating to the First School District of the State of Pennsylvania* (Philadelphia: Crissy & Markley, 1861), 15.

84. *Digest of the Acts of Assembly*, 17.

85. *Eighteenth Annual Report of the Controllers of the Public Schools for the City and County of Philadelphia, Composing the First School District of the State of Pennsylvania; With Their Accounts* (Philadelphia: Printed by Order of the Board of Control, 1836), 6.

86. *Nineteenth Annual Report of the Controllers of the Public Schools for the City and County of Philadelphia, Composing the First School District of the State of Pennsylvania; With Their Accounts* (Philadelphia: Printed by Order of the Board of Control, 1837), 6.

87. *Nineteenth Annual Report of the Controllers of the Public Schools*, 7.

88. Harry S. Silcox, "Delay and Neglect: Negro Public Education in Antebellum Philadelphia, 1800–1860," *Pennsylvania Magazine of History and Biography* 97 (October 1973): 456.

89. Silcox, "Delay and Neglect," 457.

Conclusion

1. Jean Barth Toll and Mildred S. Gillam, eds., *Invisible Philadelphia: Community through Voluntary Organizations* (Philadelphia: Atwater Kent Museum, 1995), 695.

2. See, e.g., Michael Katz, *The Irony of Early School Reform: Educational Innovation in*

Mid-nineteenth Century Massachusetts (Boston: Beacon, 1968); Samuel Bowles and Herbert Gintis, *Schooling in Capitalist America: Educational Reform and the Contradictions of Economic Life* (New York: Basic Books, 1976).

3. See, e.g., Maris A. Vinovskis, "Trends in Massachusetts Education, 1826–1860," *History of Education Quarterly* 12, no. 4 (Winter 1972): 501–29; Carl F. Kaestle and Maris A. Vinovskis, *Education and Social Change in Nineteenth-Century Massachusetts* (Cambridge: Cambridge University Press, 1980); Ira Katznelson and Margaret Weir, *Schooling for All: Class, Race, and the Decline of the Democratic Ideal* (New York: Basic Books, 1985); Michael Katz, Edward Stevens, and Maris Vinovskis, "The Origins of Public High Schools," *History of Education Quarterly* 27, no. 2 (Summer 1987): 241–58. See also the more recent work of historians such as Hilary J. Moss, *Schooling Citizens: The Struggle for African American Education in Antebellum America* (Chicago: University of Chicago Press, 2009); and Kabria Baumgartner, *In Pursuit of Knowledge: Black Women and Educational Activism in Antebellum America* (New York: New York University Press, 2019).

4. Robert Owen to Joseph Lancaster, January 6, 1811, box 2, folder 1, Lancaster Papers, American Antiquarian Society, Worcester, Massachusetts.

5. *Eighth Annual Report of the Controllers of the Public Schools of the First School District of the State of Pennsylvania; With Their Accounts* (Philadelphia: Printed by Order of the Board of Control, 1826), 6.

6. Carla L. Peterson, *Black Gotham: A Family History of African Americans in Nineteenth-Century New York City* (New Haven, CT: Yale University Press, 2011), 5; Leslie M. Harris, *In the Shadow of Slavery: African Americans in New York City, 1626–1863* (Chicago: University of Chicago Press, 2003), 138–39.

7. Ruth Wallis Herndon, "Poor Women and the Boston Almshouse in the Early Republic," *Journal of the Early Republic* 21, no. 3 (Fall 2012): 349–81; Monique Bourque, "Women and Work in the Philadelphia Almshouse, 1790–1840," *Journal of the Early Republic* 32, no. 3 (Fall 2012): 383–413.

8. R.D.O., "Cause of the People," *Mechanics Free Press*, September 26, 1829, 1.

9. David J. Rothman, *The Discovery of the Asylum: Social Order and Disorder in the New Republic* (New York: Little, Brown, 1971); Michael B. Katz, *In the Shadow of the Poorhouse: A Social History of Welfare in America* (New York: Basic Books, 1986); Gary B. Nash, "The Social Evolution of Preindustrial Cities, 1700–1820: Reflections and New Directions," *Journal of Urban History* 13 (February 1987): 115–45; Robert E. Cray Jr., *Paupers and Poor Relief in New York City and Its Rural Environs, 1700–1830* (Philadelphia: Temple University Press, 1988); Billy G. Smith, ed., *Down and Out in Early America* (University Park: Pennsylvania State University Press, 2004).

10. Carl F. Kaestle, *Pillars of the Republic: Common Schools and American Society, 1780–1860* (New York: Hill & Wang, 1983), 41; Lawrence A. Cremin, *American Education: The National Experience, 1783–1876* (New York: Harper & Row, 1980), 396.

11. Carl F. Kaestle, ed., *Joseph Lancaster and the Monitorial School Movement: A Documentary History* (New York: Teachers College Press, 1973), 47.

Index

abolition, 29, 123–124, 128
Adams, Eric, ix–xi
Adams, James, 130
Adams, John Quincy, 66
Adelphi School, 85–86, 91, 116, 164
African Free Schools (New York), 125, 129, 184, 194; attendance, 77–78, 109–110, 115, 119, 125, 127–128, 151; curriculum, 77, 122–123, 156; discipline, 48–50, 103, 112–115; exhibitions, 69–72; origin, 29; racism, 71, 104, 113, 123, 130–131; teachers, 95, 113, 123, 130, 159
African Mutual Instruction Society, 121
Aimwell School, 31
Allen, Richard, 29, 78, 115
Allen, William, 67–68
Andrews, Charles C., 113, 128–130, 156
apprenticeship, 11, 98–99, 193
architecture, classroom, 51–53

Baker, Edward, 86, 88, 93, 96–97, 149–150, 181
Bassett, Burwell, 66
Baumgartner, Kabria, 121
Beadie, Nancy, 107, 161, 182
Bedford, Duke of, 12, 14–15, 18
Bell, Andrew, 11
Bender, Thomas, 25
Boese, Thomas, 3, 5
Bolivar, Simon, 173, 177
Booker, Cory, ix
Boonshoft, Mark, 106, 134
Borough Road School, 10–12, 17, 20, 68, 86, 193
Bourque, Monique, 104
British and Foreign School Society, 14, 16–20, 41, 175

Calhoun, John C., 65–66
Catholicism, 5, 175–176
child labor, 118–120
Christie, Chris, ix
classical languages, 58–59, 155, 157–158

classroom architecture, 51–53
classroom discipline, 38, 41–42, 46–50, 102–103, 111–114, 134–135, 154
classroom technology, xii, 11, 51–55; telegraph, 37, 53
Clay, Henry, 63, 66, 73
Clinton, De Witt, 27, 28, 31, 163; educational experience, 192; praise of Joseph Lancaster, 2; relationship with Joseph Lancaster, 63; support for Lancasterian system, 22, 24–25, 61–62, 66, 75–76, 83, 189–190
Coleridge, Samuel Taylor, 111
compulsory schooling, 118, 120
Controllers of the Public Schools (Philadelphia), 21, 79, 109–111, 184; admissions policies, 163; attendance, 76, 114–115, 117–118; budget, 151; relationship with Joseph Lancaster, 81
Cornish, Samuel, 115–116, 124–127
Cremin, Lawrence A., 6
Cries of London (book), 33
Cries of New-York (book), 33
Cries of Philadelphia (book), 33

Dabel, Jane A., 126
Dale, William A. Tweed, 41, 47, 55
DeVos, Betsy, ix–x
discipline, classroom, 38, 41–42, 46–50, 102–103, 111–114, 134–135, 154
Donaldson, Arthur, 30
Dublin, Thomas, 107
Dwight, Timothy, 152

Eddy, Thomas, 14
education, girls', 45, 86–88, 122, 158
education, mathematics, 45–46, 72, 153
emulation, 47–48
Erie Canal, 63, 75–76, 190
expulsions, 113–114

Ferguson, Ebenezer, 88
Fowle, George, 94–95

Fowle, William B.: Boston school, 2, 139, 154–156, 192–193; pedagogy, 45–46, 47, 53; publications, 41, 46
Franklin, Benjamin, 31
Freedom's Journal (newspaper), 116, 120–127
Free School Society, 149; attempts to retain teachers, 83–84, 98–100; budget, 56, 89–93, 100, 138, 161–162; change to Public School Society, 138–139, 167–168, 184; discipline, 49–50, 111–114, 116–117; enrollment, 68–69, 77, 109, 163–164, 180; origins, 14, 26, 28–29; publications, 41, 52; relationship with Joseph Lancaster, 173, 179; schools, 64; teacher-payment schemes, 93–95, 100, 159, 166; teacher training, 96–97; tuition payments, 165–168, 182

George III, King, 10, 14, 18, 148
George IV, King, 177
Gilfoyle, Thomas, 26
girls' education, 45, 86–88, 122, 158
global Lancasterian movement, 1–2, 9, 14–15, 174–175
Gloucester, Stephen, 122
Go, Sun, 108
Greek language instruction. *See* languages, classical
Griscom, John, 55

Harris, Leslie M., 194
Hawthorne, Nathaniel, 75
Hebrew language instruction. *See* languages, classical
Holt, David, 144
houses of refuge, 118
Hutcheson, Francis, 34

indigenous children, 65–66
international schools. *See* global Lancasterian movement

Jackson, Andrew, 177
Jones, Absalom, 29
Jones, Richard, 143–149, 173–174
Justice, Benjamin, 35, 108

Kaestle, Carl F., 74; on funding, 160–161, 182; on impact of Lancasterian movement, 6, 196; on numbers of public schools, 31, 78; on roots of public education, 8, 28, 196; on school attendance, 107–108

labor, child, 118–120
Lambert, Henry, 27
Lancaster, Elizabeth (senior), 143–149
Lancaster, Elizabeth "Betsy" (junior), 142–149, 173–174
Lancaster, Joseph, 63–64, 86–88, 102–103, 137–138, 150; abuse of students, 2, 7, 12, 18–19, 68, 193; childhood, 10; death, 1–3, 172–173, 178–179; dispute with Andrew Bell, 11; family, 66, 87–88, 141–149; financial crimes, 2, 11, 15–16, 68, 176, 193; in Caracas, 173–178; in Montreal, 178; religion, 7
Lancaster, William, 143–149
Lancasterian movement, global, 1–2, 9, 14–15, 174–175
languages, classical, 58–59, 155, 157–158
Latin instruction. *See* languages, classical
Lindert, Peter H., 108
literacy education, 35, 42–46, 53–55, 69, 103, 128, 178
Locke, John, 10, 34
Lovell, John E.: Lancaster family life, 143–149; New Haven school, 3, 139, 152–154, 192–193
Lowell, Massachusetts, mills/factories in, 63, 179–180

Mann, Horace, 5–6, 183, 197–198
Manumission Society, 29, 31, 77, 104, 123–124, 130–131, 184
mathematics education, 45–46, 72, 153
Mexico, 174
Missing, John, 94
Monroe, James, 63, 75, 150
Moss, Hilary J., 128

Neem, Johann N., 108
New Harmony, Indiana, 73–74
New Lanark, Scotland, 63, 75
New York African Society for Mutual Relief, 29
New York Female Association, 29, 31

Opal, J. M., 47
orphan asylums, 21
orphans, 163
Ould, Henry, 141–142
Ould, Robert, 95, 109, 133, 141–142
Owen, Robert, 73–74, 75, 194

Panic of 1819, 86, 106, 145
Parrish, Ann, 31

Pennsylvania Abolition Society, 29
Peterson, Carla L., 194
Philadelphia Society for the Establishment and Support of Charity Schools, 28, 79, 90–91
Philadelphia Society for the Instruction of Indigent Boys. *See* Philadelphia Society for the Establishment and Support of Charity Schools
Pickton, Charles, 94
Pickton, Susan, 94
Place, Francis, 18–19
Public School Society. *See* Free School Society
punishments. *See* classroom discipline

Quaker religion. *See* Society of Friends

Reese, William J., 33, 69
religion in public schools, 8, 11, 26, 28, 31, 58, 78–79
Rhees, John L., 41
Ronaldson, James, 111
Royal Lancasterian Society. *See* British and Foreign School Society
rural schools, 8, 104–108, 190–191, 195, 199
Rush, Benjamin, 74, 91

Schlesinger, Arthur Meier, 106
schooling, compulsory, 118, 120
slavery, 123–124, 128
Smith, James McCune, 129
Smith, William, 93
Society of Free People of Colour for Promoting the Instruction and School Education of Children of African Descent, 29

Society of Friends (Quakers), 7, 10–11, 21, 31, 67, 78–79, 176
Somerville, Lord, 12, 14–15, 18

tax funding, 131, 135, 160–162, 181–182, 191, 197
teacher pay, 85, 86, 93–95, 152, 155, 159–160, 166
teacher training, 58, 86–88, 95–97, 150, 158–160, 183–184, 197
Teasman, John, 123–124
technology, classroom, xii, 11, 51–55; telegraph, 37, 53
Tigall, Sarah, 159
Tolley, Kim, 141
tuition payments, 28, 29, 131, 135, 153, 154–155, 160, 163–168, 182, 191

Vaux, Roberts, 69, 131–132, 160, 194; Board of Controllers of Public Schools, 79–80, 111, 118; budget, 57; on child labor, 118–120; philanthropy, 21, 90; praise for Lancasterian schools, 21–22, 24; relationship with Joseph Lancaster, 63, 67, 86–88, 143, 177–178; teaching experience, 21, 192
Vinovskis, Maris A., 107
vouchers, 164–165

Wales, Elisha, 164–165
War of 1812, 106
Whiteman, Betty, 27
Williams, Peter, 125
Winfrey, Oprah, ix

Zuckerberg, Mark, ix–x

Milton Keynes UK
Ingram Content Group UK Ltd.
UKHW030837250824
447326UK00020B/101/J